# Social Functions and Economic Aspects of Health Insurance

# Huebner International Series on Risk, Insurance, and Economic Security

**J. David Cummins, Editor**
The Wharton School
The S. S. Huebner Foundation for
Insurance Education
University of Pennsylvania
Philadelphia, Pennsylvania, USA

**Series Advisors:**

Dr. Karl Borch
Norwegian School of Economics and
Business Administration
Dr. Phelim P. Boyle
University of Waterloo, Canada
Dr. Jean Lemaire
Université Libre de Bruxelles, Belgium
Dr. Akihiko Tsuboi
Kagawa University, Japan
Dr. Richard Zeckhauser
Harvard University, USA

**Previously published books in the series:**

The objective of the series is to publish original research and advanced textbooks dealing with all major aspects of risk bearing and economic security. The emphasis is on books that will be of interest to an international audience. Interdisciplinary topics as well as those from traditional disciplines such as economics, risk and insurance, and actuarial science are within the scope of the series. The goal is to provide an outlet for imaginative approaches to problems in both the theory and practice of risk and economic security.

# Social Functions and Economic Aspects of Health Insurance

**William A. Rushing**
Vanderbilt University
Nashville, Tennessee

**Kluwer•Nijhoff Publishing**
a member of the Kluwer Academic Publishers Group
Boston / Dordrecht / Lancaster

Distributors

for the United States and Canada: Kluwer Academic Publishers,
101 Philip Drive, Assinippi Park, Norwell, Massachusetts 02061, USA

for the UK and Ireland: Kluwer Academic Publishers, MTP Press Limited,
Falcon House, Queen Square, Lancaster LA1 1RN, UNITED KINGDOM

for all other countries: Kluwer Academic Publishers Group, Distribution
Centre, Post Office Box 322, 3300 AH Dordrecht, THE NETHERLANDS

Library of Congress Cataloging-in-Publication Data

Rushing, William A.
  Social functions and economic aspects of health insurance.
  (Huebner international series on risk, insurance, and
economic security)
  Includes Index.
  1. Insurance, Health—United States.  2. Insurance, Health—Social
aspects—United States.  I. Title. II. Series.
HD7102.U4R86  1986       368.3′82′00973       86-7297
ISBN 0-89838-219-X

Copyright © 1986 by Kluwer • Nijhoff Publishing, Boston

Printed in the United States of America

# Contents

CONTENTS                                            vii

# Social Functions and Economic Aspects of Health Insurance

# 1 INTRODUCTION

Statistics published by the U.S. Department of Commerce (1980) indicate that in 1977 we spent 8.1% of our gross national product (GNP) on life, health, property-casualty, and other forms of insurance. An additional 5.7% was used to pay the Social Security tax, which is another form of insurance premium, for a total of 14.8% of the GNP.[1] Although insurance had its historical origin in marine insurance, it has now developed into one of the major industries of the American economy and extends into many areas of economic activity. One area where growth has been particularly strong is the medical sector. Health insurance is a major institution in all industrialized countries.

It became a government responsibility in 1883 when Bismarck introduced a compulsory program of health insurance for industrial workers in Germany. Programs for workers in various industrial and income categories soon followed in other European countries—Austria (1888), Hungary (1891), Norway (1909), Servia (1910), Great Britain (1911), and Russia and Romania (1912) (Rubinow, 1913:250). Programs in these countries were extended in subsequent years, and other countries in Europe followed with their own programs. Consequently, today most industrial countries have universal or near-universal health insurance coverage. In the United States the issue of national health insurance has been seriously debated since just prior to World War I, and polling data since the 1930s show that a substantial majority of the public has been supportive of such a program (Erskine, 1975). Health insurance coverage

1

of the population is not as extensive as in other industrial countries, though many members of the most vulnerable groups, the elderly and the poor, are covered by government insurance (Medicare and Medicaid). Also, a 1982 national survey indicates that about 90% of the population has some form of health insurance (Aday, Fleming, and Andersen, 1984), though the quality and comprehensiveness of the coverage varies. Approximately 68% of all medical expenses in the United States is paid by insurance, and 90% of hospital expenses, the most burdensome of all medical costs, is paid by insurance (Gibson and Waldo, 1982).

Depite the popularity, health insurance is being severely criticized. The criticisms are several.

Private companies have been criticized because of reimbursement defaults and delays (Guarino and Trubo, 1974). Some claim that private insurance companies "siphon off billions of dollars of people's money for health care" in the form of overhead expense (administrative costs, executive salaries, advertising and sales promotion) and profits that could otherwise be spent directly on medical care (Bodenheimer, Cummings, and Harding, 1974:595–596). Another criticism is that even with public and private insurance health insurance is often inadequate so that costs of medical care are catastrophic in too many cases (Bodenheimer, Cummings, and Harding, 1974). Others believe that coverage provided by Medicare and Medicaid is insufficient particularly as these programs have been cut back in response to escalating medical costs and tighter budgets (see Krauss, 1977:168–173; and Davis and Rowland, 1983). The investigators of the 1982 national survey who found that only about 10% of the population had no form of health insurance felt that this was unacceptable (Aday, Fleming, and Andersen, 1984). According to these criticisms, health insurance should be more extensive. Further, some believe the coverage should be open-ended, with the insurance carrier paying for all services. The individual should

> ...purchase insurance that pays benefits in services rather than cash indemnity. When claims are made under a service plan, the insurer pays the hospital and doctor directly, usually in full for all services stipulated in the policy (Guarino and Trubo, 1974:61).

At the same time, third-party reimbursement for medical care has been criticized for this very open-ended feature. Reimbursement on a "cost-plus" basis in which charges are based on the cost of services plus a percentage for profit has come under serious criticism on the grounds that it causes the cost of health services to rise.

While most of these criticisms are directed to commercial carriers, other criticisms are directed at public or government insurance. Government insurance has been criticized for increasing both the cost and the impersonality of care. "As government has paid a larger share of the nation's medical bills, both patients and physicians complain of rocketing costs and of the increasing impersonality of medicine" (Friedman and Friedman, 1980:87). While some economists, such as Martin S. Feldstein, claim that private and public insurance both raise the cost of medical care (Feldstein, 1971, 1977, and 1978), others, such as Milton and Rose Friedman, seem to believe that government insurance increases costs whereas private insurance does not, because in a national insurance system "there would be no connection between what you would pay and the actuarial value of what you would be entitled to receive, as there is in private insurance" (Friedman and Friedman, 1980:194). In public insurance what you get is not what you pay for. Cross-national evidence would indicate, however, that the rising costs of medical care are not related to the way medical care is financed; the cost of medical care has risen at a rapid rate in almost all industrial countries despite different plans of reimbursemant (see Abel-Smith, 1967; Organization for Economic Cooperation and Development, 1967; Glaser, 1970; and White, 1975). For example, in Great Britain, a country with universal health insurance, national expenditures on health care as a proportion of GNP has grown less than expenditures in the United States. From 1960 to 1976, expenditures as a proportion of GNP increased by 53% in Great Britain and 62% in the United States (Simanis and Coleman, 1980). Furthermore, there is no evidence in national health statistics, such as life expectancy at birth, that the dominance of the private sector in health insurance produces superior medical benefits. In 1978, the life expectancy for England and Wales was 70.2 years; for the United States it was 69.5 years (U.S. Department of Health and Human Services, 1981:116). Not all private carriers are profit makers, with Blue Cross/Blue Shield being the most prominent example. While many believe nonprofit plans siphon fewer profits off medical care, some claim that nonprofit plans, such as Blue Cross/Blue Shield, have been primarily responsive to the financing needs of the hospitals (e.g., for construction and expensive technology) and have neglected the financial and medical needs of subscribers (Law, 1981).

Clearly, then, there is no consensus on the positive and negative aspects of health insurance, public or private. However, much of the recent criticism, particularly as it has emanated from economists, is that health insurance increases the cost of medical care, though as the somewhat differing positions of Feldstein and the Friedmans indicate, economists are not always in complete agreement on the issue with respect to private versus public insurance. Underlying the economists' general argument is the contention that health insurance leads to irrationality in the demand and supply characteristics of medical and hospital care. Health insurance "distorts" market mechanisms. The general argument is not limited to health insurance but applies to insurance in general.

When insurance plays a role in the market, economic transactions are mediated by a third party. Policyholders pay premiums into a common pool out of which funds are paid to individual policyholders during periods of crisis. In this way the individual doesn't suffer the full economic consequences of his purchasing behavior but is able to shift the uncertain but potentially very costly burden to all policyholders. This lessens the discipline and restraint imposed by the market. When purchasing an insured good or service, one is less constrained to weigh its cost or to compare it with that of alternative goods and services (e.g., automobile repair against the purchase of some other good or service). In addition to the relaxation of market restraints, overhead expenses of the insurance carrier must be included in the premium, as must profits in the case of commercial carriers. For these reasons, the average policyholder pays more than he or she would without the insurance. Therefore, according to one line of economic thinking, the purchase of insurance is not rational economic behavior. The result is higher prices, or inflation. Some attribute inflation in today's world altogether to the growth of insurance: "At bottom, inflation [in today's society] was caused by the inability of our political institutions to restrain the growth of insurance within tolerable limits. The increased insurance necessitated much higher costs, both in the public and private sectors" (Aharoni, 1981:186).

The argument has been directed strongly against health insurance in recent years. Since health insurance lowers out-of-pocket expenses, many critics say people are less apt to question the need for services that suppliers (e.g., physicians) prescribe or recommend. Also, since a third party pays for all or a proportion of the care, suppliers may be less restrained in recommending expensive services. Insurance reduces cost consciousness of both the public and the supplier. Some criticisms focus more specifically on the nature of the coverage, namely, reimbursement based on cost, as noted above. Third parties frequently pay what the suppliers say the cost of the care is, usually with some percentage increase, rather than some predetermined rate. Many argue that this keeps the restraints on the cost of medical care too weak.

Despite the disparate views reflected in the criticisms of health insurance—some contending that coverage is too extensive, others that it is not extensive enough—there is nevertheless a common issue. All focus on the medical benefits and economic costs. Some emphasize that costs are too high, others that the benefits are too low. Considering the wide divergence of views, the debate over the net medical benefits and economic costs would be impossible to resolve to everyone's satisfaction. There will be no attempt to do so in this book. Effort will be made instead to point out the limited nature of this debate and to show that the assessment of health insurance should involve the analysis of social consequence as well as the calculation or estimation of medical benefits and economic costs. Health insurance may have important social consequences even if the medical benefits are most limited and the economic costs extremely high.

The conceptual framework for the analysis is in the tradition of structure-function analysis of social anthropology and sociology. This framework views the institutions of society in terms of the consequences for the psychological functioning of individuals and the social cohesion and integration of society. In contrast to the economic theorist, the functional theorist does not view irrational behavior as necessarily undesirable. Behavior that distorts market forces and drives up market prices may still have significant social and psychological utility. Indeed, some of the most important forms of behavior, at least in terms of their effect on societal functioning, may be irrational. The rain ritual performed by members of a preliterate society is the classic example. Such behavior is clearly not rational in the sense that the behavior accomplishes what it is intended to accomplish. At the same time, the ritual may alleviate anxiety surrounding uncertain events, and it may have important psychological consequences accordingly. One thesis of this book is that health insurance has similar consequences for the natives of contemporary societies. In this sense, the purchase of health insurance is ritualized behavior.[2]

Other functional theorists argue that ritual, though "irrational," performs a more important service to society than simply alleviating anxiety. By bringing members of society together for a common purpose, it reduces a sense of difference between them and, therefore, contributes to the cohesion of society. A thesis of this book is that health insurance also promotes social cohesion, though the specific mechanism by which it does so is different. It reduces conflict and the potential for conflict in the health-service sector (e.g., between providers and patients), different social classes, and members of the same kinship unit, thus promoting cohesion between them. Thus, health insurance may not only have important psychological consequences for individuals (e.g., by reducing anxiety); it may have important collective consequences for society. For well over half a century, sociologists, social commentators, and social philosophers have decried the decline of social integration and cohesion in modern society. The cause has been variously attributed to class conflict, urbanization, and technological change. At the same time, institutions exist which promote integration and cohesion. Health insurance is such an institution.

The growth of health insurance, and of insurance more generally, represents a major way that economic relations have been reshaped and reordered in the twentieth century. It reflects the increased orientation to what Yair Aharoni (1981) has called "The No-Risk Society." In contrast to a highly competitive economy which operates in accordance with free and unregulated market forces, numerous regulations have been introduced to protect industry from the competition and risk of an unregulated market. Legislation and subsidies which protect industries and workers from foreign competition have been introduced. In general, the context of economic action has increasingly moved away from a free market in which individuals make choices at the risk of uncertain consequences to one in which there are more restraints on an individual's economic action as well as the action of others which may significantly affect one's economic outcomes. Outcomes are more predictable and less uncertain as a result. Restraints imposed by regulation, legislation, and subsidies spread costs among the many and the benefits among the few. For example, all taxpayers pay for farm subsidies, but the benefits flow primarily to farmers. Similarly, people socialize or spread risk by paying insurance premiums. All policyholders pay a certain sum in return for protection against an uncertain disaster, which occur to a very few policyholders. Thus, as with other institutions (e.g., farm subsidies) insurance spreads the costs and concentrates the benefits. The pooling of resources this way (all policyholders paying into a common fund) may encourage the development of two contradictory trends.

On the one hand, it may be related to the development of a collective or social ethic rather than an individual ethic, namely, a concern with collective welfare and social order. "Whereas in the nineteenth century insurance ministered primarily to the needs of economic man, in the twentieth century it became one of the main instruments by which law created a welfare-minded society" (Kimball, 1960:301). Consequently, the insurance industry and laws governing that industry are said to have "contributed to the most significant twentieth century change in the overall power structure of a society in which public policy shows a living and increasing concern for social income and costs" (Kimball, 1960:311). Insurance is a mechanism by which society assumes responsibility for the individual's welfare. Consequently, "the dynamic of an insurance-oriented society [is] toward a greater social direction and administration" (Kimball, 1960:311).

On the other hand, because individuals (policyholders) are dependent on each other only because they are dependent on a common source of funds, the actions of each have no direct and immediate influence on the actions and outcomes of others. Further, policyholders (including taxpayers) are usually strangers. As a result, individuals are less apt to be inhibited in their behavior because of the adverse effect their behavior may have on others. They may be less careful in preventing insured events from occurring, as when industrial managers do not eliminate occupational hazards which endanger workers' health, or purchasing more and more expensive goods and services for which one is insured, as with medical care. The result is weak social control, or what insurance analysts and economists call "moral hazards."

Insurance contributes both to individualistic and collective outcomes. At the individual level, it provides protection against uncertainty and the unpredictability when outcomes depend on the operation of free market principles. "The attitudes closely connected with the growth of insurance law...was the...insistence upon an ordered and secure [rather than unpredictable] existence" (Kimball, 1960:303–304). Insurance thus alleviates anxiety and worry about the unanticipated consequences of one's behavior. At the collective level, it may go hand in hand with a concern for the welfare of others, as, for example, the requirement of compulsory automobile insurance and compulsory universal health insurance. Or, by providing access to medical care health insurance helps to facilitate the integration of individuals in society because the result of medical care may allow people to participate in normal activities of society. Also, since health insurance helps to assure that no one is denied medical care for economic reasons, it helps to preserve and reduce conflict between individuals and groups, thus promoting social cohesion.

The significance of insurance to modern societies, therefore, is not purely economic and financial. First of all, insurance, private and public, extends into areas of human enterprise that are not exclusively economic in nature, though one need not be an orthodox Marxist to appreciate that much of what we generally consider social behavior has an economic dimension. As Spencer L. Kimball observed over 20 years ago, "most human activity" has "insurance implications" (Kimball, 1960:301); the fact that we may now spend upward of 15% of GNP on insurance suggests the validity of this statement. More significantly, as noted, insurance, and especially health insurance, has important social benefits regardless of its adverse economic consequences.

For the most part, however, insurance has been ignored by sociologists. Although economists have also given it little attention,[3] some macroeconomic and microeconomic analysis has been conducted. At the macroeconomic level, the general relationship of expenditures for insurance to national savings and investment and to the gross national product has received attention, and the role of the insurance industry in the mobilization of capital, and the impact of this on the bond market and home and commercial mortgage markets as the interest rate fluctuates, are widely recognized; these issues are frequently commented on in monthly, weekly, and daily financial journals. (For a discussion of insurance from a general macroeconomic perspective, see Cummings and Weisbart, 1976; Pfeffer and Klock, 1974:253–271; and Nelli and Marshall, 1969.) Nevertheless, there has been very little effort to bring insurance explicitly into macroeconomic theory.

At the microeconomic level, problems in conceptualizing insurance are most difficult. (For general discussions, see Pfeffer, 1953, and Pfeffer and Klock, 1974:229–252.) The motivational basis for buying and selling products is, of course, crucial in microeconomic theory, and the motive for purchasing insurance poses problems at the outset. The motive economists usually attribute to the purchase of insurance is the reduction of economic risk, so that in purchasing insurance one exchanges a small definite loss (the premium) "in order to eliminate the possibility of a large but improbable one" (Pfeffer, 1953:146). The formulation attributes greater accuracy to actuarial accounting than is really warranted (Pfeffer, 1953:5). If the accounting were valid, one would purchase insurance in accordance with the mathematical probability of the risk. There are two specific problems here.

First, as Pfeffer and Klock (1974:239:252) note, the purchase of insurance is motivated by feelings of anxiety and uncertainty rather than being guided by the principles of mathematical probability and the calculation of risk. The correspondence between the facts and our awareness of them is far from perfect. Furthermore, even if insurance were purchased on the basis of (postulated) mathematical probability, behavior would not be rational because of this. Quite the contrary. Blanchard has observed that when one wants to transfer risk to an insurer in order to approximate certainty, it is *possibilities* rather than probabilities that are important since, "if the premium rates are accurate [that is, if the actuarial forecasts are correct], the odds are against the insured,...for the [insurance company] must collect more in premiums than it expects to pay out in losses, in order to meet the expense of operating the insurance business." Consequently, the person "who buys insurance on the principle of insuring against the loss most likely to happen (most probably) is on unsound [nonrational] ground" (Blanchard, 1965:9).

Second, unlike the role of pricing in creating aggregate demand for most products, the role of price is of secondary importance in the purchase of insurance because demand is a function of anxieties and uncertainties rather than rational calculation (Pfeffer and Klock, 1974:249). This further complicates the problem because anxieties and uncertainties are difficult to quantify (Pfeffer and Klock, 1974:246). In addition, because reliable insurance is so important to so many people, it has come to be viewed as similar to a public utility, subject to price regulation like most public utilities.[4] The price is not altogether a function of free market forces which, ideally, are the result of rational motives.

Consequently, when economists do treat insurance, they are apt to treat it in terms of a discount function or as creating imperfections in the market. According to the discount function, the insurance premium protects against risk, and assuming the accuracy of actuarial statistics, the premium is a substitute for risk. The only risks remaining to study are the residual ones, which in essence removes insurance from the purview of economic theory.[5] This approach is especially relevant to the study of entrepreneurship.[6]

As to market imperfections, some economists emphasize the role of insurance in distorting supply and demand. Because insurance protects against risks, some types of insurance may encourage suppliers to supply more of a particular product and buyers to purchase more of it than would be the case if insurance did not exist. As a result, marginal utility functions are distorted from their "optimum" functions, and the relationship between supply and demand deviates from its "optimum" relationship—that is, from what the relationship would be if buyers and sellers were rational and at risk. In this approach, then, insurance is irrational and viewed as having negative economic consequences for society.

In contrast, the approach of this book is that insurance, and particularly health insurance, has important positive social consequences for society. In some respects insurance is inherently social, such as when the protection of another party is central, as with life insurance. Some analysts have gone further and suggested that insurance is an important way society alleviates some of the social problems inherent in an industrial society—such as providing worker compensation for workers who are victims of industrial accidents and preventing the destitution of widows and children upon the death of the male head on whom they are economically dependent (e.g., Pfeffer, 1967; Nellie and Marshall, 1969). Hence the view that insurance is a social and not just an economic or financial institution is not new. Neither is the view that insurance has integrating and cohesive effects for society, which is a major thesis of this book, altogether new (e.g., Kimball). However, the explicit linkage of this thesis with structure-function theory is more explicit in this book than in other treatments.

## Outline of the Book

Chapters 2 and 3 set the background for chapters 4 through 7, which constitute the core analysis of health insurance as a social institution. In chapter 2 the network of relations between policyholders is described and viewed as a form of pooled interdependence, as formulated by Thompson (1967). The relationship of pooled interdependence to moral hazards is outlined. Moral hazards are viewed as due to weak social control inherent in pooled interdependence; the argument is made that moral hazards are not so much the result of insurance per se but of the way the relations between policyholders are structured. In essence, they result from the absence of a sense of mutual aid and moral community among policy-holders, stemming from pooled interdependence.

Chapter 3 reviews the potential benefits derived from medical care. In the past 10 years or so, medical care has come under rather close scrutiny with respect to questions about the value of the benefits from increasingly large national expenditures for health services. Answers to the questions are ambiguous and opinions are conflicting. The high value the public puts on medical care is the result of social definition as much if not more than from proven medical benefit. Also, most agree that medical care, or at least the perceived need for it, is often filled with fear and anxiety. Sometimes medical care actually generates fear and anxiety; in other instances it may alleviate those states. Sometimes fear and anxiety precipitate the seeking of medical care. The presence of anxieties as well as the confusing and ambiguous nature of the benefits of medical care and the technical nature of medical care do not provide clear guides for people when they need or think they may need medical care. These factors do not encourage rational decisions in seeking medical care.

Chapters 4 and 5 review the possible reasons people pay so much for insurance to assure that medical care, the benefits of which are so questionable, is available to them. Factors include, in addition to the belief that medical care promotes health, the belief that it promotes economic efficiency, the reduction of economic insecurity, the cultural imperative that medical care is a fundamental human right, and advances in medical technology. The review identifies possible causes of health insurance as it has evolved in industrial societies and indicates that health insurance is the result of cultural and social forces as well as medical and economic factors. Chapters 4 and 5 provide material on which chapters 6 and 7 build. These chapters contain the structure-function analysis of health insurance as a social institution.

Chapter 6 begins by reviewing the idea that marginal economic utility functions are distorted by health insurance. The distortion is itself viewed as a major motivating factor in the purchase of health insurance. A distinction is drawn between the sacred and profane, and medical care is viewed as different from an ordinary economic commodity since it is characterized by properties of both the sacred and the profane. This accounts for much of the ambiguity, conflict, and debate associated with medical care, health policy, and health insurance. The point is made that although health insurance does inflate the cost of medical care, people obtain more than just medical care from the increase in costs. They experience reductions in medical, economic, and moral anxieties, and this provides the psychological foundation for health insurance.

In chapter 7 consequences of health insurance for society are outlined. Health insurance is viewed as helping to contribute to the integration and cohesion of society and to a reduction of conflict between groups in society. The distinction between economic and social policy is drawn. The importance of health insurance for preserving the traditional social bond between practitioner and patients, for reducing class conflict and contributing to employee morale, for reducing conflict between generations, and for retaining strength in an already weak family unit by reducing interpersonal conflict between family members are outlined. The implications of the analysis for the Social Security program and for theories of economic and social exchange are reviewed.

The analysis of health insurance from the perspective of theories of social exchange is extended in chapter 8, which addresses the issue of inflation and the conflict between economic and social outcomes of health insurance. Exchange theory provides a perspective for recognizing much of the strain and potential conflict between sectors of the population with respect to the disproportionate distribution of medical care. At the same time, when health insurance is viewed in terms of its sociological consequences—in terms of its integrative and cohesive functions—serious qualifications are indicated for recommendations that health insurance should be reduced because of the very limited benefit it may produce, that is, the very large expenditures for such small proportions of the population. Increases in social integration and social cohesion are important benefits of health insurance, and these are to be reckoned in the analysis of the higher costs of medical care that health insurance generates. Suggested ways of dealing with the inflationary consequences of health insurance are reviewed, with particular attention given to increasing the visibility of the connection between medical benefits received and costs incurred.

The final chapter provides a perspective on the future. It contends that with future developments in medical manpower and technology, changes in the demographic characteristics of the population, and increases in the proportion of the population who are disabled, forces are already in place that will exert strong upward pressure on national expenditures for medical care in the future. This will lead to an increase in the demand for health insurance. This trend is in opposition to cost containment policies and recommendations that medical care be "rationed" and health insurance coverage be reduced. The implications of these conflicting trends for society are reviewed. Detailed attention is given to the relations between the elderly and preretirement generations. While much of the history of health insurance may be understood by viewing it from the perspective of conflict between social classes, the current forces make conflict between generations more important than class conflict in the years ahead. Health insurance will be the focal point of social and economic conflict in the future, and relations between generations will be central in this conflict.

## Notes

1. Source of data is U.S. Department of Commerce (U.S. Bureau of the Census, 1980:260, 343, 548, 552, and 557). Data are reported for 1977 because this is the latest year for which the U.S. Department of Commerce reports premium income for the three forms of insurance: life, health, and property-casualty. The percentage underestimates actual expenditures since it does not include expenditures for all forms and types of insurance (e.g., burial, veterans' life insurance) and is based on reports of institutions and thus excludes data from nonresponding institutions. Figures for health insurance premiums paid in 1977, derived from the *Source Book of Health Insurance, 1981–82* (1982:28), are higher than those reported in the Department of Commerce publication (2.73% of GNP versus 2.48%). Also, for 1978, *The Value Line Investment Survey* indicates we spent 9.7% of the GNP on property and casualty insurance premiums alone, versus only 3.8% reported by the Department of Commerce. In any case, even if 14.8% of GNP underestimates actual expenditures, it is nevertheless substantial. Furthermore, inspection of figures for years beyond 1977 indicates that except for life insurance premiums, insurance expenditures increased faster than GNP. Thus, the expenditure for insurance as a percentage of GNP in 1977, regardless of the exact figure, is probably higher today. The figures reported here are very close to those reported by Greene (1977:107). He reported that based on *Life Insurance Fact Book* private and government premiums totalled $268 billion (cited in Ahroni, 1981:77). Since GNP was $1,918 billion in 1977, premium payments amounted to 13.56% of GNP. In 1985, a journalist (Bogdanovich, 1985) reported that, according to the National Insurance Consumer Organization, 11.1% of Americans' disposable income is spent on private insurance premiums.

2. Zelizer (1979) refers to life insurance as a "secular ritual," though not so much in connection with reducing the risk and uncertainty of death but of assuring that provisions are made for those left behind (Zelizer, 1978:54–55).

3. As Pfeffer and Klock (1974:239) remark about economics in general: "the literature of economics has very little discussion of insurance despite the fact that insurance is one of the largest financial institutions in the United States."

4. The insurance industry itself is partly responsible for the social role of insurance and its subsequent regulation. "The insurance industry sought to convince the American public of the virtues of the insurance idea, and in so doing, insurance leaders quite unintentionally subverted their own most cherished wish—a free enterprise, private profit economy. Insurance was inherently mutual, and the dynamics of an insurance-oriented society was toward greater social direction and administration. It was one of the striking anachronisms of the twentieth century that the individualistic insurance man was, in fact, one of the chief apostles of the socialization of risk" (Kimball, 1960:311).

5. Pfeffer (1956:146) states: "If the insurance premium can serve to eliminate all insurable risks, then the residual risks of the economic system are properly the only subject for studies of the entrepreneurial function." Elsewhere he and Klock state more generally: "Economists have neglected insurance because economic theory generally assumes perfect knowledge and static analysis in its models. Economists usually assume demand and supply functions that are instantaneous with perfect flexibility of adjustment. But insurance exists because knowledge is imperfect and adjustments to change are somewhat uncertain."

"A theory of economics that is static in nature requires no discussion of insurance...The economist deals with uncertainty by discounting for it. He can use a discount function as a substitute for the uncertainty situation. In effect, he ignores the uncertainties related to insurance by assuming that he can determine the discounted value of cash flows required for insurance premiums. The premium is treated as a substitute for risk, and if discounted in this fashion the net result is a simple movement of the appropriate curve. The economist contends that there is no more reason to focus on the foregoing movement of the curve than on other shifts (e.g., movements caused by advertising, education, etc.). Thus, insurance is treated as an institutional topic" (Pfeffer and Klock, 1974:240).

6. "If, for example, one is planning on building a new factory, the risk that the factory may be destroyed by fire before it has been fully depreciated, is exactly calculable. Now it is clear that actuarial principles of insurance apply to all cases of risk, as we have defined it. Insurance is, indeed, the technique which has been devised to relieve the entrepreneur of risk. Risk of loss, can be, and normally, is insured against: it is not relevant to the study of entrepreneurial behavior" (Keirstead, 1953:18).

## References

Abel-Smith, Brian. *An International Study of Health Care Expenditure and Its Relevance for Health Planning*. Geneva: World Health Organization, 1967.

Aday, Lu Ann, Gretchen V. Fleming, and Ronald M. Andersen. *Access to Medical Care in the U.S.: Who Has It, Who Doesn't*. Chicago: Pluribus Press, Inc., 1984.

Aharoni, Yair. *The No-Risk Society*. Chatham, NJ: Chatham House Publishers, Inc., 1981.

Bodenheimer, Thomas, Steven Cummings, and Elizabeth Harding. "Capitalizing on Illness: The Health Insurance Industry." *International Journal of Health Services* 4 (Fall 1974):583–598.

Blanchard, Ralph H. *Risk and Insurance and Other Papers*. Lincoln: University of Nebraska Press, 1965.

Bogdanich, Walt. "Coverage Provided by Specialty Insurance is Relatively Expensive, Seldom Necessary." *The Wall Street Journal* 65 (August 28, 1985): 21.

Cummins, J. David, and Steven N. Weisbart. "The Role of Insurance in the United States Economy." *Chartered Property and Casualty Underwriters Annals* 29 (1976): 123–140.

Davis, Karen, and Diane Rowland. "Uninsured and Undeserved: Inequities in Health Care in the United States." *Milbank Memorial Fund Quarterly* 61 (Spring 1983):149–176.

Erskine, Hazel. "The Polls: Health Insurance." *Public Opinion Quarterly* 39 (Spring 1975):128–143.

Feldstein, Martin S. "Discussion of Inducement and Impediments for Private Corporate Investment in the Delivery of Health Services." In Gordon K. MacLeod and Mark Perlman (eds.), *Health Care Capital: Competition and Control*, pp. 225–227. Cambridge: Ballinger Publishing Company, 1978.

Feldstein, Martin S. "The High Cost of Hospitals—and What to do About It." *The Public Interest* 48 (Winter 1977):40–54.

—————. *The Rising Cost of Hospital Care*. Washington, DC: Information Resources Press, 1971.

Friedman, Milton, and Rose Friedman. *Free to Choose*. New York: Avon Books, 1980.

Gibson, Robert M., and Daniel R. Waldo. "National Health Expenditures, 1981." *Health Care Financing Review* 4 (September 1982):1–34.

Glaser, William A. *Paying the Doctor*. Baltimore: The Johns Hopkins University Press, 1970.

Greene, Mark R. *Risk and Insurance*, 3rd ed. Cincinnati: Southwestern Publishing, 1977.

Guarino, Richard, and Richard Trubo. *The Great American Insurance Hoax*. Los Angeles: Nash Publishing, 1974.

Keirstead, B.S. *An Essay in the Theory of Profits and Income Distribution*. Oxford: Basic Blackwell, 1953.

Kimball, Spencer L. *Insurance and Public Policy: A Study in the Legal Implementation of Social and Economic Public Policy, Based on Wisconsin Records, 1955–1959*. Madison: The University of Wisconsin Press, 1960.

Krause, Elliott A. *Power and Illness: The Political Sociology of Health and Medical Care*. New York: Elsevier North-Holland, Inc., 1977.

Law, Sylvia A. "Blue Cross—What Went Wrong?" In Peter Conrad and Rochelle Kern (eds.), *The Sociology of Health and Illness: Critical Perspective*, pp. 280–303. New York: St. Martin's Press, 1981.

Light, Ivan H. *Ethic Enterprise in America*. Berkeley: University of California Press, 1972.

Nelli, Humbert O., and Robert A. Marshall. *The Private Insurance Business in the United States Economy*. Atlanta: Department of Insurance, Georgia State College, 1969.

Organization for Economic Cooperation and Development, *Studies in Resource Allocation*, No. 4. *Public Expenditures on Health*. Paris: OECD, 1977.

Pfeffer, Irving. *Insurance and Economic Theory*. Homewood, IL: Richard D. Irwin, Inc., 1956.

——————. "The Role of Insurance in Solving Social Problems." *Best's Fire and Casualty News* (June 1967):14–22.

Pfeffer, Irving, and David R. Klock. *Perspectives on Insurance*. Englewood Cliffs, NJ: Prentice Hall, 1974.

Rubinow, I.M. *Social Insurance*. New York: Henry Holt and Company, 1913.

Simanis, Joseph G., and John R. Coleman. "Health Care Expenditures in Nine Industrial Countries, 1960–76." *Social Security Bulletin* 43 (January 1983):3–8.

*Source Book of Health Insurance Data*. Washington, DC: Health Insurance Association, 1982.

*The Value Line Investment Survey, Ratings & Reports*, edition 12, 35 (June 20, 1980).

Thompson, James D. *Organizations in Action*. New York: McGraw-Hill, 1967.

U.S. Bureau of the Census. *Statistical Abstract of the United States, 1980*, 102nd ed. Washington, DC: U.S. Government Printing Office, 1980.

——————. *Statistical Abstract of the United States, 1980*, 101st ed. Washington, DC: U.S. Government Printing Office, 1980.

U.S. Department of Health and Human Services. *Health, United States—1981*. Washington, DC: U.S. Government Printing Office, 1981.

White, Kerr L. "International Comparisons of Medical Care." *Scientific American* 233 (August 1975):17–25.

Zelizer, Viviana A. Rotman. *Morals and Markets: The Development of Life Insurance in the United States*. New York: Columbia University Press, 1979.

# 2 INSURANCE, SOCIAL RELATIONS, MORAL COMMUNITY, AND THE COST OF MEDICAL CARE

In the analysis of any group or collective unit, sociologists examine the social relations and the rules or norms that regulate the behavior of individuals toward each other. In some groups individuals are dependent on each other in a number of ways, so that social relations are diffuse with obligations of members to each other extending over a range of areas, as in kinship relations. Individual allegiance to other members and to the group as a whole may be strong. Social allegiance and commitments may be reinforced by the norms of conduct, which stipulate that one's behavior must follow rather narrow channels and be in conformity with the community morality. Such morality generally requires that members of the group come to the aid of others in time of need. The needs of others and of the group itself compete with the needs of the individual.

In other groups, relations may be more specific, with an individual's commitment to others limited to a narrow range of interests and behavior, such as the commitment of an employee to an organization. Allegiance to the collective may be weak; because the norms that regulate conduct are so specific, a sense of strong community morality is lacking. Norms that guide behavior become formalized and are contractual in nature.

These terms have been used to describe the distinction between traditional or preindustrial society and modern or industrial society. Durkheim (1949) pictured preindustrial societies as integrated in terms of "mechanical solidarity," where the division of labor is very limited and people resemble each other in attitudes, values, and beliefs. Members

17

of society subscribe to the same norms, and the "collective conscience" or community morality is extensive and strong. Mechanical integration or solidarity is said to be strong in these societies because the community of norms is so strong that most people "mechanically" conform to them. Social control is very strong and problems of deviance are rare. The polar opposite of this type of society is one that is integrated in terms of "organic solidarity," in which integration is based on interdependence. The division of labor is extensive, and there are a variety of subgroups with different cultures. Integration is achieved because the actions of one individual and subgroup (e.g., occupation) have important consequences for the actions of other individuals and subgroups and for the group as a whole. Consequently, the parts of society are bound together not so much by feelings of allegiance and moral ties but by mutual dependence and exchange. In pre-industrial society dependence takes a somewhat different form. Individuals are dependent on a common resource, such as a collective harvest or hunt, which they share.

Other formulations have described the difference in the two polar societies in terms of *Gemeinschaft*, in which relations are informal and diffuse, and *Gesellschaft*, where relations are formal and specific. Other formulations refer to it as a difference in the dominance of primary and kinship relations versus secondary relations, and still others to a difference of status, in which social relations and social commitments are informal, and contract, where commitments are in written form and formalized by legal statutes.

In this chapter I will examine social relations and the problem of a moral community among insurance policyholders in terms of these distinctions. The precise formulation will depart somewhat from general formulations as outlined. These polar distinctions traditionally made in sociology are usually made to gain a general understanding between societies and groups. For example, from the perspective of social control, the distinction pertains to problems or methods of social control across the gamut of behavior (and attitudes). In this chapter the focus will be far more narrow. The focus will be on how social relations among the insured encourage the same exact behavior that the insurance is designed to protect the insured against. Although the analysis of such behavior is usually considered the province of economists and insurance analysts, a sociological perspective on such behavior will serve to enhance our understanding of it.

## Insurance and Social Relations

As noted in the first chapter, growth of insurance has proceeded at a rapid pace during the past century, with some referring to the twentieth century as the "age of insurance" (Kimball, 1960) and the "no-risk society" (Aharoni, 1981). Different explanations could be given for such growth. Growth of public insurance programs has no doubt been in response to political forces, with different groups in society wishing to protect their risks with subsidies from the government. No doubt such growth is also due to the fact that people have learned that insurance is a way to protect themselves against unexpected crises (see Aharoni, 1981). Also, as Kimball (1960) notes, the dominant image and philosophy of society has moved away from economic man and a laissez faire philosophy to social man in which there is greater concern for the welfare of society and the integration and solidarity of the collective. While these analyses indicate that the growth of insurance occurred along with significant social changes, they do not indicate the particular character of the relationships and the nature of the moral community that emerge among individuals who together socialize or spread risks.

There are a variety of schemes that fall under the rubic of insurance. Shippers who paid a fee to an underwriter in return for the underwriter assuring payment for the value of the cargo in the event of piracy or shipwreck was a form of insurance. Lloyd's operates on the same principle today. Using its capital and that of its investors, it insures oil tankers, air cargos, satellites, and other commercial ventures in return for a premium. In this way the shipper or satellite owner has his investment protected against accident. While this type of insurance is similar to other types of insurance which are designed to reduce risk, it is not the type I am addressing in this book. Rather, attention is directed to the situation where a number of policyholders pay into a common fund which assures their own protection against crises rather than to the situation when a single individual or corporation purchases an individual policy from an underwriter or several underwriters. Specific attention at the moment is in the nature of the social relations that exist among the many policyholders, such as among members who have a common health insurance plan. James D. Thompson's distinction between types of interdependence will provide the necessary concepts to see the nature of these relations.

Thompson (1967) distinguishes three forms of interdependence: reciprocal, sequential, and pooled. In reciprocal interdependence, the actions of each individual or unit have implications for the actions of other individuals and units so that relations are in a more or less constant process of adjustment and readjustment. This situation exists in many modern organizations, in which the actions of various departments and persons must be coordinated. Examples would include surgical teams, research teams, and air flight crews. At the same time, it also exists in traditional societies: "Even in the most traditional societies, intensive interdependence probably is widespread; indeed, it would seem to be characteristic of the family or kinship unit wherever it acts as an entity: for traditional methods of producing food, shelter, and clothing still call for coordinate action in response to weather, accidents, invasions, stubbornness of the family's ox, or escape of the family goat" (Rushing and Zald, 1976:276). While Thompson does not deal with the issue, social control is built into the structure of relationships in reciprocal interdependence. If an individual or department does not perform so as to facilitate the performance of other individuals or departments, sanctions are imposed by those parties who are adversely affected. Exchange takes place on a continuous basis, and when the return of one party is less than expected, the affected party may respond by changing its rate of return. The terms of exchange may therefore change. Intensive interdependence resembles Durkheim's conception of organic solidarity. It exists when individuals and parts of a larger unit are heterogneous, where units are bound through exchange between them, and where the actions of one affects the actions of others and of the functioning of the whole. The complex of interdependencies and exchange relations become increasingly important in holding the group together, in comparison to individuals conforming to the same norms, as in mechanical solidarity.

Sequential interdependence exists when the action of one unit follows upon and is dependent on the action of another unit. The prototype of this interdependency is the assembly line. While it is an important basis of interdependence in many organizations, it will be of no concern to us at this point.

The third form of interdependence, pooled interdependence, exists when

> the unit contributes to the group and receives from it but there need be no specific beneficiary for its contributions nor need its members know the specific sources of its benefits. A member contributes to an undifferentiated system and collects from that system, and in some cases has no personal acquaintance with those on whom he depends, or who depend on him. We might refer to this as a "common-wealth" situation, and in the modern society it obviously is the basis for such things as public taxation for public parks or policy protection, and also for insurance programs, public or private (Rushing and Zald, 1976:268).

It is clear from this quote that relations among members of a common insurance plan are characterized by pooled interdependence, though relations among policyholders need not be limited to pooled interdependence, as, for example, when policyholders belong to the same workgroup in which work activities necessitate mutual dependence or when certain members are from the same kinship unit, and thus, mutually dependent with respect to a range of activities and responsibilities.

Although Thompson argues that both pooled and reciprocal interdependence exist in modern society and traditional society, he contends that there has been a progression from societies based predominantly on pooled interdependence to societies based predominantly on reciprocal interdependence. "One can interpret the sweep from...primitive to peasant to modern [societies] in terms of changing interdependencies. The historical movement has been from interdependence organized around common resources [that is, pooled interdependence] to interdependence organized around specialized exchange, and now to interdependence organized around the intensive application of knowledge [reciprocal interdependence]" (Rushing and Zald, 1976:279). Observe that this would appear to be contrary to the views of Kimball (1960) and Aharoni (1981) who see insurance, and thus pooled interdependence, as growing in a linear trend, at least during the twentieth century. Before attempting to reconcile what would appear to be conflicting perspectives, a discussion of pooled interdependence and social control is in order.

## Pooled Interdependence and Social Control

In pooled interdependence each unit is dependent on a common resource but not dependent directly on other units who share in that common resource. Community hospitals in the United States approximate a form of pooled interdependence. They are dependent on the same basic resource, the hospitalizing physicians. As Schroeder and Showstack (1979:122) state: "Hospitals...find themselves in a position of having to compete for the same market, the hospitalizing physicians." Unlike other public services, such as fire, police, and education, hospitals are usually not organized in a system in which different units perform different roles (e.g., as academic versus vocational education) and where personnel are transferred to different units in the system as they are needed. Usually the relationship between hospitals is not such that cooperative relations exist among them and where each strives to complement and enhance the performance of the others. Each hospital is a "free standing" institution with little cooperation with other hospitals. They are dependent on each other only through their dependence on a common resource; there is little exchange between them. The actions of each do not have a restraining influence on the other. For example, the introduction of a facility in one hospital is apt to lead to the duplication of that facility in a hospital across the street. The duplication of hospital and excess hospital capacity are well known and have been the object of several public policies which have attempted to create cooperative relationships or a system of relations among hospitals (as well as other health-care units). Such policies point to a need for reciprocal interdependence—where hospitals complement each other's actions rather than stand in a competitive relationship with each other (Rushing, 1984).

As noted, Thompson views the historical sweep from a traditional society to modern society as a movement away from pooled to reciprocal interdependence. He observes, however, that reciprocal interdependence exists everywhere among kinship units. In primitive societies and the mutual-aid societies, group life is organized around diffuse, informal relations between people who have similar values, attitudes, and beliefs. Such societies are integrated in terms of what Durkheim called mechanical solidarity, that is, in terms of rules and norms to which most persons in society automatically conform—or meet the wrath of community if they do not. This moral community is also the basis for helping individuals and families during periods of crisis. While pooled interdependence exists in the sense that members are dependent on the same resources (common crop yields; yields from hunting, fishing, and gathering; or shelter), the way in which these resources are shared is based on reciprocal give and take.

In strict pooled interdependence, relations between interdependent parties have a specific and narrow basis. Interdependence is usually between strangers, among whom there are few direct exchanges. In the case of insurance, most policyholders do not know each other, and direct exchange between them does not occur. Rather, exchange is mediated by a contractual relationship with a third party. Consequently, the actions of interdependent units are not restrained by the actions of each other, and there is limited basis for social control accordingly. Excessive behavior, as in the duplication of facilities in nearby hospitals, for example, is apt to be the result. In the case of insurance, excessive behavior is referred to as "moral hazards."

Technically the term moral hazards means that insurance may encourage the event against which it is designed to protect. An obvious example is arson, which would occur less frequently if buildings were not insured against fire. A less dramatic but more frequent example is when individuals obtain more medical care and hence generate greater medical expense than their conditions may warrant. The relationship between such behavior and pooled interdependence is this: each policyholder pays into a common fund and is only slightly adversely affected by the actions of other policyholders, so there is less apt to be community scrutiny of individuals or punitive reactions to their misconduct. Indeed, since policyholders frequently do not know who their fellow policyholders are, they are not apt to know who the excessive users are. (In reciprocal interdependence where individuals usually know on whom they are dependent, misconduct is more often seen and the identity of the individual known.)

Although moral hazards have not been viewed as a problem of social control stemming from the nature of pooled interdependence, they are a commonly recognized feature of insurance. They are also commonly recognized as *inherent* in insurance. However, they are inherent in insurance only if pooled interdependence stands alone, that is, in the absence of reciprocal interdependence. While the two types of interdependence have been discussed as though they were concretely separate forms of interdependence, they are analytic distinctions and both may exist in the same concrete situation. This may be illustrated by insurance in primitive societies, mutual-aid societies in Europe, and ethnic groups in the United States.

## Primitive Societies

Primitive societies are organized in large part around group survival. Problems of subsistence are common to all members of society who are also dependent on a common source of subsistence, whether this be growing crops, fishing, or hunting and gathering. At the same time, activities concerned with subsistence and for dealing with crises are conducted jointly with cooperation and give and take among the natives. Such activities are regulated by rules which assign joint responsibilities to persons in different roles. "Group survival often depends on inventing modes of cooperation in calamities, ways of redistributing the take to unsuccessful hunters, and rules for assigning responsibilities for support in case of death or illness" (Gilder, 1982:130). Because of the smallness of society and the limited resource base, all depend on common resources. Thus reciprocal interdependence is merged with pooled interdependence in day-to-day activities as well as during periods of crisis. In contrast, in modern society, except in those instances of community emergencies during natural disasters (e.g., floods), day-do-day living and coping with crisis is largely an individual responsibility. Crises are guarded against not through the establishment of rules assigning responsibilities in joint efforts but by socializing risks. People pay into a common fund from which they may receive benefits during periods of crisis. Pooled and reciprocal interdependence are divorced. The result is the problem of moral hazards. Today, "millions of citizens are coming to believe that their best chance of striking it rich comes not...from health, but from opportune disability

...Most fundamentally, people experience a steady erosion of the link between conduct and its consequences, effort and reward, merit and remuneration" (Gilder, 1982:113). This is because insurance against risk is not built into the structure and organization of group life. The moral code that people come to the aid of individuals in trouble is eroded as is the concern with how one's conduct may adversely affect the fate of others. One does not see that he or she has been helped by others (fellow policyholders) during periods of crisis. Hence feelings of mutual dependence and allegiance do not exist. By the same token, people do not see how their own actions and crises have an adverse influence on people who may be perfect strangers; premiums of fellow policyholders may increase but this is mediated by a third party so that one does not usually see that his or her own actions and circumstance may contribute to the added expense of others. Pooled interdependence does not have the underlying support of reciprocal interdependence, as in small primitive societies.

## Mutual-Aid Societies of Europe

Although government health insurance is usually traced to the introduction of a national compulsory program in Germany in 1883, it actually had its European origin in industry-wide and locally-based mutal-aid societies, some of which date to the thirteenth century (Light, Liebfried and Tennstedt, 1986:78) The formal national and compulsory systems developed out of these societies. Rubinow stated in 1916: "The beginnings of systematic sickness insurance are to be looked for in cooperative efforts of workers themselves [in the form of mutual relief or mutual aid]...thus a system of [national compulsory] insurance grew up out of a system of mutual help" (Rubinow, 1916, 224). By the time compulsory government insurance programs were introduced,

> Europe was covered by a network of...voluntary associations.... Associations of working men (and to a smaller extent other social groups such as salaried employees, farmers, etc.) for purposes of mutual aid and mainly in the cases of sickness, had reached a very substantial part of Europe's population. And these associations have played a very important role in European life. For that reason they have long attracted attention of government and legislation (Rubinow, 1934:171–172).

These associations were not eliminated by the new government plans. On the contrary, they were incorporated into the state programs.

Only when no such associations exist[ed] [did] the general government authorities undertake [the functions of mutual-aid societies]. In other words, the German state did not destroy anything in carrying its national plan of insurance through. It left the existing mutual-aid institutions, recognizing their tremendous educational as well as administrative value, and compelled the organization of many similar new ones.... All types of existing sick-benefit organizations were, therefore, pre-served, and where none existed, new ones were to be organized (Rubinow, 1916:250).

Similarly, Gilbert (1960: chapter 6) observed that the National Health Insurance plan of 1911 in England did not replace the "friendly societies" so much as it incorporated them into a national system of health insurance.

Thus, government plans were built on mutual-aid societies, first in the form of subsidies, and then eventually as their replacement. Because the resources of the voluntary societies were so limited, their replacement by more systematic government plans was considered necessary. The societies were financially unstable, had weak management, and had no actuarial accounting. Also, since they were organized along neighborhood, community, occupational, or industry lines, even in the aggregate they failed to provide protection for the total population:

the voluntary principle was found wanting, primarily for two reasons; first, because it failed to make insurance universal, and left without protection those most in need of it; second, because it failed to lift the burden of the working class as such, as long as the state remained aloof, satisfying itself with the policeman's function of control and regulation. The rapid growth of this voluntary form of subsidies, proved not only the great need of this form of social protection, but also the inability of the workingman to provide it by his own means (Rubinow, 1916:249).

At the same time, the transformation to government programs led to qualitative changes in social relations. Gradually, as government programs replaced the mutual-aid societies (the "friendly societies" of England, the "*Societés de Secours Mutuel*" of France).

...relationships became more formal, acquired the character of a contractual obligation, contributions to them became more of a premium and less of a voluntary contribution out of the goodness of one's heart (Rubinow, 1934:171).

Government insurance served to put relations between "policyholders" on a contractual basis and the basis for interdependence moved from reciprocal interdependence to pooled interdependence. Since reciprocal interdependence more than pooled interdependence promotes feelings of solidarity and collective allegiance, the decline in reciprocal interdependence led to a decline in moral community and, by implication, to an increase in the problem of social control via moral hazards.

> The enormous advantage of these friendly or mutual benefit societies was claimed to be that they build up character at the same time that they yielded necessary financial assistance. Most of these claims are eminently sound. There is no doubt that the average intelligence, moral and economic strength of members of these organizations in all countries is very much higher than of the workingmen outside these organizations (Rubinow, 1916:231).

Thus, when viewed from the perspective of the needs to which mutual-aid societies and government programs responded and the types of social relations that prevailed, the relationship between mutual-aid societies and government insurance programs represents a paradox. Both responded to the same needs, and the more systematic and comprehensive national programs were a natural development out of the less systematic, more narrowly based mutual-benefit programs; from the standpoint of building institutions and responding to the needs of the population, the relationship between the two responses is one of continuity. But in terms of social relations a qualitative tranformation occurred. Mutual-aid societies were based largely on relations among persons in a local setting in which the needs of individuals are known and can be responded to spontaneously by other members. While the government programs may assure that the needs of more persons are met on a more systematic basis, the response is not as spontaneous as it is when "insurance" is organized on a local basis and intertwined with moral community. "Any degree of compulsory government control, it was argued [by those who defended mutual-aid societies], might interfere with the development of the small village or neighborhood sick-benefit society, which naturally arises out of local needs and may be the seeds of a stronger [social] institution" (Rubinow, 1916:237). While something is gained with the introduction of government insurance, something is also lost.

The role of reciprocal interdependence and moral community, and the absence of the moral hazard problem, is particularly clear among mutual-aid societies of American ethnic groups.

## Mutual-Aid Societies Among American Ethnic Groups

In the eighteenth and nineteenth centuries, black Americans formed mutual-aid societies in order to provide aid for members during sickness and death. Thus risks were shared by members of the society, and the benefits were concentrated on those who were victims of crisis. The society "scrutinized the life conduct of members and expelled many for loose living" (Light, 1972:153). Consequently, "the first insurance enterprise among Negroes had the rather large and difficult task of fostering the advance in morals as well as the economic advancement of the group" (Trent, nd:16). In other words, insurance was organized around a moral community. Individuals were obligated to live righteous lives and to come to the aid of others in time of need. With the coming of modern insurance, this changed:

*Not*

*M.H.*

> Church beneficials and mutual-aid societies dominated black insurance until 1880. Thereafter, both congregational and mutual-aid societies gave way to fraternal orders which offered "features." The church beneficials never recovered their earlier importance.... Between 1880 and 1910 the fraternal orders experienced their "Golden Age." The expansion of fraternalism in this period was largely attributable to the discovery of "added insurance to the other benefits they offer their members.".... Unlike the earlier church beneficial societies, the fraternal insurers were regional and national in scope.... More organizations permitted the fraternal orders to pay higher benefits than those possible in purely local organization such as the church beneficials. Members paid a premium to the national order, and the national order provided individual members with insurance protection. Impersonal administration replaced face-to-face mutual aid.... The businesslike organization of fraternal insurance tended to shift the basis of operation from assessment to actuarial insurance and from noncontractual to contractual obligation. Actuarial insurance encouraged the passive participation of persons whose only connection to the lodge was the premium payment. Diffuse, affectively charged social obligation to persons gave way increasingly to specific contractual obligation to an organization. The fraternal community took on the characteristics of a *Gesellschaft* (Light, 1972: 153–155; quotation marks in original but source of quote not indicated).

A moral community organized around mutual aid disappeared and was replaced with contractual relationships based exclusively on pooled interdependence. "In the legal-reserve insurance companies, the 'social and moral' element was entirely suppressed. The commercial insurers made no attempt to influence the conduct of those who paid their premiums regularly. The businesslike attitude obviously precluded the development of moral solidarity among those insured by a particular company" (Light, 1972:159). The only thing the insured had in common (other than common background, ethnic heritage, and so forth) was the fact that they paid into the same fund and were dependent on that fund during periods of crisis. This does not lead to a sense of moral commitment to others with respect to outcomes that are insured against. Because insurance was on an ecoıic contractual basis, "poor blacks were covered. . .only as long as they ᵖᵘd regular premiums." But among mutual-aid societies, "so long as one's friends or relatives were alive, one could depend on their help in a crisis" (Light, 1972:162). Because of the reciprocal interdependence characteristic of these societies, the problems that a person's crisis created for others were known and visible to the victim. This inhibited any tendency to feign misfortune in order to receive unearned benefits. The norms of a moral community alleviated the problem of moral hazards

More than just moral norms were involved, however. The fact that members of mutual-benefit societies were frequently known to each other and were expected to come to other member's assistance in time of need made for reciprocal interdependence. The fact that these societies had "the old idea of insurance as a philanthropic measure of relief" and "their purpose [as] charity, not business" (Commons, 1919:801) did not mean that economic interdependence did not also keep the problem of moral hazards within bounds. The economist John R. Commons, a strong advocate of universal government health insurance, observed that members "assess themselves, and if expenses go up, their assessments go up." Consequently, members "are careful to watch their members and to prevent them from feigning sickness and getting the benefits fraudulently" (Commons, 1919:801). Commons may have been unaware of the cost of moral hazards that could accompany government-sponsored health-insurance programs, but his view of the mechanism of social control among members of mutual-benefit societies was certainly insightful.

Control of moral hazards through reciprocal dependence is particularly clear in the analysis of the mutual aid of the fong, clan, and kenjinkai among the Chinese and Japanese. "In fong, clan, and kenjinkai, provisions for social welfare took the form of nonactuarial mutual-aid. When a member was in trouble, others helped him with goods in kind, services, and money.... [The] moral communites [were] intensely solidary and mutually supportive" (Light, 1972:160). The groups were small so that members in need of help could not anticipate windfall rewards during times of crisis or the pretense of crisis. At the same time, benefits were extremely valuable. "If sick, a member could expect friends to operate his store or get him into a hospital for treatment.... If he were unemployed, a member's friends would help him find a job." Insurance companies which replaced mutual-aid societies did not provide these diffuse relations and offer these services. "The insurance company would provide the wherewithal to purchase goods and services; but friends could provide goods in kind and services for free. Obviously there could be no question of chiseling benefits from fong or kinjinkai, because one did not chisel from friends and friends were sure to know when one claimed benefits one did not deserve." This changed with the development of insurance companies based on pooled interdependence because "fraudulent insurance claims did not affect friends directly" (Light, 1972:161).

Today, Chinese and Japanese in America also have revolving credit societies, called the *Tanomoshi* and *Hui*, in which members pool their resources and provide credit to individuals to help them establish businesses. The specific relations based on pooled interdependence from these societies are reinforced by more diffuse relations.

> Japanese-Americans' membership in *Tanomoshi* is limited strictly by the geographical regions of birth in Japan, and by the region in Japan from which one's ancestors came. Among the Chinese-Americans, membership in a *Hui* is limited to those within the kinship network. Thus one can only be born into a *Tanomoshi* or a *Hui*, and one can never escape from the network of familiar, communal, social, religious, and economic ties that bind these groups together. If a member should fail to make good on his obligation, members of his family would certainly take up his obligation or else pay the very high price of having all branches of the family shut out of the economic and social network of the community (Ouchi, 1981:73).

It is now possible to reconcile Thompson's contention that there has been a progression from societies based relatively more on reciprocal interdependence with the argument that there has been an increase in the growth of insurance, which is characterized by pooled interdependence. First of all, as already noted, in simple societies and the mutual-aid societies of ethnic groups, reciprocal interdependence strengthens ties based on pooled interdependence and fosters the development of a moral community. Individuals are submerged in groups. In modern society, individuals are more detached and only loosely connected with groups, sometimes even their kinship units. The division of labor has also increased, so that there are many nations, organizations, and occupations doing different things on which other nations, organizations, and occupations depend. At the national, organizational, and occupational levels, reciprocal interdependence has increased. Furthermore, such interdependence may have significant consequences for individuals who are powerless to change the actions that large collective units may take. Indeed, the actions of one unit may have consequences for another unit and this, in turn, has implications for the welfare of individuals. For example, the closing of an automobile assembly plant in Dayton affects tire plants in Toledo, and the individual workers in both are adversely affected. Members of either group cannot do much if anything to improve their own employment situations or the situation of the other group. They can, however, protect themselves against unemployment with unemployment insurance. Although individual workers in Dayton and in Toledo are not related in terms of mutual aid and reciprocal interdependence, they are related in terms of pooled interdependence. The resulting interconnectedness is fragile, however.

People have probably not shifted to greater socialization of risk through insurance programs because they are less risk-adverse than in the past. What has happened is that individuals can no longer protect against risk as much through relationships based on reciprocal interdependence. The range and strength of diffuse relations (e.g, kinship relations) has decreased. People have therefore turned more to pooled interdependence as a result, though relations of mutual aid continue to exist in attenuated form among kinship units. Many of the reciprocal interdependencies that do exist today are due to broad social, political, and economic forces that are beyond the control of individuals. This itself creates uncertainty and the need for pooled interdependence. "Any single decision is seen today as both influenced by and influencing other decisions. Interdependence in a national economy is the result mainly of urbanization and technological complexities" (Aharoni, 1981:8). Living in close urban quarters and in an economy where decisions in one sector or region have major implications for other sectors and regions, individuals are buffeted about by events and processes over which they have no control. They turn to pooled interdependence for protection. This, however, is a thin social bond.

This in turn has implications for moral community. Whether relations of mutual aid deteriorated and were replaced by insurance or whether insurance drove out relations of mutual aid could be debated. Probably each had an effect on the other. The point is, however, that the transformation to relations based more on pooled interdependence has important implications for the place of the individual in society, his (her) allegiance and commitment to others, and to the presence of a moral community.

> ...there is enough general truth in the depiction of American society as mobile, urban, individualistic, atomized, secular, and rationalist that the old modes of private assistance and religious discipline no longer can suffice. The insurance companies drove out the parochial charities, funeral societies, and mutual-aid groups by offering much larger benefits at far lower cost, while at the same time extended coverage to citizens of the new international economy and secular rationalistic culture who lacked reliable affiliations to church, kin, and com-

munity. Where the division of labor was expanded and specialized, new modes of cooperation were formed to accomodate it (Gilder, 1982:134).

The new modes of cooperation take the form of pooled interdependence with the attendant problems of social control, namely, moral hazards.

The moral hazard problem has led some authorities, such as Martin S. Feldstein, to conclude that health insurance, or at least hospital insurance, has undoubtedly been the single most important factor in the escalation of medical costs in the United States in the recent past. (Feldstein's analysis is reviewed in chapter 6.) The foregoing analysis is not necessarily inconsistent with this, though it does indicate that moral hazards and weakened social control are not inherent in insurance, but only in insurance programs, such as those existing in modern society where relations are characterized by pooled interdependence. It is pooled interdependence rather than insurance per se that leads to the moral hazard problem.

Although there has been a historical movement toward pooled interdependence with respect to the assurance of medical care and protection of great economic loss due to the receipt of such care, the effect of pooled interdependence on the moral hazard problem is not the same in all countries. Even if insurance coverage is approximately the same in most industrial countries, national expenditures for medical care vary widely. The adverse effects of pooled interdependence may be moderated by the cultural values and patterns, institutions of society, and the nature of the medical care system. Comparison of Japan and the United States make the point clear.

## Health Insurance and Expenditures for Medical Care in Japan

It is estimated that the United States spent approximately $1,500 per person for medical care in 1984, whereas Japan spent only about $500 (Macrea, 1984:18). Although expenditures for medical care as a percentage of the gross national product have continuously risen over time in Japan (from 1955 to 1974), and may be due to increases in insurance coverage (Ohmura, 1978:497), the percentage for the United States has also risen and has been substantially higher for all years (Ohmura, 1978).[1] At the same time, evidence would indicate that the Japanese are at least as healthy as the Americans (see next chapter). Views vary on the adequacy of health-insurance protection provided for the Japanese. Some argue that in comparison to the plans of Western Europe, Japan's coverage is inadequate.

an's level of insurance payments from medical and pension insurance is insufficient. In the case of medical insurance, total amount of medical expenses incurred is paid to the insured, while 70 percent of such expenses is paid to the family members of the insured (as to National Health Insurance, only 70 percent of medical expenses incurred is paid to both the insured and the family members of the insured). Thus, 30 percent of incurred medical expenses must be paid by the patient when the patient is one of the family members of the insured (in the case of National Health Insurance, whether the patient is the insured or one of the family members of the insured). When hospitalized, in general, special charges for beds and fees for nurses have to be paid. Such a heavy burden on the patient is almost non-existent in the developed countries of the West (The Tsuneto Yano Memorial Society [Yano-Tsuneto Kinenkai] under the direction of Ichiro Yano, 1980:386).

However, others believe that the "average [Japanese is] extremely well protected against medical expenses through national health insurance schemes" (Whitaker et al., 1974:136). Some believe the coverage is superior to that for Americans. William Caudill concludes that "Japan has a national health insurance system with extensive coverage including, for example, up to three years of hospitalization for mental illness in private hospitals, and cheap, easily available abortion, while the United States largely relies on an antiquated and costly system of private health insurance" (Caudill, 1976:162).

The fact is, however, that insurance coverage for Japan and the United States is quite similar. Although a recent national survey of the United States (Aday, Fleming, and Andersen, 1984) indicates that in 1982 about 90% of the population is covered by health insurance in comparison to a reported figure for Japan of virtually 100% (Christopher, 1983:237), the level of coverage is approximately the same. Total personal expenditures paid by private insurance and the government in the United States in 1980 was 66.2% (U.S. Department of Health and Human Services, 1981:202). This is almost identical to the percentage for Japan given by Christopher (1983:237), who concludes that "as a general rule, health insurance in Japan pays only about two-thirds of a patient's bills...."[2]

In sum, it appears that virtually all Japanese citizens have some form of health insurance, which is higher than in the United States and about the same for many other industrialized countries. The amount of total coverage, however, is less than that in most industrialized countries but approximately what is in the United States. Certainly in comparison to the United States, if health insurance is an important (some say the single most important) factor in national expenditures on health care, the expenditures in Japan should be about on par with those in the United States when in fact they are much lower.

Furthermore, the Japanese view of mild illness and the way others should respond to persons with mild physical complaints suggest that the expenditures in Japan would be even larger than expenditures in the United States.

### Cultural Values and Behavior Patterns

On the basis of a review of the evidence of personality studies of the Japanese, Caudill reports "a strong hypochondriacal tendency" among the Japanese (Caudill, 1976:163). He also states, but gives no data, that for the adults "the average number of days taken off from work because of sickness is considerably greater in Japan than in the United States." He believes that since the general health of Japanese and Americans is comparable, "this indicates a more lenient attitude by Japanese employers about time off for sickness, and a greater amount of self-indulgence concerning minor illnesses on the part of the Japanese" (Caudill, 1976:161). He believes that illness behavior and self-indulgence is related to general expectations about individual behavior and to behavior patterns that are encouraged during infancy. "I am struck by the fact that the responses of infants are in line with general expectations for behavior in the two cultures: in America, that the individual should be physically and verbally assertive; and in Japan, that he should be physically and verbally restrained" (Caudill, 1976:166). Whereas the Japanese mother is indulgent when the child has a minor illness, the American mother "encourages her child to care for himself" (Caudill, 1976:175). In summarizing, he concludes: "Japanese tend to be hypochondriacal and to have permissive and sympathetic attitudes about the occurrence and treatment of minor illness. Behavior in infancy and early childhood seem to presage and lay the groundwork for these adult attitudes toward the body and treatment of its ills" (Caudill, 1976:175).

This "hypochondriacal tendency" and the permissive attitudes of others toward illness would seem to be inconsistent with the low expenditure on health. This tendency and level of insurance coverage would suggest that expenditures for medical care would be much higher, at least in comparison to the United States. Other factors are important in level of expenditure, however. In particular, Japan is unique among industrialized countries in retaining a strong kinship structure.

### Kinship Organization

Traditionally, extended kinship ties have been strong in Japan. The emphasis is not just on lineal authority and family line but on the family as a corporate unit, so that in some instances members of the unit may not themselves be blood-related to other members. (This is reflected in the mutual-aid societies of the Japanese-American, as described above.) This is not just a matter of tradition but is also related to present-day economic realities. "Present Japanese wages and salaries are seldom sufficient to permit an individual to live 'by himself.' They reflect an underlying premise that the individual is part of a corporate family unit to which all members are able to contribute financially" (Caudill and Scarr, 1974:55). This is related in two ways to illness, medical care, and possibly to expenditures.

First, family relations reinforce the hypochondriacal tendencies mentioned above. On the basis of interview responses to a set of picture cards, Caudill concludes "that minor illness in Japan has a very egosyntonic quality. People rather welcome the chance to be mildly sick if this involves staying at home and being cared for by others" (Caudill, 1976:174). The relationship of interdependence among family members and personality is indicated in the following quote from Caudill (1976:164, 165):

> Both the enjoyable and communicative (symbolic) aspects of mild illness rest on the assumption that family members consider themselves as an interdependent group in which the needs of one member will be taken care of by another.... the Japanese have a somewhat different set of attitudes toward and behavior concerning body management than Americans. These differences occur within the context of rather different personality structures in the two countries—the emphasis in Japan on the interdependency of people, the use of physical rather than verbal communication, and the expectation that it is legitimate to rely and presume upon the benevolence of others.

It is not clear why the hypochondriacal tendency among the Japanese and the tendency of others to be sympathetic to minor complaints apparently do not create upward pressures on the costs of medical care. It may be because the caring is done by family members, and indeed, in light of the evidence, the rewards of being cared for by family members may give rise to the apparent tendency to make a great deal about minor problems and illnesses. While there are no data comparing Japan with other countries with respect to the comparative frequency with which they visit physicians when they are ill, one national survey in 1969 reported "that of the total number of disease and injuries occurring, 60 percent of the cases consulted either a physician or a dentist and 35.5 percent treated themselves with home remedies" (Whitaker et al., 1974:135). The "home remedies" would have probably involved the caring activities of other members of the household.

Second, elderly members of households are cared for by younger members. This has traditionally been the case, but even today family elders continue "to elicit obedience, deference, and economic support from their grown children. . . . at no time in the past hundred years has there been a period in which the demands or rights of the elders. . .been simply neglected or cast aside by the growing children" (Goode, 1975:324). Extended family relations and not just ties based on economic interdependence are still strong. Even today, "the number of families in which grandparents have never lived with their children and grandchildren is relatively small" (Wagatsuma, 1977:185). Industrialization has no doubt brought about changes in family life (Samuna, 1978). Nevertheless, in a survey of 160,000 "young people," a total of 83.5% indicated their intention to support their parents unconditionally ("no matter what"— 29.8%) or with some qualification ("as much as my financial situation allows"—53.7%). Only 2.8% "wanted their parents to support themselves or to rely upon public facilities and welfare programs" (Wagatsuma, 1977:185). Another survey, which compared youths and adults in Germany, Japan, and the United States, produced the following results. Respondents were asked, "Is it preferable for parents to live with their adult children?" For Japanese, 71.2% of youths and 70.2% of adults replied affirmatively in comparison to 23.0% and 11.5% of American youths and adults, and 13.3% and 17.7% German youths and adults (Wagatsuma, 1977:186, table 2). The difference is not just in sentiment and attitudes; intergenerational ties as reflected in living arrangements are stronger in Japan. For example, only 14.3% males and 10.2% females above 60 live alone or only with their spouse in Japan, while about 60% of males and 50% females do so in the United States, and in some other Western countries the percentage is higher (Wagatsuma, 1977:186). "A majority of elderly Japanese (80.3% males and 82.7% of females) live with their married or unmarried children, while comparable figures for Western societies run about 30 percent or less" (Wagatsuma, 1977:186).

While neither the presence of strong collateral and lineal ties reveal anything, as such, about the relationship between illness and medical expenditures, they are certainly suggestive. First, as noted above, in contrast to the United States (and perhaps other Western industrial countries as well), there is a strong tendency in Japan to rely on family members for caring activities, though the tendency may not be as strong today as in the past (Samuma, 1978). Despite a greater apparent fear about illness, the Japanese may be less reluctant to consult professional healers when they have a mild illness. The relations of kinship apparently moderate the moral hazard problem that inheres in relations based on pooled interdependence as in modern health insurance plans. Second, since illness increases with age and since the elderly are more apt to live with younger family members, family members are relatively more apt than professional healers to care for older relatives in Japan. The national savings in medical expenditures may be substantial. It may be a major reason the number of physicians per capita is so low.

### Number of Physicians and Organization of Medical Care

Among 13 industrialized countries, Japan has the fewest physicians per capita (see next chapter), and this may also be a factor in her comparatively low expenditure for medical care. The fewer the physicians, the less the medical care, and, hence, the less serious moral hazards are apt to be. Since so many health services are initiated by physicians, fewer physicians would be expected to lead to lower expenditures (see Rushing, 1985).

In addition, the organization and financing of medical care are such that restraints are put on the cost of medical and hospital services. There are restraints on physicians hospitalizing patients that do not exist in many other countries, particularly the United States. There are fewer hospital beds per capita for one thing (Ohmura, 1978:493–494 and Tanaka, 1978:481). In addition, patients receiving hospital care are treated by hospital-based physicians (Broida, 1978). Therefore, a doctor who refers "his patients to a hospital [normally loses] all control over, and thus any income from, that patient. Consequently, there [is] a tendency among practitioners to delay hospitalization of seriously ill patients until the last possible moment" (Whitaker et al., 1974:137). Since hospital care accounts for such a large proportion of medical expenses, this restraint could amount to substantial savings in medical expenditures. In addition, "doctors' fees and hospital costs...are set by the government [and therefore] are kept relatively low..." (Christopher, 1983:237; see also Ohmura, 1978:487). One specific consequence of this is to keep the number of hospital personnel per 100 beds relatively small (Tanaka, 1978:481).[3]

When making comparisons between complex societies, conclusions as to the reason why one country differs from the others on one variable must be made with extreme caution. No one factor would probably account for all the difference. So it is with the cost of medical care. The lower health-service expenditure for Japan is no doubt due to a variety of factors. While the available evidence is fragmentary, certain conclusions are indicated. The lower medical costs in Japan are probably related to family, to the response that physical complaints elicit from others, and to the availability, organization, and financing of medical care. The lower cost of medical expenditures in Japan could not be due to a lower level of health insurance coverage since the coverage is as comprehensive as in the United States, though not as comprehensive as in most other industrial societies. Thus, the role of health insurance must be specified with respect to a number of other variables. This is consistent with the conclusion of other studies which have found no particular relationship between national expenditures and method of financing of medical care (Glaser, 1979; White, 1975; and Organization for Economic Cooperation and Development, 1977). Even when the social relations of insurance plans are viewed in terms of pooled interdependence, which creates problems of social control (that is, moral hazards), the extent of the problem, as reflected in national expenditures for medical care, varies depending on the broader culture and institutional context. Hence, any conclusion that health insurance itself is the single most important factor in the rising cost of medical care is a gross overstatement.

### Private and Public Insurance

In concluding this chapter, a few words about the differences between private and public insurance are in order. The social relations that are formed by modern insurance plans and pooled interdependence are essentially the same whether the insurance is private or public. The network of relations so formed connect individuals only to the extent that they are dependent on common resources. There is no direct relationship between them by virtue of this dependence. Private no less than public insurance leads to weak or nonexistent feelings of allegiance and commitment to those with whom one is interdependent. With the qualification that the effect of any structural form will be modified by the broader culture and institutional context in which the form exists, both private and public insurance create problems of social control, that is, moral hazards. They also have similar psychological effects and similar consequences for social integration and cohesion.

There are differences between the two types of insurance, to be sure. Public insurance is more apt to be introduced, or at least to be rationalized, in terms of the public interest. Another difference is that private insurance premiums are based, or tend to be based, on actuarial experience and projections, though the actuarial data and projections are far less precise than is commonly assumed. In general, there is a direct relationship between the cost of the premium and the risk involved. An automobile driver with a poor driving record pays a higher premium than one with a good record; a person with a chronic health condition or a history of a chronic condition pays a higher premium than a person in good health, and sometimes the former cannot get insurance at all, or if he (she) does, the insurance may not cover the preexisting condition or cover it only after a period of time has lapsed. In private insurance effort is made to bring premiums into line with the risks insured against and the probable benefits received. This is much less the case with public insurance, such as for unemployment, disability, and sickness, or for old-age assistance. While in some instances the level of benefits depends to some extent on the premiums (or taxes) paid, as with old-age assistance in the Social Security program, the protection or potential benefit provided by public insurance is more apt to be the same for all policyholders.

Another difference is that whereas both public and private insurance socialize risk and redistribute wealth, only public insurance is directed at specific groups in need. For example, public health insurance may distribute medical care across age and economic groups on the basis of need, but there is no such effort to do this with private health insurance. This difference is related to another difference, and this is that the recipients of benefits from public insurance do not always pay premiums. For example, Medicaid provides medical care for the indigent, but the premium (tax) for such care is paid by other members of society. In private insurance, to be a recipient of benefits one must be one of the premium payers (or in some instances, a dependent of a payer).

Such differences are important from the standpoint of public policy and are the source of much political debate. Some persons are philosophically opposed to public insurance programs, whereas others believe that commercial insurance carriers exploit the public. The motives behind the two types of insurance may be quite different; public insurance is intended to redistribute income, wealth, and opportunity as well as raise the level of health and productivity of a nation, whereas the motive behind private insurance is to make a profit. But in terms of consequences for social relations, moral community, and social control and moral hazards, differences are matters of degree rather than kind. Private insurance probably guards against moral hazards somewhat better than public insurance, at least for certain types of insurance, by raising premiums to bring them in line with the risks. In general, however, the nature of social relations and social control is the same. This is particularly true for health insurance since so much private health insurance is based on the actuarial experience of groups (e.g., employees of organizations) rather than of individuals.

Therefore, the premiums of individuals who have chronic illnesses, or whose dependents have chronic illnesses, pay the same premium as persons whose risks are less. For these reasons, as well as the fact that in both private and public insurance reimbursement for medical services in the United States has been traditionally shaped largely by fees and charges that are customary in a community and by what providers of services say they should be, both private and public insurance have similar social consequences. Of course, public insurance is more apt to lead, or is intended to lead, to the redistribution of medical care, and it is more apt than most forms of private insurance to encourage individuals to identify with a collective unit (the state of society). While these differences are noted in subsequent chapters, similarities rather than differences are emphasized.

## Notes

1. Ohmura (1978) observes that the figures for medical care expenditures for Japan are not strictly comparable to those of the United States. The Japanese figures include expenditures for items that are not included in the figures for the United States, so that if they were included in U.S. figures the difference in expenditures would not be as large. After making adjustment in the U.S. figures, Ohmura's figures indicate that, as a percentage of GNP, when expenditures reported for the United States are made comparable to those for Japan, they are about 15% lower on the average for the years 1955–1974. U.S. figures used in the calculation are from Worthington (1975).

2. There are three types of medical insurance in Japan. One plan is for establishments that have five or more regular workers. These plans are administered either by the government or by a licensed health society. In 1971 over 16 million workers and their dependents were covered by this type of plan. Another plan exists for work establishments which employ more than 300 workers. Upon approval of the Ministry of Health and Welfare and the concurrence of at least half their employees, employers may form a health insurance society. Nearly 21.2 million workers and their dependents were covered by this plan (Whitaker et al., 1974:166). By the end of 1979, 71.5 million, or about 62% of the population, were covered by the first two plans in connection with employment, and 44.6 million, or about 38%, were covered by the national insurance plan (Statistics Bureau of Japan, 1982:121; see also Steliske, 1982).

3. These factors along with those of cultural values and kinship organization serve to highlight a potential intersection of medical technology, as it relates to increases in the cost of medical care, and other factors. While insurance may encourage the use of more new technology in medical care, as Feldstein (1971) contends, other factors are involved. The financial restraint on hospitals is one obvious factor. In addition, however, the fact that the health status of the Japanese is better than that of most other industrial countries (see next chapter) indicates that other factors are probably more important than medical technology in the health of a nation. Along with the section on kinship organization, the lower cost of medical care may suggest that the apparently more rational response (increases in sophisticated technology) in the United States is really not the most rational at all because it leads to a much higher economic cost for a small return in terms of health status. It might also suggest that comparable health outcomes for the population may be achieved by cohesive

kinship units as well as by sophisticated and expensive technology; and it may suggest, even more than studies of preliterate societies by anthropologists, that the extended cohesive kinship unit is a functional alternative to health insurance in reducing uncertainty and risk concerning illness and its economic consequences. Strengthening the kinship unit in modern society and having sick people cared for more in the home would reduce the cost of health services. However, if this is not a policy option, the role of health insurance in preserving the strength of a weak family unit becomes evident. Figures on Japan's capital investment in medical technology and how Japan compares with other industrialized countries are not available, though the use of technology has increased over time (Ohmura, 1978:494), and this appears to be related to the growth of insurance coverage (see Broida and Maeda, 1978). According to Aaron and Schwartz (1984:71), Japan has as many computer tomography scanners as the United States though it has only half as many people. This suggests that the difference between Japan and the United States in medical expenditure would not be in Japan's lower investment and utilization of medical technology.

## References

Aaron, Henry J., and William B. Schwartz. *The Painful Prescription: Rationing Hospital Care*. Washington, DC: The Brookings Institution, 1984.

Aday, Lu Ann, Gretchen V. Fleming, and Ronald M. Andersen. *Access to Medical Care in the U.S.: Who Has It, Who Doesn't*. Chicago: Pluribus Press, 1984.

Aharoni, Yair. *The No-Risk Society*. Chatham, NJ: Chatham House Publishers, Inc., 1981.

Broida, Joel H. "Case-Study of Physicians' Practice in the Ambulatory Medical Care Setting—Japan." *Social Science and Medicine* 12A (November 1978): 555–561.

Broida, Joel H., and Nobuo Maeda. "Japan's High-Cost Illness Insurance Program: A Study of Its First Three Years, 1974–76." *Public Health Reports* 93 (No. 2, 1978):153–160.

Caudill, William. "The Cultural and Interpersonal Context of Everyday Health and Illness in Japan and America." In Charles Leslie (ed.), *Asian Medical Systems: A Comparative Study*, pp. 159–177. Berkeley: University of California Press, 1976.

Caudill, William, and Harry A. Scarr. "Japanese Value Orientations and Culture Change." In Takie Sugiuama Libra and William P. Lebra (eds.), *Japanese Culture and Behavior: Selected Readings*, pp. 37–89. Honolulu: The University Press of Hawaii, 1974.

Christopher, Robert C. *The Japanese Mind: The Goliath Explained*. New York: Linden Press, Simon and Schuster, 1983.

Commons, John R. "A Reconstruction Health Program." *The Survey* (September 6, 1919):798–834.

Durkheim, Emile. *The Division of Labor in Society*. Glencoe, IL: The Free Press, 1949.

Feldstein, Martin S. *The Rising Costs of Hospital Care*. Washington, DC: Information Resources Press, 1971.

Gilbert, Bentley B. *The Evolution of National Insurance in Great Britain: The Origins of the Welfare State*. London: Michael Joseph Limited, 1960.

Gilder, George. *Wealth and Poverty*. New York: Bantam Books, 1982.

Glaser, William A. *Paying the Doctor*. Baltimore: The Johns Hopkins University Press, 1970.

Goode, William J. *World Revolution and Family Patterns*. New York: The Free Press, 1975.

Kimball, Spencer L. *Insurance and Public Policy: A Study in the Legal Implementation of Social and Economic Public Policy, Based on Wisconsin Records, 1835–1959*. Madison: University of Wisconsin Press, 1960.

Light, Donald W., Stephen Liefried, and Florian Tennstedt, "Social Medicine vs. Professional Dominance: The German Experience," *American Journal of Public Health* 76 (January 1986):78–83.

Light, Ivan H. *Ethnic Enterprise in America*. Berkeley: University of California Press, 1972.

Macrae, Norman. "Health Care International." *The Economist* 290 (April 28, 1984):17–34.

Organization for Economic Cooperation and Development (OECD). *OECD Studies in Resource Allocation*. No. 4. *Public Expenditures on Health*. Paris: OECD, 1977.

Ohmura, Junshiro. "Analysis of Factors Affecting the Need and Demand for Medical Care." *Social Science and Medicine* 12A (November 1978):485–496.

Ouchi, William G. *Theory Z*. Reading, MA: Addison-Wesley Publishing Company 1981.

Rubinow, I.M. *Social Insurance*. New York: Henry Holt and Company, 1934.

——————. *The Quest for Security*. New York: Henry Holt and Company, 1934.

Rushing, William A. "Social Factors in the Rise of Hospital Care." *Sociology of Health Care* 3 (Fall 1984):27–114.

Rushing, William A., and Mayer N. Zald (eds.). *Organizations and Beyond: Selected Essays of James D. Thompson*. Lexington, MA: D.C. Heath, 1976.

Samura, Kiyoski. "The Japanese Family in Relation to People's Health." *Social Science and Medicine* 12A (November 1978): 469–478.

Schroeder, Steven A., and Jonathan A. Showstack. "The Dynamics of Medical Technology Use: Analysis and Policy Options." In Stuart H. Altman and Robert Blendon (eds.), *Medical Technology: The Culprit Behind Health Care Costs?*, pp. 178–212. Washington, DC: U.S. Government Printing Office, 1979.

Statistics Bureau of Japan. *Statistical Handbook of Japan*. Tokyo: Prime Minister's Office, 1982.

Steslicke, William E. "Development of Health Insurance Policy in Japan." *Journal of Health Politics, Policy and Law* 7 (Spring 1982):197–226.

Tanaka, Tsuneo. "Medical Care in Japan, Yesterday, Today, and Tomorrow." *Social Science and Medicine* 12A (November 1978):479–483.

The Tsuneto Yano Memorial Society (Yano-Tsuneto Kinendai) under the supervision of Ichira Yano. *Nippon: A Chartered Survey of Japan—1980–81*. Tokyo: Kokusei-Sha, 1980.

Thompson, James D. *Organizations in Action*. New York: McGraw-Hill, 1967.

Trent, W. J., Jr. "Development of Negro Life Insurance Enterprise." Cited in Ivan H. Light, *Ethnic Enterprise in America*, p. 153. Berkeley: University of California Press, 1972. No publisher or date cited.

U.S. Department of Health and Human Services. *Health, United States—1981*. Washington, DC: U.S. Government Printing Office, 1981.

Watasuma, Herosi. "Some Aspects of the Contemporary Japanese Family: Once Confusian, Now Fatherless?" In Alice S. Rossi, Jerome Kagan, and Tamara K. Heraven (eds.), *The Family*, pp. 181–201. New York: W.W. Norton and Company, 1977.

Whitaker, Donald P., et al. *Area handbook of Japan*. 3rd ed. Washington, DC: U.S. Government Printing Office, 1974.

White, Kerr L. "International Comparisons of Medical Care." *Scientific American* 233 (August 1975):17–25.

Worthington, Nancy L. "National Health Expenditures, 1929–1974." *Social Security Bulletin* 37 (January 1975):3–19.

# 3 MEDICAL CARE: ACTUAL EFFECTS AND PUBLIC PERCEPTION

The rapidly escalating costs of medical care over the past quarter century, from 4.5% of the gross national product GNP in 1955 to 10.6% in 1984 (Levit, et al., 1985), has directed attention increasingly to aspects of the delivery, organization, and financing of medical care. Critics have claimed that there is excessive and unnecessary use of tests and procedures, too much duplication of facilities, and large inefficiencies in the organization of health services. Critics frequently focus on the "nonsystem" of medical care in which the various parts are not linked in a coherent pattern in which there is rational control over the allocation of resources. Many contend, therefore, that national resources employed in the medical area could be used better (that is, more rationally) if they were employed in other sectors. Others charge that it is the public's utilization of medical care that is irrational in that public expectations of the medical sector are frequently unrealistic. Still others claim that we spend too much for medical care for what we get, some contending we get little if any benefit at all, and a few believe the care we get does more harm than good. In this chapter I will review these issues by examining what people and society apparently do get from medical care and how people view its value. While this does not deal with health insurance per se, the review will be drawn upon in chapters that follow. It will help to put the role of health insurance in proper perspective.

In the 1970s a number of writings and studies suggested that medical care is much less effective than the public and many members of the medical sector appear to believe. In 1972, in an influential work, A. L. Cochrane (1972) calls attention to the fact that many conventional medical procedures and much medical technology are commonly used in medical practice when the effectiveness of those procedures and technology has not been demonstrated. Cochrane recommended, and many have supported the recommendation, that diagnostic and treatment procedures be subjected to more careful study. They should be scientifically studied using random clinical trials and proven to be effective before they are accepted in medical practice. In another assessment, David Mechanic concludes that there is an "overall lack of definitive evidence as to which health care practices really make a difference in illness outcomes. While standards for processes of care are readily formulated, it is difficult to demonstrate for most facets of care that such process norms have any clear relationship to outcomes that really matter" (Mechanic, 1978:331). He, too, urges more systematic study of medical procedures before they are adopted in practice.

Note that the argument is not that modern medical care is ineffective, but rather that the effectiveness of much medical care is simply not known and that medical care is not as effective as it *could* be (and more costly than it needs to be). Appropriate testing of new medical technology would be a corrective to the wasteful use of ineffective (or even harmful) procedures. The implication is that with better evaluation studies the outcomes of medical care—health and longevity—could be raised.

### The Historical Decline in Mortality Rates and Ill Health

In analyzing historical changes in mortality and morbidity, others come to quite different conclusions. For example, René Dubos (1959, 1968) argues that the achievement of health is an illusive goal. Effective medical care simply contributes to the development of a new set of diseases in society which replaces another set. The conquering of infectious diseases and the reduction of acute disease by medicine, which have also led to an extension of life expectancy, resulted in an increase in chronic disease and residual disability (disablements which accompany the effective treatment of chronic conditions). Modern medicine is a paradox (Somers and Somers, 1961); while life is preserved for an increasing proportion of the population, it is accompanied by increases in the proportion of the population who are also chronically ill and disabled.

> The demand [for medical care] grows rather than diminishes, despite all that has been achieved in the last fifty years, and shows little sign of slackening in the

foreseeable future. Old diseases have been mastered, but new ones take their place and the total burden of disease remains (Poynter, 1963:3).

The view that medical care leads to better health is called a mirage (Dubos, 1957).

In a particularly careful and thorough analysis, Thomas McKeown (1976) examines mortality rates since 1830 for England and Wales and convincingly demonstrates that declines in mortality from most infectious diseases began long before effective therapies (immunizations and antibiotics) were available. He contends that such declines were due primarily to increases in the food supply and nutrition; to the elimination of environmental hazards—namely, improvements in environmental hygiene, such as sewage systems, purification of water, and more sanitary preparation of food (e.g., pasteurization of milk); and to a reduction of population growth through reductions in the birth rates. Much that has been attributed to modern medicine was not due to modern medicine at all, or at least only a very small proportion was. While McKeown does not deny that clinical procedures need more careful study, he believes that improvements in clinical treatment will play a minor role in a nation's health.

In an analysis of the decline of mortality for infectious diseases in the United States from 1900 to 1973, McKinlay and McKinlay (1977) come to a similar conclusion. They find that almost all of the decline in mortality occurred in all but one of the diseases (poliomyelitis was the only exception) before medical treatments (e.g., penicillin for scarlet fever) were even introduced. Evidence indicates that the decline in mortality over time has not been due much, if at all, to curative medical care. If the mortality rate is taken as an index of a population's health, evidence challenges much traditional scientific and popular thought and leads to a "fundamental challenging heresy of modern times" because it states "that medical care (as it is traditionally conceived) is generally unrelated to improvement in the health of populations (as distinct from individuals)" (McKinlay and McKinlay, 1977:405). Particularly telling is the McKinlays' analysis of the relationship between the trend of expenditures for medical care and the decline in mortality. They observe that "*the beginning of the precipitate and still unrestrained rise in medical care expenditures began* [about 1955] *when nearly all (92 per cent) of the modern decline in mortality this century* [as of 1977] *had already occurred*" (McKinlay and McKinlay, 1977:414; authors' emphasis).

Despite the mounting evidence, the McKinlays observe that such evidence is often dismissed "as unthinkable in much the same way as the so-called heresies of former times. And this is despite a long history of support in popular and scientific writings as well as from able minds in a variety of disciplines" (McKinlay and McKinlay, 1977:405), though the evidence presented in most writings is not as compelling as that provided by McKeown and the McKinlays.

An argument used to counter this "heresy" is that the analysis is based on mortality data, which many consider to be flawed; they contain considerable error (e.g., misdiagnosis). The McKinlays observe that such error may not be as serious as is often thought, and in any case, mortality statistics have been used to *support* the view that medical care improves a population's health. If data are accepted as valid when they are thought to support one position, they must be accepted as valid when they support the opposite position:

> if such data constitute acceptable evidence in support of the presence of medicine, then it is not unreasonable, or illogical, to employ them in support of some opposing position....double standards of rigor seem to operate in the evaluation of different studies. But surprisingly, those which challenge prevailing myths or beliefs are subject to the most stringent methodological and statistical scrutiny, while supportive studies, which frequently employ the flimsiest impressionistic data and inappropriate techniques of analysis, receive general and uncritical acceptance (McKinlay and McKinlay, 1977:412).

Finally, a comprehensive study of the National Health Service in England from its inception in 1948 to the middle to late seventies sponsored by the United Kingdom Department of Health and Social Security (reported as The Black Report) found that greater availability of health services had not diminished class differences in ill health and death. It concluded that this was due to class differences in social and economic factors (income, education, housing, diet, employment, and conditions of work) rather than to class differences in health services (Gray, 1982). Since there has been a decline in the death rate and ill health in the population overall since 1948, the implication is that the decline has been due far more to overall improvements in living and working conditions than to medical care. (On this general point, see Fuchs, 1974.)

Therefore, studies of the historical decline in mortality and ill health provide virtually no support for the view that medical care has accounted for the decline in mortality and morbidity rates over time.

## Cross-National Evidence

The evidence against medical care is not limited to historical studies of mortality statistics. Differences between contemporary societies yield the

Table 3–1.  Health Care Expenditure as Percent of Gross National Product and Infant Mortality Rate for 1975 and 1976 for Nine Countries

| Country | Health care expenditures (1975)[1] | Infant mortality rate (1976)[2] |
|---|---|---|
| Australia | 7.0 | 14.3 |
| Canada | 7.1 | 14.3 |
| France | 8.1 | 12.5 |
| Federal Republic of Germany | 9.7 | 17.4 |
| Netherlands | 8.6 | 10.5 |
| Sweden | 8.7 | 8.7 |
| United Kingdom | 5.6[3] | 14.0 |
| United States | 8.4 | 15.2 |
| Japan | 4.0[4] | 9.3 |

[1]Source of data: Simanis and Coleman, 1980.
[2]Source of data: U.S. Department of Health, Education, and Welfare 1978:178. Data for Australia and Canada are for 1975.
[3]Data for England and Wales.
[4]Source of data: U.S. Department of Health, Education and Welfare, 1978:381.
*rho* = .18

Table 3–2.  Health Care Expenditures as Percent of Gross National Product and Physicians per 100,000 for 13 Countries

| Country | Physicians per 100,000 | Infant mortality rate[2] |
|---|---|---|
| Canada | 17.3 (1976)[1] | 14.3 |
| Australia | 13.9 (1972) | 14.3 |
| Sweden | 17.1 (1975) | 8.7 |
| England and Wales | 13.1 (1974) | 14.0 |
| Netherlands | 16.6 (1976) | 10.5 |
| German Democratic Republic | 19.1 (1976) | 14.1 |
| German Federal Republic | 19.9 (1975) | 17.4 |
| France | 14.7 (1975) | 12.5 |
| Switzerland | 19.1 (1976) | 10.5 |
| Italy | 20.6 (1974) | 19.1 |
| Israel | 28.7 (1973) | 22.9 |
| Japan | 11.8 (1975) | 5.3 |
| United States | 17.8 (1976) | 15.2 |

[1]Figure in parentheses is for latest year. Source of data: U.S. Department of Health, Education, and Welfare (1978:338).
[2]Source of data: U.S. Department of Health, Education, and Welfare (1978:178). Infant mortality for Australia and Canada for 1975.
*rho* = 0.66

47

same conclusion. International comparisons for industrialized countries indicate that the national resources devoted to health care are not positively related to health status measures, such as lower infant mortality, the most widely used single index of health status for large populations. For eight such countries, the Spearman rank correlation (*rho*) between mortality rates and national expenditures on health care is 0.18 (see table 3–1), and for 13 countries, the *rho* is 0.66 for number of physicians per 100,000 population (see table 3–2). The correlations are *opposite* in directions to what one would expect if level of medical care had a beneficial effect on infant mortality. However, for 12 industralized countries, the rank correlation is negative though weak (−0.20) for hospital beds per 1,000 population (see table 3–3).

The global index of infant mortality is, of course, only one criterion to use in assessing the effectiveness of medical care (Levine, Feldman, and Elinson, 1983). Also since differences in infant mortality are a function of a number of things for societies as diverse politically, culturally, and economically as those in tables 3–1, 3–2, and 3–3, conclusions are to be drawn with care. Even so, it is reasonable to expect at least modest

Table 3–3. Number of Hospital Beds per 1,000 Population and Infant Mortality Rate for 12 Countries

| Country | Hospital beds per 10,000 | Infant mortality rate (1976)[2] |
|---|---|---|
| Canada | 5.7 (1975)[1] | 14.3 |
| United States | 4.9 (1976) | 15.2 |
| Sweden | 7.2 (1975) | 8.7 |
| Netherlands | 4.8 (1976) | 10.5 |
| German Democratic Republic | 8.5 (1976) | 14.1 |
| German Federal Republic | 7.0 (1975) | 17.4 |
| France | 8.1 (1974) | 12.5 |
| Switzerland | 5.8 (1976) | 10.5 |
| Italy | 7.4 (1974) | 19.1 |
| Israel | 3.4 (1976) | 22.9 |
| Japan | 6.4 (1975) | 9.3 |
| Australia | 6.7 (1977) | 1.43 |

[1]Figure in parentheses is for latest year. Source of data: U.S. Department of Health, Education, and Welfare (1978:376).

[2]Source of data: U.S. Department of Health, Education, and Welfare (1978:178). Data for Australia and Canada for 1975.

*rho* = −0.20

negative correlations between such an index and medical resources. (Similar results are obtained for life expectancy; results not shown.) Despite their limitations, mortality rates of a society are important criteria against which the effectiveness of medicine is to be assessed. Mortality rates of society are, after all, the sum of individual mortality. But such rates do not decline as total investments in medical care and medical resources increase. From this perspective, investments in and use of medical care would appear, on balance, not to be very rational. Since total use of medical care and the health status of society are unrelated, on average the individual's use of medical care will not have a positive effect on his health, or at least on his longevity. A more rational way for people to invest in health might be to spend more money on improving diets, making changes in the environment, and developing programs to change personal and social behavior.

## The Special Case of Japan

Among all industrialized countries, Japan spends less of its gross national product on medical care and has fewer physicians per capita than any other country (see tables 3–1 and 3–2), and it ranks seventh among 12 countries in number of hospital beds per 1,000.[1] At the same time, it resembles other industrialized countries in its illness patterns and compares most favorably with respect to death rates and life expectancy. In pre-industrial societies the predominant form of illness is infectious disease, which declines with the progress of industrialization. Japan has followed the same decline, except the decline has been steeper, occurring over a briefer period of time. For example, deaths per 1,000 caused by tuberculosis declined from 1,908 in 1935 to 1,464 in 1950, to 154 in 1978, and 72 in 1978 (The Tsuneto Yano Memorial Society [Yano-Tsuneto Kinenkai] under the supervision of Ichiro Yano, 1980:386). Along with this, the decline in the mortality rate for persons 65 and over has been steeper than other industrialized countries (U.S. Department of Health and Human Services, 1981:22) and infant mortality has declined at a much faster rate since the early thirties than any other country in the world (see the Tsuneto Yano Memorial Society [Yano-Tsuneto Kinenkai] under the supervision of Ichiro Yano, 1980:286).

It might be argued that Japan's overall decline in mortality is because Japan has a lower proportion of older people than most other industrialized countries. However, even after the death rate has been standardized by age, Japan ranks with Sweden and The Netherlands in having the lowest rate in the industrial world (The Tsuneto Yano Memorial Society, [Yano-Tsuneto Kinenkai] under the supervision of Ichiro Yano, 1980:283), and for men 65 and older it has the lowest ago-adjusted male death rate of any industrial country in the world (see U.S. Department of Health and Human Services, 1981:22). The decrease in the death rate has occurred for all age groups. In addition, life expectancy for newborn Japanese males in 1979 was 73.5 years versus 69.9 for the United States (U.S. Department of Health and Human Services, 1983:104).

Other patterns have also developed in Japan that are common to industrialized countries. The frequency of diseases and injuries increased from 63.6 per 1,000 in 1965 to 109.4 in 1979 (Statistics Bureau of Japan, 1982:124). Now cerebrovascular disease, cancer, heart disease, and other diseases of old age are increasing due, in large part at least, to the fact that the population is aging. Also, the "frequency-of-illness rate" (reported number of sick people per 1,000 persons) has shown a continuous increase. In 1970 it reached 13.6, which is about twice what it was in 1960 (Whitaker, 1975:133). While this increase may be due to a variety of factors (e.g., better statistics), "it may also be evidence that health did not keep pace with the improvement in longevity" (Whitaker, 1975:133), a phenomenon commonly attributed to advanced industrialized countries.

Human crowding and pollution that accompany industrialization are more severe in Japan than other countries since a population of approximately 120 million today is crowded into 20% of the land area suitable for habitation, which itself is much smaller than most other industrialized countries. The resulting air pollution has probably led to the high incidence of respiratory disease (asthma, bronchitis, and emphysema) (Whitaker, 1974:140). In addition, the number of psychiatric patients almost doubled between 1961 and 1970 (Whitaker, 1974:137).

Therefore, common to other industrial countries, Japan's rate of infectious disease has decreased, the infant mortality has declined dramatically as have the death rates of all age groups, and life expectancy has risen to top-ranking for countries in the world. At the same time, chronic and debilitating diseases have increased. In health-relevant matters, Japan resembles other industrialized countries. In comparing the United States and Japan, Caudill (1976:159) states that both

> ...are highly urban and industrialized, both have well-developed medical systems, and both are plagued with the myriad problems of modern societies: urban deterioration, overcrowding, a lengthening lifespan with an attendant shift from the infectious to chronic diseases, and the bleakness of retirement and old age.

Some of these changes may, of course, have been due to changes in medicine; it has been noted that Japan has a well-developed medical system (was Yamamoto and Sawaguichi, 1975). However, the illness patterns are also characteristic of other industrialized countries, and, as we have seen, there is no particular correlation between the resources a society devotes to medical care and the health status of the population. A more likely explanation is that the increase in longevity is due largely to a decrease in infectious diseases, which was the result of environmental changes, and the increase in chronic disease is the result of an aging populaton, residual disability resulting from the successful treatment of chronic diseases from which people would have died at an earlier time, and possibly to some environmental pollution.

To summarize, Japan's expenditure for health services as a proportion of the gross national product is much less than most industrial nations and far less than that of the United States. Despite this, it surpasses almost all other countries in measures of health status. Japan thus exemplifies the fact that there is no apparent positive correlation among industrialized countries in national resources devoted to medical care and the medical well-being of the population as a whole.

## Is Curative Medicine Irrelevant?

One is tempted to concude, therefore, that medical care may have become or may be in the process of becoming more or less irrelevant for health. The historical change in disease patterns has been influenced very little if at all by curative medicine, and most dominant illnesses today—chronic disease—are not curable by medical procedures. In a review of medical research sponsored by the National Institutes for Health, Springarn's comments are relevant, though she does not necessarily subscribe to the conclusion about the general ineffectiveness of medical care. She states that

> ...doctors know that some people run a greater risk of falling victim to heart disease if they eat diets rich in animal fats or smoke excessively. But they feel they have not been especially successful at helping them change such lifestyle habits; on the contrary, there has been a rise especially in the number of women and teenagers who smoke in the United States.
>
> Historically, the most successful disease prevention and control programs like mosquito spraying or rat control or mass immunization have been directed at communicable disease and most often done for people, or in the case of immunization to them. [According to McKeown's evidence, immunization efforts have not been as successful as this statement seems to suggest.] Now

disease prevention, particularly chronic disease prevention, requires that
patients enter into a therapeutic alliance with their doctors. They need not just
become aware of the necessity for certain actions, but to take such actions for
themnselves (Springarn, 1976:63).

Such comments indicate a radical change may be needed in medical
care. Carlson (1975), Fuchs (1974), and Illich (1976) believe, in disagree-
ment with McKeown's analysis, that medicine has in the past contributed
significantly to the health status of populations and to a decline in the
mortality rates for entire societies; but they agree with McKeown that
there is less need for technical curative medical care today. Carlson
believes that medicine has become or will soon become more or less
irrelevant while Illich argues that it actually produces more harmful effects
for health than curative effects (see also Mendelsohn, 1979). Fuchs is less
critical but nevertheless argues that health and longevity are far more a
function of life-style than of technical medical care. Despite certain
differences between the three and between them and McKeown concerning the role of medicine, all agree that the future mortality rate and health
of the population will be largely a function of things other than curative
medical care. The socioeconomic environment, life-style, and social
behavior will be far more important.

The thesis that health is more a function of environmental factors is not
new; it has been advanced by advocates of public health and social
medicine for over a century. Moreover, the criticism of medicine,
particularly along the lines of Carlson and Illich, is not new. McKeown
observed that "at least since the time of Montaigne, the notion that
treatment of disease may be useless, unpleasant, and even dangerous, has
been expressed frequently and vehemently" (McKeown, 1976:ix). John
Knowles (1976:60) states that in the colonies, physicians were viewed
"with a mixture of fear, contempt and amiable tolerance." Paul Starr
observes that up to the twentieth century medicine was generally held in
ill repute.

> In the nineteenth century, some leading scientists held that virtually all existing
> drugs and treatments were of no use, and that the sick had no other hope than
> the healing power of nature. This doctrine was known as therapeutic nihilism
> (Starr, 1981:435).

Over a century ago, Oliver Wendell Holmes told the Massachusetts
Medical Society, "I firmly believe that if the entire materia medica as now
used could be sunk to the bottom of the sea, it would be all the better for
mankind—and all the worse for the fishes" (Holmes, 1861:39). In 1912,
the distinguished biologist Lawrence Henderson remarked that "for the

first time in human history, a random patient with a random disease con-sulting a doctor chosen at random stands better than a 50/50 chance of benefiting from the encounter" (quoted in Marmor, 1970:5). At about the same time medicine was described in a way that Carlson believes is still valid today: "There is a great difference between a good physician and a bad one, yet very little between a good one and none at all" (Carlson, 1975:20). With the advances in new drugs and improvements in the quality of medical education, in the aftermath of the Flexner report[2] (Flexner, 1910), Hirschfield says that by the 1920s "medical care became for the first time in history more than a questionable benefit" (Hirschfield, 1970:28). (In light of McKeown's and McKinlays' analyses, one must wonder, how-ever, whether the "more than a questionable benefit" in the 1920s was due to developments in medicine or to changes external to medicine.) A difference between the therapeutic nihilism of the nineteenth century and the disbelief in medicine today, according to Paul Starr, is that today "the net effectiveness of the medical care as a whole, rather than particular treatments, is called in question" (Starr, 1981:435). Another difference between the conclusions of earlier critics and those of many modern critics is that the latter are based on a systematic review of the evidence and are not based on personal experience and limited to personal opinion. In any case, as Starr states, "most serious critics of the system now doubt that medical care does much good for our health" (Starr, 1981:435). While such criticism may resemble views held in the nineteenth century, it is a radical departure from the view held by almost everyone in modern times until the 1970s, and by a very large proportion of the lay public today.


## Contrary Evidence?

All the evidence on the relationship between medical care resources and mortality rates is not negative, however. In a study of states for 1960, Auster, Leveson, and Sarachek (1969) report negative, though statistically insignificant, relationships between medical care resources (physicians and hospital beds per capita) and the mortality rate for the white population. Silver (1972) reports mixed results for the relationship between physicians per capita and mortality for racial and sex categories for states and SMSAs. Hadley (1982) investigates relationships for 400 county groups, grouped similarly to the way state economic areas are designated. He investigates the relationship between three medical care measures—total stock of medical care resources (number of physicians, nurses, and occupied hospital beds), the utilization rate of age-sex-race categories or cohorts, and Medicare expenditures per Medicare enrollee. Only for the latter measure does he find a negative relationship with mortality rates for 12 age-race-sex cohorts. Hadley believes, however, that the Medicare expenditures measure is a more valid measure of medical care and, on this basis, concludes that an increase in medical care does have a favorable effect on a population's health status, as indexed by the morality rate. He further notes that the magnitude of the coefficients in his study is approximately the same as those reported by Auster and others and by Silver. He does not note, however, that the medical care variables for which he fails to find a favorable effect on mortality are the kinds of variables for which Auster and colleagues and Silver *do* report small favorable effects (negative coefficients), not all of which are statistically significant. Hadley's assumptions and reasoning about the greater validity of Medicare expenditure per enrollee as a measure of medical care may be correct, but his findings can hardly be considered as exactly consistent with those of Auster and associates and Silver. In general, it would appear that the results of cross-sectional studies of nations, states, SMSAs, and county groups provide little support for the belief that more medical care lowers the mortality of the population.

At the same time, there has been a significant decline in mortality in recent years, and some believe it is not implausible that medical care has played a significant role in this decline (e.g., Levine, Feldman, and Elinson, 1983:397). Infant mortality declined from 29.2 per 1,000 live births in 1950 to about 11.2 in 1982 (U.S. Department of Health and Human Services, 1983:100), and it has declined by more than 50% since 1965, the year of Medicare-Medicaid legislation. Table 3–4 (first row) shows a decline in the death rates since 1970, most of it due to reductions in deaths due to chronic disease, particularly diseases of the heart (an exception is cancer, for which there has been no decline) (U.S. Department of Health and Human Services, 1983:105). Medical care may indeed have played a significant role in these declines. It is important to note, however, that since the sixties, substantial changes have also occurred in public policies other than Medicare and Medicaid that might have decreased death rates. The average monthly number of persons receiving food stamps increased from 425,000 in 1965 to 22,431,000 in 1981 (U.S. Bureau of the Census, 1984:131). This has probably contributed to improved nutrition for the poor and elderly, and particularly for the poor and elderly who might have chronic disease, thus increasing their physical ability to sustain chronic disease. Housing assistance has also risen, and this has raised the quality of life and living environment, thus reducing the risk of death from chronic disease. In addition, changes in personal behavior (e.g., reduction in smoking), eating habits (lower cholesterol intake), and environmental and traffic laws may have reduced the risk of death and disability. Furthermore, while there have been decreases in mortality due to some causes, there have been increases due to other causes. Death rates from cirrhosis of the liver, accidents, suicide, and homicide have increased. It is generally assumed that these increases have been due more to changes in personal and social behavior than to anything else. However, it is altogether possible that the decreases in *other* death rates are also due to changes in behavior.

Others have noted that it is possible that the death rates for small subpopulations may decline as a result of medical care, but that this will not be reflected in the index of mortality for the total population. For example, the lives of victims of end-stage kidney disease are clearly extended through transplants and hemodialysis, but the number involved is too small to have a statistically significant effect on the mortality rate of the entire population. Waitzkin cites a program of prenatal care and delivery services for predominantly Black and Latino pregnant women in a section of East Oakland. The infant mortality rate for geographic areas in which the services were concentrated declined in four years, though the infant mortality rate for East Oakland as a whole did not change (Waitzkin, 1983:31–32). Still, one may argue that if mortality and life expenctancy for the entire nation or community were the most important criteria against which medical care is to be assessed, some may want to question the value of programs, particularly if they are extremely expensive that have little effect on the health status of the entire community or nation. Waitzkin also reports that a medical care program specifically for farm workers in rural California had positive results for that population (Waitzkin, 1983:31), and Gordis (1973) reports that for census tracts in Baltimore, rheumatic fever among children decreased 60% in areas where comprehensive care programs were introduced but remained unchanged in areas where such programs did not exist. At the same time, in a longitudinal study, Benham and Benham (1975) show that increased utilization of physician and hospital services had no significant positive effect on health status, as indexed by a variety of indices. Thus, despite the fact that perceived morbidity is the one single factor most closely correlated with utilization of medical care in a number of countries (Kohn and White, 1976), there is no compelling evidence that utilization actually decreases morbidity rates or increases the health status of populations.

Of course, there are some conditions for which immediate medical care is essential to prevent permanent disability or death. Organ transplants, implants, and hemodialysis are obvious examples, as are treatments for victims of automobile accidents, gunshot wounds, and occupational hazards, as well as surgery for acute appendicitis, gall stones, and hernias.

Still one may argue that programs resulting in safer driving habits, stricter traffic laws, greater enforcement of occupational safety regulations, and the decreased availability of handguns would have a greater impact on the mortality and disability rates of the population than medical care. But in light of the urgency of the need, such arguments at the time of need would be pointless. For example: "No argument and no logic will convince terrified parents that the resources needed to treat their child would be more rationally allocated to prevention" (Carlson, 1975:29). It may be the terror and not the physical conditions per se that people respond to and which physicians must try to alleviate. Success in this regard would not affect morbidity or mortality rates of course; and because of the small proportion of the population requiring such urgent care to prevent disability or death, successfully managing the physical conditions would not be reflected in morbidity and mortality rates either. Moreover, the level of success in urgent or emergency care is not known, though some evidence suggests that it may not be very good. For example, one study based on process evaluation reported that only 27% of the visits to the Baltimore City Hospital emergency room were given effective care, 60% were given ineffective care, and 13% were given neither effective nor ineffective care; similar findings were reported for the hospital emergency room at Johns Hopkins (see Brook and Stevenson, 1970; and Brook, Berg, and Schechter, 1973). Such results are not inconsistent with the claim that medical care actually generates more illness than it does cure (Illich, 1976), and they are clearly consistent with the evidence that medical care may have little effect on morbidity and mortality rates. The overall curative effect of medical care may not be very strong.

At the same time, few would actually advocate the elimination of all medical care. Most critics would probably agree that morbidity and death rates would increase if all medical care were eliminated, even after the iatrogenic effects were taken into account. The central issue would seem to be that once a certain level of medical care has been reached, additional care has little if any positive effect on physical well being. In a recent review of several studies of the relationship between health and medical care, Valdez (1986:4) concludes that "the general consensus among medical care experts seems to be that more medical care, beyond some necessary level, does not produce better health." Exactly what the "necessary level" is no one can say with assurance, but most who have examined the relationship between health and medical care would agree that we are far beyond that level in the United States.

## Other Criteria for Assessing the Effectiveness of Medical Care

Even if death rates, life expectancy, and morbidity rates are the ultimate criteria against which medical care for entire nations and communities is to be assessed, other criteria are also important. People obtain medical care for reasons other than to extend their lives, and the outcomes of medical care are not limited to life extension and cure. Obviously, most medical care is not an immediate life-or-death matter, and successful treatment would not be expected to affect the length of time an individual lives. Further, most medical care is not even concerned with serious illness or injury. Much treatment is for minor ailments.

### Minor Ailments

Lewis Thomas, biologist and former Dean of the Yale School of Medicine, contends that physicians and their families make fewer physician visits, have fewer check-ups, and have less surgery than the general population. This, he believes, is not because they are any less ill than the general population but because physicians and their wives know "the great secret," namely, "that most things get better themselves. Most things, in fact, are better by morning" (Thomas, 1972:762). In other words, most of the things we go to physicians for we could very well ignore—with no physical harm to ourselves. These visits are different from those in which no physical problem is present; they would be self-corrective in short order. The numbers involved may be great. According to John Knowles, former professor of medicine at Harvard Medical School, general director of Massachusetts General Hospital in Boston, and the president of the Rockefeller Foundation, "Some 80 percent of the doctor's work consists of treating minor complaints and giving reassurance. Common colds, minor injuries, gastrointestinal upsets, back pain, arthritis, and psychoneurotic anxiety states account for the vast majority of visits to clinics and doctors' offices" (Knowles, 1976:62). The high percentage of physician visits for minor (or nonexistent) physical conditions may be the major reason the correlation between illness and morbidity variables and utilization of physician services is so low; Mechanic (1983:603) reports that typically studies show that morbidity explains only about 16–25% of the variance in physician contacts, and some studies report considerably less than this (e.g., the international study by Kohn and White, 1976). In any case, measures of the effectiveness-ineffectiveness of medical care might need to

include outcomes of treating minor conditions. It would be most difficult
to justify the amount of expenditures we make for health services in terms
of such criteria, however.

## Medical Judgment as the Reason for Seeking Care

A major reason, perhaps the most important reason, that people seek
medical care is becasue they visited a physician in the first place. A
peculiarity of medical care is that persons who purchase it usually cannot
evaluate its quality and, indeed, they may be unable to assess whether they
need more of it, as in so many instances of hospitalization.

People frequently comply with the physician's decision because of their
faith in physicians, not because they themselves decide this is the best use
of their money. In an overwhelming number of cases physicians no doubt
think it is in the patients' best interests to do as they recommend.
However, there is enough evidence of variation in elective surgery and
level of hospitalization among different populations to make any observer
wonder whether the consequences of much of the treatment recommended
by physicians produces a cure. The treatment may not have been needed
in the first place.

## Improvement in Role Functioning

Others argue that the major outcome of medical care is not cure but,
rather, improved functioning (Levine, Feldman, and Elinson, 1983:400–
401)[3]. For example, a 65-year-old arthritic patient may be able to walk
unaided with no pain and engage in normal social activities with a total hip
replacement; a 55-year-old man who has suffered cardiac arrest is able to
return to work after treatment; a 40-year-old diabetic housewife is able
to function unimpeded in the roles of mother and housewife with medical care. Much may be said for the role medicine plays in raising the
functioning level of individuals. There are, however, two qualifications.

First, it is not known exactly how successful medical care really is in
promoting improved functioning, though in individual cases the result is
unquestionable. Second, and more problematic, many of those who are
functioning at less than optimum may do so precisely because of the
medical care they have received in the past. By successfully treating
chronically ill persons, medical care may decrease the mortality rate but
increase the proportion of the population who are residually disabled. The
patterns in table 3–4 are consistent with this statement. The first row gives

Table 3–4. Death Rates and Activity Limitations Due to Chronic Disease for Selected Years, 1970 to 1981

| | 1970 | 1971 | 1972 | 1973 | 1974 | 1975 | 1976 | 1977 | 1978 | 1979 | 1980 | 1981 |
|---|---|---|---|---|---|---|---|---|---|---|---|---|
| Death Rate[1] | 714 | | | | | 630 | | 601 | | | 585 | 572 |
| Percent Limited in Activity[2] | 11.6 | | 12.7 | | | | 14.3 | | 14.3 | | | 14.4 |
| Percent Limited in Major Activity[2] | 9.1 | | 9.6 | | | | 10.8 | | 10.6 | | | 10.9 |
| Average Restricted Activity Days Per Person[3] | 14.3 | 15.7 | | 16.7 | 16.5 | 17.9 | 18.2 | 17.8 | 18.8 | 19.0 | 19.1 | 19.1 |

[1] Number per 100,000 population (age adjusted). *Source:* U.S. Department of Health and Human Services, 1983:97.
[2] *Source:* U.S. Bureau of the Census, 1975:87; 1978:20; 1980:117; and 1984:124.
[2,3] A restricted day is a day a person cuts down on his or her usual activities for the whole day because of illness or injury. Includes bed-disability, work-loss, and school-loss days. *Source:* U.S. Bureau of the Census, 1976:88; 1978:117; 1980:123; and 1984:121.

the death rate from chronic disease, which decreased from 1970 to 1981. The other rows are based on interview surveys of the American population conducted by the National Center for Health Statistics. The second row shows that the percentage of persons who are limited in their major activity (e.g., work if employed, school work if a student, housework if a homemaker, and so forth) also increased. The fourth row gives the average number of days individuals cut down on their normal activities during the course of the year. As can be seen, disability almost continuously increased from 1970 to 1981.[4] While it is impossible to know with absolute certainty if this is due to the increase in chronic illness that is a result of an increase in medical care, or the effectiveness of medical care, it is certainly a plausible interpretation. This is not to say that such a result is to be construed as not being worth the cost of successfully treating chronic disease; that is a matter of values and opinion. The point is that if improved social functioning is taken as an index of effective medical care, then the evidence might not be favorable. It would amount to many of medicine's successes being counted as its failure (e.g., the blind diabetic who has survived only because of medical care). The successes of medical care in raising the functional status of individuals must be viewed in light of the number of persons who function at less than normal because of the medical care they received.

### Stress and Anxiety Reduction

Writers have commented that many visits to physicians are prompted by personal stress and problems of social adjustment. For example, Sanders states that medicine offsets "the impersonality of mass society by giving people a chance to talk intimately with health personnel about matters that trouble them. The psychiatrists are those most quickly thought of in this connection, but anyone familiar with the health field realizes that health personnel of all types are viewed by those in need as confidants or as competent to give advice" (Sanders, 1963:377–378). In a study of users of a medical clinic in Israel, Shuval (1970) reports that people visit physicians for catharsis, to legitimize their failure, and for other nonmedical reasons. It is not possible to know exactly what proportion of physicians' time is involved, though Mumford (1983:43) concludes that "A succession of epidemiological surveys have rediscovered what clinicians have long known—that much of the time of most physicians is spent with patients whose primary source of distress is social or emotional rather than physical."

Other writers note, however, that illness may itself generate anxiety. It is in this connection that some actually define the primary purpose of medicine, namely, as reducing anxiety and promoting "peace of mind" about illness and symptoms of possible illness (McDermott, 1978:173; Levine, Feldman, and Elinson, 1983:402).

Anxiety may be involved in medical care in several ways. In a study of 512 mothers, Roghmann and Haggarty report that the number of medical contacts for families is less than the episodes of illness. (This would suggest that much of what people experience as pain and abnormal symptoms is actually ignored.) Roghmann and Haggarty find, however, that when symptoms appear in conjunction with a stressful event, it raises the probability about 50% that medical attention will be sought. (Roghmann and Haggarty, 1972 and 1973). (Also, when there are no physical symptoms at all, stressful events raise the probability that medical attention will be sought by about 80%.) This would indicate that much medical care is sought for reasons that may have little if anything to do which physical problems per se. The reduction of anxiety may be a prominent reason itself. Some defenders of modern medicine agree (McDermott 1978).

Perhaps the largest group of persons for whom there is an absolute need for technical medical care, or at least the perception that there is such a need, are persons who have chronic illnesses and impairments, such as diabetes, renal disease, cancer, cardiovascular disorders, and heart disease. Treatment of such persons, a high proportion of whom are elderly, often results in relief of physical pain and enhanced social functioning. Such results are not reflected in mortality statistics. This is true even when life is prolonged either because the number is so small or because the successful treatment usually only adds a few months or years to a person's life (see McDermott, 1978). While technical medical care is often considered essential for victims of chronic and debilitating conditions, the reduction of anxiety may be more important than improvement in physical health. To know that one is in good hands and that everything technically possible is being done may be reassuring to the patient and to his or her family.

Reassurance is particularly important for individuals who have symptoms which may suggest a serious and perhaps fatal disease when, as a result of medical attention, they are assured that they have nothing to worry about. According to one physician, this appears to be the most prevalent situation. "I think most of us would agree that a patient's primary feeling when he seeks medical care is an intense wish to find out that whatever it is that is wrong, it is not something that will cause him awful harm"

(McDermot, 1978:173). People don't enjoy being uncertain about serious life events; they want assurance that matters will work out. To give patients this peace of mind may require highly developed technical care.

> ...for one human being to make the judgment about another that whatever is "wrong" is not a serious threat and make that judgment stick, requires that the judge, in this case the physician, have a legitimatizing base... *Today's doctor derives his legitimatizing base, the base that permits him to dispense reassurance, from his expertise in the use of a broad spectrum of scientific and technical knowledge* (McDermott, 1978:173; author's emphasis).

Observe also that in many instances performance of this role has no curative function at all.

> For example, to examine a small lump in a woman's breast may involve the discriminating use of a considerable amount of complex technology, including such procedures as mammography, xeroradiography, termography, anesthesiology, surgery, and tissue microscopy. With the use of all or some of that technology, the outcome may be that the patient turned out *not* to have cancer. Considered solely in terms of the public good, e.g., mortality and morbidity rates, one might argue that the not inconsiderable effort here was wasted. For after all, if the woman had done absolutely nothing about the breast lump and gone off and forgotten all about it, she would have been just as well off. The investment in money and effort is essential to fulfill the doctor's purpose to help the patient toward peace of mind (McDermott, 1978:172–173; author's emphasis).

Contributing to peace of mind and reducing anxiety, rather than reducing morbidity and mortality, may be the major function of modern medicine.

The above statements don't point out, however, that the very persons who contribute to patients' peace of mind may be the same ones who disturbed their peace of mind in the first place; the anxiety that doctors reduce may have been generated by doctors themselves. And the performance of such a role is not inexpensive, as the above quotes do make clear.[5] To assure people they are not victims of some dread disease, or of successfully treating them for serious conditions requires much more than the humanizing elements of sympathy, listening, and understanding. Extreme specialization and the use of advanced technology may be required, and these lead to higher costs. They are also the things that critics say lead to care that is too impersonal and without enough human concern.

Sometimes peace of mind may be impossible to achieve for all interested parties. What is peace of mind to the patient may not be peace of mind to others, and vice versa. Reference is not just to inner conflict and turmoil associated with the all too familiar instances in which individuals are kept alive by artificial means. In addition to each of these

> ...there are thousands where, with survival impossible, death is postponed for weeks or even months with the aid of modern drugs and scientific techniques. The patient, especially if old and weary, is not always grateful, but relatives are satisfied that "everything possible has been done" (Poynter, 1973:59).

Also, in instances where expenses are extremely high, peace of mind about the patient's medical condition may be at the expense of peace of mind about financial matters. And, of course, when medical care results in the diagnosis of a dread condition, it may lead to distress.

On balance, however, while the evidence is far from definitive, it is probable that medical care does more to alleviate anxiety than it does to reduce mortality and morbidity rates. This may very well be the most important benefit of medical care, as McDermott (1978) argues.

## Public Perception and Social Definition

Considering the low probability of medical care having a positive effect on mortality and perhaps, also, on morbidity, the logical question is what do people think of it? Evidence would indicate that Americans are well satisfied with what they get from medical care. By any criterion, medicine is a most esteemed and valued social institution.

Physicians enjoy the highest status of any major occupation in the United States, and their average income places them in the upper 0.5% of the population. National surveys show that the population is overwhelmingly satisfied with medical care, and this is true for all subgroups of the population, defined by ethnicity, age, residence, region, and similar variables (see Aday et al., 1980, chapter 4; Andersen, Fleming, and Champney, 1982; and Aday, Fleming, and Andersen, 1984:38). The fact that in 1984 we spent 10.6% of our gross national production on medical care implies that as a society we place a great value on medical care—presumably life, health, and freedom from pain. This is reasoning in a circle, of course, since this says that people spend money on things they value, and if they spend a large proportion of their income on something, it indicates that they put a high value on it. Also, others argue that economic expenditure for medical care as a reflection of our value preferences is distorted because physicians rather than the public make many of the decisions and because much medical expense is paid for indirectly, by health insurance. Although these arguments have merit, the fact that the expenditures are so high and have been rising almost continuously since 1955, when they were only 4.5% of GNP, certainly suggests a high level of commitment to whatever it is that medical care provides, or is thought to provide. Since medical care is generally thought to contribute to health and longer life, such high expenditures should be reflected in the high priority the public gives to health and longer life. Evidence indicates that this is the case.

In a national survey, Campbell, Converse, and Rodgers (1976:83–84) asked respondents about the importance of various aspects of life (such as "a happy marriage," "a large bank account, so you don't have to worry about money," "an interesting job"). Seventy percent said, "Being in good health and in good physical condition" was "extremely important," and another 24% said it was "very important"; this was higher than any other aspect of life. Responses to open-ended questions in national surveys in 1959, 1964, and 1971 showed that health ranked first on a scale of social preference, and illness was mentioned more than any other fear. For the respective years, 56%, 54%, and 44% mentioned good health for self and family in reply to a question about hopes for the future, and 65%, 52%, and 44% mentioned illness for self and family among their fears. By way of comparison, percentages who hope for a better standard of living and fear a lower standard of living are much less (Cantril and Roll, 1971:19). In the 1982 National Survey of Access to Medical Care (Aday, Fleming, and Andersen, 1984), respondents were asked to select the *one* area from a list of 10 areas (education, defense, energy, welfare, health, public transport, environment, unemployment, housing, and social security) in which they favored additional federal spending. After being asked for their choice, respondents were asked for their second choice. Health was selected by 21% as the first choice and by 22% as the second choice. The 43% was higher than that for any other area.[6] Therefore, the high priority we give to health in our stated values is consistent with the amount of money we spend on medical care in an apparent attempt to maintain our health.

The public seems never to get enough medical care. The perceived need for medical care is high and apparently has been high for many years. At one time some authorities thought that after a certain level of medical need had been met, the need, or at least the perceived need, would stabilize or decline. They thought

> ...that the phenomenal growth of medical services everywhere [was] a transitional phase, that the heritage of disease carried over from the wretched conditions of the masses in the nineteenth century first had to be cleared out of

the way before a stable level of medical care could be reached when, with a healthier life assured for all, there might even be a reduction (Poynter, 1974:4).

Actually the reverse has happened, with perceived need for medical care increasing rather than decreasing. Thus:

More hospitals, more doctors, more research, and much more money will be demanded. How much is spent will ultimately depend on how much can be afforded rather than on needs, for these seem to be limitless (Poynter, 1974:4).

Despite efforts to reduce the cost of government insurance programs, public opinion seems to be supportive of more rather than less spending. A 1978 national survey found that 71% agreed with the statement that "better health care, which saves lives and makes the sick healthy, is worth almost any price" (Harris, 1978:12); however, only 49% of physicians agreed with this statement. In addition, a full 84% "generally agreed" with the statement that "We are a rich country and could afford to spend more money to improve the quality of health care." Health is a high priority among Americans, and despite the questionable benefit of so much medical care for our health, we have apparently not reached the limits on the amount we will spend on such care.

Therefore, although there is little basis for expecting most of the medical care people receive to have a positive effect on health, the social definition states otherwise. And people act on the basis of their definitions of situations regardless of their validity. For example, more than a few have noted the public's unrealistic expectations of medicine. Hence, large expenditures are made for the purchase of medical products, the effectiveness of which is not known and which, in fact, may have no value for the physical health of most people at all (e.g., see Cochrane, 1972). This may be hard to believe for the vast majority of people, but it is not all that surprising. Human history is full of examples in which soical definitions differ from the underlying reality. Nevertheless, it will be worth exploring for a moment why in this particular case social definitions differ so much from the underlying reality.

We have already noted that seeking and receiving medical care is pervaded with anxiety and that one of the functions, perhaps the dominant function, of medicine is to alleviate such anxiety. People with what appear to be possible symptoms of illness may actually respond more to the anxiety than to physical symptoms per se when they seek medical care. Consequently, beliefs and expectations may be unrealistic and irrational. This is not unusual for people who are under emotional stress, fear, and uncertainty; such conditions sometimes even lead to superstition and magic. In 1942 Talcott Parsons wrote that society's response to medical care resembled magic. He stated (Parsons, 1949:204, no. 10):

> ...the field of health is, in spite of the achievements of modern medicine...a classical example of this type situation [that is, one resembling magic]...Even though...magic in a strict sense is not prominent, there is an unstable succession of beliefs which *overemphasize the therapeutic possibility* of certain diagnostic ideas and therapeutic practice. The effect is to create an *optimistic bias* in favor of successful treatment of disease....(emphasis supplied)

To a substantial degree, then, the unrealistic expectation and high utilization of medical care may be prompted largely by anxiety associated with illness and medical care. People believe or hope that medical care may extend their lives, cure their illnesses, and prevent or eliminate their disablements when, in fact, it is able to accomplish less than the public believes. Public attitudes and behavior are not very rational when it comes to medical care.

This is not to say that unrealistic expectations are responses to social definitions that are unrelated to underlying aspects of medicine. Advances in medical technology since World War II may have influenced the social definition of medicine and raised the hopes of people unrealistically. With the huge increase in national investments in medical research shortly after World War II to the 1960s, the public and Congress became concerned that too little of the new technology and forms of treatment were being diffused to the public (Springarn, 1976:63). Congressional support for medical research, which grew enormously in the quarter century after World War II, was based on the expectation that federal funds for research would subsequently be translated into successful treatments for the "dread" diseases—heart, cancer, stroke (Strickland, 1972). The public became aware of many amazing developments and apparent breakthroughs in medical research. Expectations as to practical outcomes sometimes were unrealistic as a result. "Popular stories of open-heart surgery, of transplantation of kidneys and other organs, and of magical prostheses have made it hard to accept that any illness should still lead to long-term permanent disability" (Sidel and Sidel, 1983:90). The fact that some dramatic possibilities exist may lead to the refusal to admit that any condition is truly disabling, and to place the blame on medicine when it is. "Over the past 30 years there has been a marked change in the expectations of the public toward health and toward health care...First, there is the rising expectation that one will avoid dying at least until one's sixties, and, particularly, that one will avoid dying of infectious diseases. [Consequently], the feeling...is that medical care system (for the individual patients) or the health care system (in the case of an outbreak) has somehow not done its job" (Sidel and Sidel, 1983:89).

Others view the social definitions and unrealistic expectations of medicine as perpetuated by the medical sector. Lewis Thomas states, for example, that "there are not nearly as many forms of effective technology as the public has been led to believe" (Thomas, 1973). Carlson and Illich go further. Carlson states that "because medicine has failed to encourage the patient to assume the responsibility for health, the public craves more and more services. . . The public has been convinced that human suffering is a disease that medicine can cure" when, in fact, medicine can contribute very little to this objective (Carlson, 1975:37). Illich (1976) expresses the view that the public places a strong value on medical care because health is no longer considered an individual responsibility. In Illich's terms such responsibility has been "expropriated" by medicine. Similarly, Carlson states that "medicine has fostered a profoundly dependent public," which, he says, "searches for cures that do not exist" (Carlson, 1975:37). The self interest of the medical professional may be involved. Mechanic states: "Although the facts may show little benefit from surgical interventions, technological innovations, or expensive new approaches, the self-interested retort of the professional who insists that the procedure saves lives usually carries the day." At the same time, he observes that the professional's self interest is not inconsistent with the public perception of medical care. "The irony is that the reasoned decision not to use [expensive services which may have no medical value], given the public perception of such technologies, makes physicians who choose such a course vulnerable to allegations of incompetence and malpractice." Therefore: "However jaundiced the medical care experts have become about the excesses, inefficiencies, ineffectiveness, and irrelevance of much of medical care, the fact is that the public does not share this perspective" (Mechanic, 1981:2).

Further, new technological developments actually stimulate fears and anxieties which encourage unrealistic expectations. New developments may cause the certainty of a dread fate to be replaced with glimmers of hope and an uncertain fate. Slim hopes and uncertainties may reawaken anxieties, leading in turn to expectations that are unrealistic. However, the development of new technologies within medicine are probably insufficient in themselves to cause false expectations. Probably in all societies some anxiety is associated with illness and this contributes to unrealistic expectations of what healers can actually accomplish. But such expectations may be especially anomalous in a society where medicine has a scientific base and uses so much sophisticated technology, as Parsons' insight of over 40 years ago suggests.

To conclude, the review in this chapter suggests that the common belief that people seek medical care to improve their health and extend their lives is a gross oversimplification, if not a distortion. It also challenges the belief that medical care contributes greatly to health and longevity. These beliefs are sometimes true, of course. People often do seek medical care when they have an objective need for it, and the care is frequently beneficial— health is restored, injuries are healed, and life is saved. There is increasing evidence, however, that people seek medical care for things that may have nothing or very little to do with health (particularly physical health) and that the consequences of medical care, on average, contribute little to a reduction of morbidity and disability or an increase in life expectancy. On the basis of a cross-national study, an economist, Joseph Newhouse, concludes that

> ...medical care services at the margin have less to do with common measures of health status such as mortality and morbidity and more to do with relief of anxiety, somewhat more accurate diagnosis, and heroic measures near the end of life (Newhouse, 1976:123).

The nonmedical benefits of medical care would appear to be more important than the strict medical benefits.

## Conclusion

Answers to questions about the reasons people use medical care and about the outcomes of that care are not as simple as many suppose. People seek medical care for a variety of things—for minor ailments that would go away in due course, to alleviate anxiety (with or without accompanying possible symptoms of physical illness), for unexpected acute disorders and injuries, and for chronic illness. In most instances, a certain amount of anxiety is involved. As for outcomes, in many cases medical care clearly has positive medical benefits; even those who question the value of medical care and view it as largely irrelevant for physical welfare in general would admit to that. At the same time, there is mounting evidence which, while not definitive, does indicate that, overall, the outcomes of medical care may be of very limited or even questionable benefit for physical health. Despite this, the cost of medical care is great and is increasing, and in individual cases it is sometimes staggering. In terms of tangible health benefits, it is hard to justify such large expenditures. The argument that people, on balance, get a bargain from their expenditures for health services is simply not evident from existing data. While everyone would agree that the elimination of all health services would in time lead to an increase in mortality and morbidity rates, the best that can be concluded is that health benefits from continued increases in health services are most questionable. As an Organization for Economic Cooperation and Development study states:

> ...indicators of the community's general health status...tell a mixed story and in a very real sense society simply does not know what it is getting for its money (Organization for Economic Cooperation and Development, 1977:83).[7]

Despite this, three conclusions about medical care would seem to be indicated. They will be drawn upon in subsequent chapters.

First, much illness (or the perception of probable or possible illness) and its treatment is fraught with fear and anxiety. Anxiety may be the precipitating factor that leads people to seek medical care, and it may also accompany the medical prognosis, treatment, and treatment outcome, including the financial consequences. Regardless of whether one views the primary role of medicine as anxiety-reducing and as contributing to peace of mind, few will deny that distress is associated with much illness and medical treatment. And anxiety and fear are not conducive to rational decision-making, particularly to decisions that lead to long-term benefit.

Second, if the questionable benefit (and possible irrelevance and harmful nature) of so much curative medical care were widely accepted, the level of anxiety associated with illness and medical treatment would mount; and the basis for making rational decisions would be even weaker. Individuals would then be forced to choose between (1) doing nothing and therefore accepting what they believe to be an unpleasant or frightening fate, and (2) adopting a course of action in which the outcome has a low probability of being beneficial to them, and indeed, where an even more frightening state is not out of the question. Under such circumstances it is difficult to imagine people rationally weighing alternative courses of action. The issue of irrationality in medical care is thus not just one of inefficiencies, duplication, and waste in the allocation of society's resources. It is also one in which the context in which individuals decide to seek medical care is characterized by elements which make rational decisions difficult if not impossible. It is little wonder that people almost blindly comply with physicians' decisions.

Third, the lack of firm evidence that medical care does in fact make a systematic difference in health and longevity is not generally recognized by the public. Access to medical care is strongly valued. This, in turn, is more a matter of social definition—of what people think is important—than of demonstrated medical reality. Even if the case for medical care were not as

70 FUNCTIONS AND ASPECTS OF HEALTH INSURANCE

weak as much of the evidence and opinion of many knowledgeable persons indicate, the social definition of medical care is clearly at variance with what most people can realistically expect to get from it. As with many social definitions, the resulting behavior may have little rational basis.

To conclude, what is known about medical care would indicate that medical care frequently involves fear and anxiety, that little empirical evidence indicates that its cost systematically leads to tangible physical outcomes that are proportional to the cost, and that the social definition that it is a valuable service prompts its use as much if not more than its demonstrated value for health and longer life. This is the state of affairs that provides the context for making decisions about purchasing health insurance to assure that medical care is available.

## Notes

1. Figures for Japan are not exactly comparable to those for the United States, for which no adjustments are made in table 3–1. All counties except Japan use the United Nations System of National Accounts. While this raises a question about the comparability of the figures, Ohmura's analysis indicates that to make the figures comparable would result in about a 15% decrease in expenditures reported for the United States for the years 1955–1974 (Ôhmura, 1978). Such an adjustment for the United States, and other countries, would have virtually no effect on the rankings in table 3–1.

2. The so-called Flexner report was the result of a study of medical education in the United States and Canada commissioned by the Carnegie Foundation for the Advancement of Education. The report recommended higher standards of medical education, stronger relations between medical schools and universities, and greater professionalization of medicine.

3. Levine, Feldman, and Ellinson (1983:401) seem to take this as indicating an affirmative answer to the question, "Does medical care do any good?" It does not follow, of course, that just because people seek help from others for a problem that, by the fact alone, they will be any better for the experience. One could just as well say the same thing for faith healers, some ministers, chiropractors, or others who profess to have special abilities to cure physical ailments.

4. Death rates in table 3–4 are adjusted for age whereas figures for disability are not. However, since the percentage of persons 65 and over who experienced activity limitation decreased only slightly from 1969–1970 to 1981 (U.S. Bureau of the Census, 1984:124), the increase in disability days is not due to an aging population per se any more than is the decline in the death rate.

5. In this connection I am reminded of a friend of mine. When my friend got his annual checkup, he was told he had symptoms that were warning of a possible heart attack and was referred to cardiologists at a nearby medical center. The cardiologists conducted similar examinations and concurred with the original physician. They said, however, that they could be more certain of their diagnosis if they performed additional tests, including an angiogram, which they also noted has a known (but small) probability of resulting in death. By this time my friend was more than slightly frightened. He therefore agreed to have the test conducted

and entered the hospital. When the tests were completed, he was told he had nothing to worry about because he was a "false positive"—he had the symptoms of the disease but not the disease. My friend, who had no health worries several days earlier, could rest easily. Physicians who had caused him undue anxiety had relieved him of that same anxiety. They also relieved him of $5,000.

6. The figure for the general population would be slightly lower than this because persons classified as poor are overrepresented in this sample, and they favor spending for health more than the nonpoor (48% versus 37.4%). Thanks to the Robert Wood Johnson Foundation for making the data available.

7. A study of 69 Fortune 500 business firms which provide health benefits to their employees indicates that this conclusion holds for business firms as well (see Sapolsky, Altman, Greene, and Moore, 1981). We will have more to say about this study with respect to health insurance in subsequent chapters.

## References

Aday, Lu Ann, Gretchen V. Fleming, and Ronald M. Anderson. *Access to Medical Care: Who Has It, Who Doesn't.* Chicago: Pluribus Press, Inc., 1984.

Aday, Lu Ann, et al. *Health Care in the U.S.: Equitable for Whom?* Beverly Hills, CA: Sage Publications, 1980.

Anderson, Ronald M., Gretchen Y. Fleming, and Timothy F. Chapney. "Exploring a Paradox: Belief in a Crisis and General Satisfaction wih Medical Care." *Milbank Memorial Fund Quarterly* 60 (1982):329–353.

Auster, R., I. Leveson, and D. Sarachek. "The Production of Health: An Exploratory Study." *Journal of Human Resources* 4 (Fall 1969):411–436.

Benham, Lee, and Alexandra Benham. "The Impact of Incremental Medical Services on Health Status, 1963–1970." In Ronald Andersen, Joanna Kravits, and Odin W. Anderson (eds.), *Equity in Health Services: Empirical Analyses in Social Policy*, pp. 217–228. Cambridge, NA: Ballinger Publishing Company, 1975.

Brook, Robert H., Morris H. Berg, and Philip A. Schechter. "Effectiveness of Non-Emergency Care Via an Emergency Room." *Annals of Internal Medicine* 78 (March 1973):333–339.

Brook, Robert H., and R.L. Stevenson, Jr. "Effectiveness of Patient Care in an Emergency Room." *New England Journal of Medicine* 283 (October 1970): 904–907.

Campbell, Angus, Philip E. Converse, and Willard L. Rodgers. *The Quality of American Life: Perceptions, Evaluations, and Satisfactions.* New York: Russell Sage Foundation, 1976.

Cantril, Albert H., and Charles W. Roll, Jr. *Hopes and Fears of the American People.* New York: Universe Books, 1971.

Carlson, Rick J. *The End of Medicine.* New York: John Wiley & Sons, 1975.

Caudill, William. "The Cultural and Interpersonal Context of Everyday Health and Illness in Japan and America." In Charles Leslie (ed.), *Asian Medical*

*Systems: A Comparative Study*, pp. 159–177. Berkeley: University of California Press, 1976.

Cochrane, A. L. *Effectiveness and Efficiency: Random Reflection on the Health Services*. London: Nuffield Provincial Hospitals Trust, 1972.

Dubos, René. *Mirage of Health: Utopias, Progress, and Biological Change*. New York: Harper & Row, 1959.

——————. *Man, Medicine and Environment*. New York: Praeger, 1968.

Flexner, Abraham. *Medical Education in the United States and Canada*. New York: Carnegie Foundation or the Advancement of Teaching, 1910.

Fuchs, Victor R. *Who Shall Live? Health, Economics, and Social Choice*. New York: Basic Books, Inc., 1974.

Gordis, Leon. "Effectiveness of Comprehensive-Care Programs in Preventing Rheumatic Fever." *New England Journal of Medicine* 289 (August 16, 1973): 331–335.

Gray, Alastair McIntosh. "Inequalities in Health and the Black Report: A Summary and Comment." *International Journal of Health Services* 12 (Summer 1982):349–480.

Hadley, Jack. *More Medical Care, Better Health? An Economic Analysis of Mortality Rates*. Washington, DC: Urban Institute Press, 1982.

Harris, Louis and Associates. *Hospital Care in America*. Conducted for Hospital Affiliates International, Inc., Nashville, TN, April 1978.

Hirschfield, Daniel S. *The Lost Reform: The Campaign for Compulsory Health Insurance in the United States from 1932 to 1943*. Cambridge, MA: Harvard University Press, 1970.

Holmes, Oliver Wendell. *Currents and Counter-Currents in Medical Science*. Boston: Ticknow & Field, 1861.

Illich, Ivan. *Medical Nemesis: The Expropriation of Health*. New York: Random House, 1976.

Knowles, John. "The Struggle to Stay Healthy." *Time* (August 9, 1976):60–62.

Kohn, Robert, and Kerr L. White (eds.). *Health Care: An International Study*. London: Oxford University Press, 1976.

Levine, Sol, Jacob J. Feldman, and Jack Elinson. "Does Medical Care Do Any Good?" In David Mechanic (ed.), *Handbook of Health, Health Care, and·the Health Professions*, pp. 394–404. New York: The Free Press, 1983.

Levit, Katharine R., Helen Lazenby, Daniel R. Waldo, and Lawrence M. Davidoff. "National Health Expenditures, 1984." *Health Care Financing Review* 7 (Fall 1985):1–35.

Marmor, Theodore R. *The Politics of Medicare*. Chicago: Aldine Publishing Company, 1970.

McDermott, Walsh. "Medicine: The Public Good and One's Own." *Perspective in Biology and Medicine* 21 (Winter 1978):167–187.

McKeown, Thomas. *The Role of Medicine: Dream, Mirage, or Nemesis?* Nuffield, England: Nuffield Provincial Hospital Trust, 1976.

McKinlay, John B., and Sonja M. McKinlay. "The Questionable Contribution of Medical Measures to the Decline of Mortality in the United States in the

Twentieth Century." *Milbank Memorial Fund Quarterly* 47 (Summer 1977): 405–428.

Mechanic, David. *Medical Sociology*, 2nd ed. New York: The Free Press, 1978.

————. "Some Dilemmas in Health Care Policy." *Milbank Memorial Fund Quarterly* 59 (Winter 1981):1–15.

————. "The Experience and Expression of Distress: The Study of Illness Behavior and Medical Utilization." In David Mechanic (ed.), *Handbook of Health, Health Care, and the Health Professions*, pp. 591–607. New York: The Free Press, 1983.

Mendelsohn, Robert S. *Confessions of a Medical Heretic*. New York: Warner Books, 1979.

Mumford, Emily. *Medical Sociology: Patients, Providers, and Politics*. New York: Random House, 1983.

Newhouse, Joseph P. "Medical-Care Expenditures: A Cross-National Survey." *The Journal of Human Resources* 12 (April 1976):115–125.

Organization for Economic Cooperation and Development. *Studies in Resource Allocation*. No. 4. *Public Expenditures on Health*. Paris: Organization for Economic Cooperation and Development, 1977.

Ohmura, Junshiro. "Analysis of Factors Affecting the Need and Demand for Medical Care." *Social Science and Medicine* 12A (November 1978):485–496.

Parsons, Talcott. "The Theoretical Development of the Sociology of Religion." In *Essays in Sociological Theory*, rev. ed., pp. 197–211. Glencoe, IL: Free Press, 1949.

Poynter, Noel. *Medicine and Man*. Middlesex, England: Penguin Books, 1973.

Roghmann, Klaus, J., and Robert J. Haggerty. "Family Stress and the Use of Health Services." *International Journal of Epidemiology* 1 (September 1972):279–286.

Roghmann, Klaus J., and Robert J. Haggerty. "Daily Stress, Illness, and the Use of Health Services in Young Families." *Pediatric Research* 7 (May 1973): 520–526.

Sanders, Irwin, T. "Public Health in the Community." In Howard E. Freeman, Sol Levine, and Leo G. Reeder (eds.), *Handbook of Medical Sociology*, pp. 369–396. Englewood Cliffs, NJ: Prentice-Hall, 1963.

Sapolsky, Harvey M., Drew Altman, Richard Greens, and Judith D. Moore. "Corporate Attitudes toward Health Care Costs." *Milbank Memorial Fund Quarterly* 59 (Fall 1981):565–585.

Shuval, Judith T. *Social Functions of Medical Practice*. San Francisco: Jossey-Bass, Inc., Publishers, 1970.

Sidel, Victor W., and Ruth Sidel. *A Health State: An International Perspective on the Crisis in United States Medical Care*, rev. ed. New York: Pantheon Books, 1983.

Silver, Morris. "An Econometric Analysis of Spatial Variations in Mortality Rates." In Victor R. Fuchs (ed.), *Essays in the Economics of Health*, pp. 161–227. New York: National Bureau of Economic Research, 1972.

Simanis, Joseph G., and John R. Coleman. "Health Care Expenditures in Nine

Industrialized Countries, 1960–76." *Social Security Bulletin* 43 (January 1980):3–8.

Somers, Herman Miles, and Anne Ramsay Somers. *Doctors, Patients, and Health Insurance: The Organization and Financing of Medical Care.* Garden City, NY: Doubleday and Company, Inc., 1961.

Springarn, Natalie Davis. *Heartbeat: The Politics of Health Research.* Washington, DC, and New York: Robert B. Luce, Inc., 1976.

Starr, Paul. "The Politics of Therapeutic Nihilism." In Peter Conrad and Rochelle Kern (eds.), *The Sociology of Health and Illness: Critical Perspectives,* pp. 434–448. New York: St. Martins Press, 1981. Originally published in *Working Papers for a New Society.* Washington, DC: Center for the Study of Public Policy, Summer 1976.

——————. *The Social Transformation of American Medicine.* New York: Basic Books, 1982.

Statistics Bureau of Japan. *Statistical Handbook of Japan.* Tokyo: Prime Ministers Office, 1982.

Strickland, Stephen P. *Politics, Science, & Dread Disease: A Short History of United States Medical Research Policy.* Cambridge, MA: Harvard University Press, 1972.

The Tsuneto Yano Memorial Society (Yano-Tsuneto Kinendai) under the supervision of Ichira Yano. *Nippon: A Chartered Survey of Japan—1980–81.* Tokyo: Kokusei-Sha, 1980.

Thomas, Lewis. "Notes of a Biology-Watcher: Your Very Good Health." *The New England Journal of Medicine* 287 (1972):761–762.

——————. "Guessing and Knowing." *Saturday Review* 55 (1973):52.

U.S. Bureau of the Census. *Statistical Abstract of the United States,* 96th ed. Washington, DC: U.S. Department of Commerce, 1975.

——————. *Statistical Abstract of the United States,* 97th ed. Washington, DC: U.S. Department of Commerce, 1976.

——————. *Statistical Abstract of the United States,* 99th ed. Washington, DC: U.S. Department of Commerce, 1978.

——————. *Statistical Abstract of the United States,* 101st ed. Washington, DC: U.S. Department of Commerce, 1980.

——————. *Statistical Abstract of the United States,* 104th ed. Washington, DC: U.S. Department of Commerce, 1984.

U.S. Department of Health, Education and Welfare. *Health, United States, 1978.* Washington, DC: U.S. Government Printing Office, 1978.

U.S. Department of Health and Human Services. *Health, United States—1980.* Washington, DC: U.S. Government Printing Office, 1980.

——————. *Health, United States—1981.* Washington, DC: U.S. Government Printing Office, 1981.

——————. *Health, United States—1983.* Washington, DC: U.S. Government Printing Office, 1983.

Valdez, Robert Otto Burciaga. *The Effects of Cost Sharing on the Health of Children.* Santa Monica: The Rand Corporation, March 1986.

Waitzkin, Howard. *The Second Sickness: Contradictions of Capitalist Health Care.* New York: The Free Press, 1983.

Whitaker, Donald P., et al. *Area Handbook of Japan*, 3rd ed. Washington, DC: U.S. Government Printing Office. 1974.

Yamamoto, Midio, and Susumu Sawaguchi. "The Development of the Social and Health Sciences in Japan." *Social Science and Medicine* 12A (November 1978):485–496.

# 4 HEALTH AND ECONOMIC FACTORS IN HEALTH INSURANCE

Government insurance was first established in 1883 in Germany, where Bismarck introduced a national health insurance program for industrial workers; other European countries followed and today most industrialized countries have some form of universal public health insurance program. In countries where publicly funded universal insurance does not exist, a combination of private and public sources makes health insurance almost universal, as in the United States where over 90% of the population has some form of coverage (Aday, Fleming, and Anderson, 1984) (though the comprehensiveness and quality of such coverage varies widely), and over 90% of hospital expenditures and approximately 68% of all health-service expenditures are paid by a third party (Gibson, Waldo, and Levit, 1983:8–9). Despite the apparent growing popularity of health insurance, it has long been controversial and in recent years has been severely criticized.

A traditional criticism is that it intervenes in the patient-provider relationship and thus leads to more impersonal care (e.g., Simons and Sinai, 1932:155). Other criticisms, though not of principle, are that commercial insurance companies are frequently slow in paying providers or reimbursing patients, have loopholes in the fine print of policies, and renege on their obligations (Guardiono and Trubo, 1974). In recent years, the most frequent criticism has probably been that insurance is responsible for increasing the cost of medical care. An aspect of this is the moral hazard problem. The criticism has been especially strong in recent years, but for many years people have realized that health insurance may encourage physicians to provide excessive care (Simons and Sinai, 1932:92). Some contend that this does not stem from moral hazards per se but from the introduction of insurance in a system of health care that operates in a market that is itself basically irrational.

> The market system in health care works effectively to absorb every additional dollar of public and private funds into increased prices, capital investment, and profits and high incomes. The market system permits each health care unit— whether physician, hospital, nursing home chain, drug company, or other provider—to develop roles based on economic demand and expected profitability rather than on any politically or technically determined assessment of the community's health needs (Brown, 1984:66).

Consequently:

> The injection of public monies (from Medicare and Medicaid) into the largely private medical market provided what seemed like unlimited revenues for physician and private hospitals to order more services and products for their patients, to finance new capital investments, and to raise their prices (Brown, 1984:65).

In this view, it is not insurance, per se, or even public insurance that causes the increase in costs. It is the particular organizational arrangements in which health insurance is introduced. Insurance does, however, leave intact and reinforce "the fiscal, organizational, and programmatic irrationalities in the present market organization of medical care." This is so because an insurance program

> . . . leaves each unit in the system independent of all other units, free to exploit the medical market to its advantages. It thus retains the basic irrationalities in our present medical care system (Brown, 1984:75).

At the same time, an institution that has grown as rapidly as health insurance must have supporters. Some argue that health insurance should be available to everyone so that medical care will not be denied to anyone; advocates of compulsory universal insurance frequently make this argument. Other people favor health insurance because it protects individuals and families against financial disaster. Still others believe that with a comprehensive health insurance plan, greater rationality and efficiency would be achieved in the medical-care system. With a few payers (or in the case of government-sponsored universal insurance, just one major payer), greater leverage could be exerted on the medical sector to reorganize along more economically efficient lines; excess capacity (excess hospital beds) could be reduced, for example. Another argument is that the need for medical care is frequently unpredictable because illness and injury are unpredictable. Thus, health insurance protects against the risks of the unexpected. Some favor health insurance, particularly government-sponsored insurance, on the grounds that it redistributes income. And still others favor insurance because it simplifies paying for medical care. People would not have to bother making separate payments to physicians, hospitals, clinics, and pharmacies. Instead, they would pay a monthly premium to the third party (government or commercial carrier) who would be responsible for seeing that all legitimate medical services were paid. Thus, health insurance has been advocated for a variety of reasons, some of which run exactly counter to the arguments of its critics. Health insurance is not a noncontroversial institution.

In this and the next chapter, I will examine several of the more prominent reasons that have been given for the existence and growth of health insurance. In this chapter, I will review possible health and economic factors; in the next chapter, cultural factors. The review and criticisms of various positions will provide background for chapters 6 and 7 in which health insurance is examined from the analytic perspective of the structure-function framework.

## Health of the Population

Many people believe that health insurance promotes and enhances health by assuring access to medical care. Public insurance programs, in particular, have been advocated on these grounds. In their review of European plans in 1932, Simon and Sinai stated that "when insurance systems are being urged upon governments one of the strongest arguments offered is that improvement in general health will follow prompt, universal medical care" (Simons and Sinai, 1932:157). Similarly, in the United States, John R. Commons, the economist, argued that health insurance would improve the population's health. He believed that "the prevention of sickness (and hence the promotion of health)...is what health insurance means" (Commons, 1919:801).

This view continues to underlie many health-insurance programs today. A study of health-care expenditures of countries in the Organization for Economic Cooperation and Development (OECD) during the seventies states: "In the vast literature of White Paper preambles to parliamentary acts, and public policy reports, there...have been two underlying concerns throughout the OECD area to justify public expenditures on health," and one of them is "an increase of the health status and well-being of the population generally" (OECD, 1977:43). (The other concern is to reduce inequalities in medical care; it is discussed in the next chapter.) Both the Simons-Sinai and the OECD studies also observe little or no movement toward meeting this objective. Simons and Sinai state:

> After the system has been adopted, one of the most amazing things to the out-side observer is the almost complete absence in the vast volume of the discussion of any reference to public health in relation to insurance. Moreover, not even the most intense partisans of insurance have ever attempted to present any statistical proof that insurance has any effect on the general death-and-sickness-rate. No sort of statistical manipulation has ever been able to show any correlation between the movements of death-rates in insurance and non-insurance countries. They have declined in both at about an equal rate, according to sanitary and health measures and other influences; but no difference in any way traceable to insurance can be discovered (Simons and Sinai, 1932:156–57).

Despite this, government insurance programs have grown continuously since this statement. The OECD study states that "despite the increase in expenditures there is no very clear evidence of declining morbidity" (OECD, 1977:86). It also states that "in a period of increasing national income and developing technology, it may be reasonable to ask how much would health standards have improved anyway, even without any public programme, and more generally this means that it is difficult to discuss the programme's 'success' in terms of the resources employed" (OECD, 1977:44). Since level of medical care and mortality and morbidity rates for populations appear to be unrelated, this is altogether understandable.

As noted in the previous chapter, some persons argue that medical care should not be assessed in terms of the mortality rate or even the morbidity rate of the population. If increased access and utilization reduces the proportion of the population operating at less than optimum functioning and reduces the proportion of persons who are in pain and discomfort, then increases in medical care have positive effects. The assumption that medical care has such effects is used by some to justify health insurance. Although Brown recognizes that increased use of medical care resulting from Medicare and Medicaid may not have led to better health, he contends that

> ...diagnostic and curative types of care are important to all people. They reduce the burden of disease by limiting it, speeding recovery, preventing or limiting disability due to illness or injury, and providing comfort and palliation. These are important benefits of improved access to and utilization of medical services...(Brown, 1984:72).

There is some evidence that increases in health insurance may in fact lead to better health. From 1950 to 1978 health insurance grew rapidly, with the proportion of health care expenditures paid by third parties increasing from 34.5% to 67.5% (Gibson, Waldo, and Levit, 1983:8). While it is hazardous to draw cause-effect connections between the growth of health insurance and decreases in mortality, significant decreases occurred in mortality rates during this period. The national age-adjusted death rate decreased from 842 per 100,000 to 606, for a 28% decrease, and life expectancy increased from 68.2 years to 73.3 years; infant mortality decreased over 50%, from 29.2 per 1,000 live births to 13.8 (U.S. Department of Health and Human Services, 1981:107, 111, and 112). Other evidence suggests somewhat more pointedly that increases in insurance may have been at least partially responsible for reductions in mortality. In 1960, before Medicare, life expectancy for persons 65 and older was 14.3, which was just 2.9% higher than life expectancy of 13.9 years at 65 in 1950. By 1970, four years after Medicare had been introduced, life expectancy had increased another 7.2% to 16.3 years (U.S. Department of Health, Education, and Welfare, 1979:90). The death rate from heart disease for persons 65 and over fell 13.9% between 1965 and 1976, which is six times the decrease of 2.3% between 1950 and 1965. In comparison, for persons 60–64 years of age (almost none of whom were covered by Medicare), the decrease was only 2.22 times greater (from 10.1% for 1950–65 to 22.5% for 1965–76) (U.S. Department of Health, Education, and Welfare, 1978:180). Furthermore, the percentage of aged Medicare benficiaries discharged from short-stay hospitals who were dead decreased by 42% from 1967 to 1976, for 9.8% to 6.9% (Helbing, 1980:29). Because of Medicare, older persons may have been admitted earlier after the onset of illness or the quality of care they received may have been better (or both). Such findings are consistent with those who believe that Medicare and Medicaid had beneficial health results (e.g., Davis and Schoen, 1978), though some would argue that the benefits are quite small in comparison to the costs. This aside, as noted in the previous chapter, increases in food supplements and other forms of assistance, along with increases in Social Security payments, beginning in 1965, probably also led to improved nutritional levels and higher standards of living, and these may have had stronger effects than medical care on the death rate. In the absence of studies with refined research designs, one can only say that some tangible health benefits occurred during the period of rapid growth in public health insurance in the United States, but not necessarily because of it.

In addition, a health insurance experiment conducted by the Rand Corporation in four communities suggests that any effect of health insurance on the health status of populations is quite small. In this experiment families were assigned to several insurance plans which varied from complete coverage (free care) to various levels of cost sharing. While adults and children in families with free care used medical care more frequently (Newhouse et al., 1981; Leibowitz, et al., 1986), with few exceptions (persons who had myopia, persons from low-income families who had high blood pressure, and anemic children from low-income families), there was no significant effect on several measures of health status (Brook et al., 1983; Valdez, 1986). All things considered, it would seem that the costs of health insurance would be difficult to defend in terms of the tangible health benefits insurance plans produce.[1]

## Economic Productivity and National Efficiency

Some advocate health insurance because they believe it raises economic productivity. It is therefore viewed as an investment in human capital. The basic argument goes back to slavery in the United States. Although there was a general distrust of medicine during the slavery period, the medical historian, Richard Harrison Shryock, observes that individuals in need nevertheless sometimes relied on physicians for help. While physicians may not have been helpful, and in fact they may have caused much harm, in times of need people were faced with dreadful consequences and, thus, physicians may have been viewed as a last resort. In any case, wealthy plantation owners wanted healthy slaves, who represented a substantial financial investment. For this reason, they were reluctant to permit slaves to engage in dangerous work [because] if a slave died, there was a loss of several hundred dollars (Shryock, 1966:167). In a further effort to preserve the well-being of their slaves, "wealthy planters would regularly employ a prominent local physician to look after their plantations. This gave slaves as good care as was then available and provided them with a rough equivalent of modern health insurance" (Shryock, 1966:167.)

Gaston V. Rimlinger believes that industrialization led to modern health insurance programs. The protection of health was an investment in human capital which people thought would lead to gains in economic productivity. With advancing economies and "the implied rise in the average productivity and relative scarcity of laborers, forms and levels of investments in human capital became profitable that were unprofitable under less-developed [economic] conditions" (Rimlinger, 1966:556). Rimlinger concludes that observations of the social insurance program in Germany by Schwedtman and Emery (1911) indicate that "German employers truly believed that social insurance had a very favorable impact on productivity" (Rimlinger, 1966:567). The idea that health insurance had significant consequences for national efficiency gained acceptance in other industrial economies. In commenting on the National Insurance Act of 1911 in England, Rimlinger states that the motivation for this program had much less to do with philanthropy than with national efficiency (and military preparedness).

> The leaders of the New Liberalism understood (*sic*) the relationship between ill health, unemployment, national economic strength, and national defense. Recruitment for the Boer War had revealed a shockingly large number of young men unfit for military service. David Lloyd-George went to Germany to observe firsthand the effects of health protection on national vitality and efficiency. It became increasingly clear that a national minimum of protection was not merely essential as a basic social right but also was a factor in the conservation of scarce human resources demanded by modern industry (Rimlinger, 1971:60).

Rimlinger notes that the link between health and national efficiency was also recognized (or assumed) by Teddy Roosevelt. Further, prominent advocates of compulsory government insurance in the United States defended health insurance on these grounds. For example, I. M. Rubinow argued in 1913 that national health insurance served the collective economic interest of the nation since experts estimated that the loss to American business through illness each year was 200 million work days and nearly $800 milion. Consequently, he believed a national compulsory program would be "an investment that will pay handsome dividends in the increase of national health, happiness, and efficiency" (Rubinow, 1913: 170). Another advocate, economist Irving Fisher, stated that he was "convinced that the great virtue of health insurance, for decades, perhaps centuries to come, will lie in the prevention of illness" and, therefore, in the reduction in economic waste and the promotion of productive efficiency (Fisher, 1917:17). In defense of health insurance, Commons stated that health was "our first and greatest asset" and "the doctor...our greatest producer of health" (Commons, 1919:800).

The twin themes—better health for the population and increased economic productivity as a result of this—were therefore central in the promotion of national health insurance schemes. Rimlinger states, "It was realized that widespread health insurance could become an important means for the improvement of the nation's health" and that economic "efficiency was the central theme of the emerging social insurance ideology" (Rimlinger, 1971:67, 70). The question of whether technical medical care did *in fact* improve the nation's health simply did not arise.

The absence of any compelling evidence that variation in a nation's health insurance program and the nation's health status and economic productivity has not deterred advocates of national health insurance schemes, of course. Supporters of such plans, as in the United States, for example, have been unrelenting. Despite repeated failures, legislation was proposed in the Congress annually from the thirties to the mid-sixties to establish some form of national health insurance plan. As in other countries, one argument was that such a program should provide medical care for those in need and, thus, improve their physical welfare. Perhaps a more frequent argument is that in comparison to other industrial countries, the United States has fallen behind with an archaic system of health insurance which does not provide coverage for the total population. Observe that in this argument no explicit connection is made between health insurance and health status of the nation. It is the *comparison* of countries in *health insurance coverage* that is central. The situation is basically the same in American industry with respect to private insurance. In a study of 69 Fortune 500 business firms, Sapolsky, Altman, Greene, and Moore (1981) found that management made no attempt to ascertain how health insurance benefits influenced worker productivity and, hence, company profits. Instead, benefits are provided that are in line with those provided by similar companies, and are usually based on "surveys of firms in the same industry or those who are said to be 'peer firms' either because of their similarly structured work forces or because of their national standing.... Thus, major benefit improvements implemented by the nation's richest or more unionized firms diffuse throughout the economy by means of a chain of interfirm comparisons" (Sapolsky, Altman, Greene, and Moore, 1981:571). Such comparisons are not unlike the comparisons critics make between the United States and most other industrial societies.

When the "test" of adequacy of a program is made by way of comparisons such as these, it reflects that the relationship between the inputs of a program and the outputs are not known. The general problem may be seen from Thompson's analysis of ways organizations evaluate their performance (Thompson, 1967). If the cause-effect relationship between inputs and outputs is known and inputs and outputs can be measured with precision, organizations can conduct efficiency tests (e.g., see how much a unit cost of health insurance contributes to a unit of worker productivity). Weaker tests are conducted when cause-effect relationships are less clear and problems of measurement exist. In this situation, organizations (and apparently national governments as well) may perform social tests—they compare what they do or what they accomplish with what other organizations do or accomplish. This is exactly what the most resourceful business firms in the United States do with respect to health insurance. The failure to evaluate health insurance programs in terms of their medical and economic worth is thus not limited to government insurance programs, which are frequently characterized as inefficient and self-perpetuating in nature. This is also true of business firms, which, according to some, have fewer inefficiencies and are less likely to perpetuate programs as ends in themselves.[2]

It is therefore altogether possible that insurance programs are not introduced primarily because of the medical and economic effects they may have or are thought to have. Other reasons may be involved. Since public and private insurance programs have grown at a steady pace for about 100 years and continue to be tenaciously fought for with no substantial tangible health benefit known to result from them during all this time, apparently other reasons have been involved. And insurance programs appear to have sustained those reasons; few people want to reduce their scope. A statement made by Simons and Sinai about government insurance programs is illuminating. They conclude that despite the apparent lack of success such programs have had in improving the health of populations, "it is plain that those who had the closest association with and have most critically observed the operations of insurance have agreed that, however imperfect it may be and however great its defects and numerous evils, the result as a whole is to be preferred to the conditions of private practice in pre-insurance times" (Simons and Sinai, 1932:163). What is the result that is "to be preferred?" Reduction of economic insecurity for individuals and families is one thing.

## Economic Insecurity

The earliest forms of health insurance were primarily concerned with alleviating severe economic adversity for individuals and families. The precarious financial position of blacks in early America is well known. As noted earlier, in the eighteenth-century blacks began forming mutual-aid societies (see Nixon, 1963, and Light, 1972) which "attempted to provide assistance to members in times of sickness and death" (Nixon, 1963:81). Still since medicine was in such a primitive state at the time, it is doubtful if mutual-aid societies were formed solely (or even primarily) to facilitate access to medical care. They were formed instead, primarily to provide assistance that was economic and social, in which individuals were cared for and families were kept together during a member's illness.

Some observers of mutual-aid societies of Europe were explicit about this. In 1916, in a discussion of the role that mutual-aid societies had performed in Europe, Rubinow stated that "the essential function [of mutual-aid societies] is the granting of a money subsidy during the duration of sickness" (Rubinow, 1913:226). Later, in commenting on state insurance programs, Rubinow stated that

> ...health improvement is not a fundamental purpose of health insurance, was not so historically, in the origin of sick benefits centuries ago, and is not fundamental logically. It is or may be a most desirable by-product of the system, but nevertheless a by-product. And even if the expectation of some enthusiasts be justified that this by-product may become more important, more valuable than the main immediate and direct purpose, it is a by-product nevertheless.
>
> The main purpose...is insurance, compensation, and restitution.... To the sick worker and his family, the first and most obvious need is compensation for wage loss due to illness. Its importance to him is even greater than the provision for medical aid (Rubinow, 1934:179).

Therefore, "the crucial test of a compulsory insurance system" is not to raise the nation's health and economic productivity but, rather, "to eliminate sickness as a cause of poverty" (Rubinow, 1916:264).

The role of health insurance in this regard was also recognized by Simons and Sinai in their study of national insurance programs in Europe. "The burden of sickness takes two forms—loss of earnings and the cost of medical care." The new government plans sought "to meet both disabilities" (Simons and Sinai, 1932:2). It is not just the unpredictable nature of illness per se that produces the need for health insurance; the economic consequences of illness are also important. Consequently, as with the mutual-aid societies, early European government insurance plans were largely in response to the economic needs of industrial and low-income workers. Simons and Sinai stated:

> Social [health] insurance is always a result of low wages. In all industrialized countries the wages of large sections of the population are so low that adequate individual protection against...crisis is impossible.... That the whole social [health] insurance problem is, at bottom, one of low wages must be recognized as a basic fact (Simons and Sinai, 1932:16).

Further,

> ...it must never be forgotten that health insurance was created to treat poverty, in which...physicians and dentists are not necessarily expert, and only took up the treatment of disease...as a means of relieving poverty (Simons and Sinai, 1932:16).

The importance of the economic functions of health insurance is apparent in the minds of most people today.

> For the individual living in a welfare state a serious illness is not the personal catastrophe it once was. He knows that his dependents will not starve or lose

their home because of his sudden loss of earning capacity and that all the medical care necessary to restore him to health will be provided without charge (Poynter, 1973:142).

The attempt to cushion the adverse economic consequences of illness is clearly reflected in the Medicare program in the United States. Advocates of the plan viewed "the aged's problem not as the inaccessibility of health services, *but the financial consequences of using those services*" (Marmor, 1970:17; emphasis in original). Hospital coverage, which is the central feature of Medicare legislation, does not provide for all the medical needs of the elderly. But it does cover the most expensive aspect of care. "The hospital benefit was designed...not so much to cope with all the health problems of the elderly as to reduce their most onerous financial difficulties" (Marmor, 1970:17).

That public insurance programs are responsive to the economic anxieties and uncertainties of the recipients is clear. Still, in universal coverage, the plan is not rational for the recipient because the average payment (or tax) is higher than the average benefit. In other plans, however, such as Medicare, the insurance is rational for the recipient. The benefits are received by one portion of the population (the elderly) and are paid for partially by another portion (payers of Social Security tax). But even the many payers are also trading a known premium for an uncertain but larger economic loss because of their family ties with recipients. This is reflected in the legislative strategy used to enact the Medicare program. For half a century prior to Medicare, universal health insurance was debated, and legislative efforts were made to establish such a program in the United States (see Harris, 1966; Hirschfield, 1970). In response to the failure of those efforts, advocates turned to a plan (later called Medicare) that would provide coverage for the elderly and paid for through the Social Security program (Marmor, 1970). Under the circumstances that existed prior to this legislation, "many of the aged [of necessity] fell back upon their children for financial assistance." This gave "Medicare emphasis upon the aged additional political appeal. The strategists expected support from families burdened by the requirement, moral or legal, to assume the medical debt of the aged relatives" (Marmor, 1970:17). Thus, taxpayers with older relatives trade a certain premium for an uncertain but potentially much larger economic responsibility. This, however, would not account for taxpaying supporters of Medicare who do not have such relatives. The explanation for this is not one of economic insecurity but is ethical in nature. It is discussed in the next chapter.

Health insurance to protect against the adverse financial consequences of illness and medical care is probably different today than in its beginning. The mutual-aid societies of American blacks and other groups in the eighteenth and nineteenth centuries were probably exclusively concerned with providing financial assistance to members and their families during the member's period of sickness. The economic assistance provided by early health insurance in Europe was probably more concerned with assuring the availability of medical care and for paying for that care, though the financial assistance for individuals and families may have continued to be foremost. But with changes in disease patterns, from a smaller proportion of acute illness and infectious diseases and a larger proportion of chronic disease and the associated residual disability, along with the development of expensive medical technology to treat those diseases and disabilities, the role of health insurance in covering the cost of medical care (including, in particular, hospital care) has increased.

There has also been a historical change with respect to the element of uncertainty in illness. Many serious illnesses and injuries are unpredictable, of course, and the cost of treatment may be great. But for the chronically ill, and this includes an increasing proportion of the population, health insurance protects against financial adversities that are less uncertain—indeed, almost predictable—in the absence of health insurance. In such circumstances, the uncertainty is not the illness and medical expense themselves, but the severity of the illness and the magnitude of the expense. Thus, the precise economic motivation for health insurance has probably changed over time. Today more than in the past insurance functions to alleviate the fear and anxiety of not being financially able to pay for medical and hospital care that is provided, of the economic adversity if one did pay, or of burdening loved ones with paying the expense if one did not pay. In this sense, health insurance is not so much to assure that medical care is available but to provide economic security in the event that such care is needed and made available. The costs in individual cases may be enormous. It has been estimated that the average cancer patient's medical expense is more than $20,000 and, according to one survey conducted by Candlelighters Foundation of Washington, D.C., the out-of-pocket costs for families with children who had cancer was $28,633 (Kotulak, 1984:19–22).

The economic motivation in health insurance has probably changed in still another way. As noted, for mutual-aid societies and early national health insurance plans in Europe, the focus was on the poor and low-income workers, who have a need for economic assistance during periods of illness. The overall standard of living is much higher today, and families have more wealth to tide them over during periods of crisis. At the same time, the proportion of the population with chronic illness has also increased. Further, the cost of medical care, if it is needed, poses a greater threat to family wealth than it did in the past.

At what point changes in disease patterns occurred and the effect of this on medical costs is difficult to pinpoint. At least one author, writing in 1934, stated that in 1926 the United States was "on the verge of abolishing poverty; yet the complaint against the heavy burden of medical care costs was rapidly rising as did the costs. Nor did they come primarily from the underprivileged, those on the borderline of poverty" (Rubìnow, 1934: 216). Shortly after this, rapid growth occurred in hospital insurance with the development of Blue Cross and Blue Shield, though this appears to be related more to the depression than to rising costs of medical care. It may have also been more a response to the needs of hospitals for capital infusion as some claim (e.g., see Bodenheimer, Cummings, and Harding, 1974) than to the medical needs of the public. Today, however, health insurance clearly does more than provide for the capital needs of hospitals. It is something that most people want. For example, in a national survey of American workers, Staines and Quinn (1979) found that 78.1% have medical, surgical, or hospital insurance in connection with employment, and 83.9% considered this their most important fringe benefit. Another 51.4% wanted their benefits extended, and 47% were even willing to exchange increases in pay for more health benefits. Health insurance is clearly a central concern to most American workers. It is used in all advanced countries to protect individuals against the economic ravages of medical care.

## Insurance as Risk Reduction

Probably the most common analytic conception of insurance is the view that it exists to reduce uncertainty. This view is common among insurance analysts and theoretical economists. In this conception, "insurance is simply protection against risk" (Cullis and West, 1979:61). It is a way individuals have of coping with uncertainty (Arrow, 1963). In return for a small certain sum (the premium), individuals guard against much larger potential losses. They are assured of income when unemployed or disabled, monetary compensation in case of fire or theft, income payments and health care during old age, and of health care expense and possible disability payments when sick. In this view, the purchase of insurance is rational behavior. The amount of the premium depends on the risk involved.

The degree of aversion to risk is often measured by the difference between the certain income an individual is willing to accept and the expected value of a random [uncertain] income. This difference might be interpreted as an insurance premium (Aharoni, 1981:29).

The conception of insurance as risk aversion is not limited to economic theoreticians. In one of the few sociological writings on insurance, Sumner and Keller (1927) link modern insurance to the motive of eliminating the arbitrary and unpredictable element in life. They contended that man has always feared bad luck and misfortune, and that this has been the basis of many social institutions in human history. They believed it was the central motive in the origin of religion. From this perspective, religion is a form of "insurance," which Sumner and Keller describe as "covering the methods of attaining security, of which the modern devices are but specific, highly elaborated, and scientifically tested examples.... [Modern] insurance is a grand device that is now a highly technical process; but its roots go further back than one would think, offhand. Man on earth, having always had an eye to the avoidance of ill luck, has tried in all ages somehow to insure himself—to take out a 'policy' of some sort on which he has paid regular premiums on some form of self-denial or sacrifice" (Sumner and Keller, 1927:749). From this perspective, insurance as a social institution may be viewed as a functional alternative (Merton, 1957) to religion, the extended family or kinship organization, and paternalistic relationships which were much stronger in an earlier social order and which provided the individual with protection against the uncertainty of misfortune and bad luck.

In an important paper on the conception of health insurance as risk reduction, Kenneth J. Arrow (1963) argues that there are two types of uncertainties with respect to the economic consequences of illness and medical care—the risk of becoming ill and the risk of incomplete or delayed recovery. Since "both losses are risk against which individuals would like to insure," the "nonexistence of suitable policies for either risk implies a loss of welfare [utility]" (Arrow, 1963:959). Consequently, "the welfare case for insurance policies of all sorts is overwhelming" (Arrow, 1963:961). (This assumes diminishing marginal utility of wealth, an aspect which is discussed below.)

Arrow's analysis as well as that of most economists is based on a theory of ideal insurance, in which premiums are computed on the cost and probability of unfortunate events. Such probabilities are assumed to enter into individual decisions as to whether the insurance premium is worth the cost. That is to say, decisions as to whether to purchase insurance are rationally calculated. However, Douglas and Wildavsky observe that research indicates, "Most people are not very good judges of probabilities. They go out of their way to get information about dangers confronting them. In addition, they do not take note of information thrust vigorously upon them. They do not make the rational calculations that they are expected to make" (Douglas and Wildavsky, 1983:74). For example, research on disaster insurance reveals that individuals do not choose optimum courses between probable losses and gains when deciding to purchase or not to purchase disaster insurance. Decisions are not made that are consistent with the individual's perception of the chance of the disaster happening, the magnitude of the disaster, and the cost of the insurance premium (Kunreuther, 1978).

With respect to health insurance, some economists argue that the purchase of extensive and comprehensive insurance is not worth what it costs (e.g., Feldstein, 1971). This, however, has no apparent effect on the actual decisions of American workers.

> Anyone who has had an opportunity to negotiate labor contracts or has had a chance to work with employees knows that . . . they all want first dollar coverage for everything, from anesthetics to a broken toe, and to override that is very difficult (MacLeod and Perlman, 1978:237).

A statement by Irwin Wolkstein about an experiment on the University of Pennsylvania faculty is even more pointed with respect to the irrational nature of health insurance decisions.

> At the University of Pennsylvania some time ago, there was a test by a now deceased health economist on whether people would pay the larger premium for a high health cost policy that really was not worth it, or save the money for a lower cost one that was more nearly worth it. After a full explanation, the faculty of the University of Pennsylvania elected the higher cost policy (Wolkstein, 1978:63).

We saw in chapter 3 that decisions about seeking medical care are frequently precipitated by anxiety and stress, and in some instances would be characterized by overreactions and irrational responses to mild or nonexistent physical symptoms. Similarly, decisions to purchase health insurance to assure the availability of medical care and to protect against adverse economic consequences of such care conform to the norm of rational calculation to a most limited extent. Decisions to purchase health insurance would thus appear not to conform closely, or even remotely, to the model of economic utility maximization.

A problem with this economic theory is that it assumes that decisions to purchase insurance are based on complete knowledge. In the real world this is far from the case. While the probability of actuarial statistics may be available, they are not known to the purchaser. More than this, theoretical formulation of insurance is apt to involve the "fallacy of actuarial perfection" (Pfeffer, 1953:5); this is, of attributing greater accuracy to actuarial accounting than is warranted. This is partly because of insurance itself. Insurance coverage changes the probabilities and, therefore, the ability of an individual to define what his risk is: "The insurer [usually] cannot define his risk, partly because the existence of the insurance causes a change in the behavior of the insured and therefore in the probabilities upon which the insurance company has hitherto relied" (Aharoni, 1981: 202). This is the moral hazard problem.

The assumption of "actuarial perfection" is a simplifying one, of course, but it is essential in economic theory because, as noted, the theory assumes that decisions to buy and sell are based on complete knowledge. Thus, in the case of insurance, one would purchase insurance in accordance with the mathematical probability of the risk. But simplifying assumption or not, the reality is that the actuarial forecasts of future morbidity and cost of medical care are apt to be very wide of the mark. This is rather dramatically revealed in the following quote concerning the consequences of the National Health Service in England.

> It may be recalled in his famous report Lord Beveridge [in 1942] anticipated an annual cost of about one-tenth of the present [1973] figure at the beginning of the service and that the cost would decline rather than increase. This assumption was based on the belief that with a reduction of disease resulting from the activities of the health service the demand for medical care would be correspondingly reduced. While it is true that many infectious diseases have been practically abolished or remarkably reduced in incidence, other diseases have increased to take their place. People are certainly living longer and so become more subject to diseases which take a long time to develop, such as lung cancer and heart disease, which are now major killers. The proportion of the population who are over 65 years of age and retired from active employment has also greatly increased and, together with young children, make the greatest demand on the services (Poynter, 1973:153).

The problem is also clear from earlier estimates of the cost of Medicare as well as the continued increase in the cost of premiums for holders of commercial insurance policies. Projections of the future costs of medical care based on actuarial forecasts are not reliable. They may be way off not just because of moral hazards but also because new technology makes treatment more expensive. Also, an increase in medical personnel and facilities may raise the volume and thus the total cost of medical care (Rushing, 1985). Environmental changes may raise (or lower) the level of morbidity unexpectedly, sometimes years after the changes were made, and this may influence the cost of health services.

Economists are not of one mind with respect to the economic utility of insurance, including health insurance. Some believe that because of transaction costs (administrative and sales expense) that are included in the premium, the utility of health insurance is not as great as Arrow's analysis might suggest (Lees and Rice, 1965). Others argue that the moral hazard raises the premium beyond the point where protection against risk yields utility (Pauly, 1968; Blanchard, 1965; and Aharoni, 1981).

Another problem with the conception that health insurance reduces economic risks and maximizes economic utility is that it views the need for medical care as occurring expectedly and with sudden swiftness. Most major needs for medical care may have occurred unexpectedly in the past, and some still occur this way today. However, in far more instances today the need for medical care is not sudden or unexpected. Even if we assume analyses such as those of Arrow's demonstrate that, theoretically, the case for health insurance is "overwhelming," this does not mean that this is the primary cause of health insurance. Indeed, in comparison to the past, it would seem that such a conception is less valid today than in the past. With the increase in the prevalence and incidence of chronic disease, more persons *know* that if their life continues medical care will be needed. Diabetics know they will need insulin therapy, and most also recognize the high probability that they will need treatment for heart problems, glaucoma, and kidney failure. (Although existing conditions are usually not covered by individual policies for a certain period of time, this is not always true for group policies and public insurance.) The change in disease patterns has led to a decrease in the degree of uncertainty in the need for medical care, although dread disease and accidental injury can still strike with unexpected swiftness. It would seem that Arrow failed to give appropriate attention to the increased proportion of medical conditions that are chronic in nature. To the extent that his analysis is valid, it would apply to a decreasing number of individuals because he views insurance as protection against the uncertainty and unpredictability of illness and recovery from illness. "On a lifetime insurance basis, insurance against chronic illness makes sense, since this is both highly unpredictable and highly significant in costs. Among people who already have chronic illness, or symptoms which reliably indicate it, insurance in the strict sense is probably pointless" (Arrow, 1963:963). It is probable, however, that these are the persons who feel the strongest need for health insurance even if, in a theoretical sense, little or no utility is derived.

In addition, Arrow's and other economists' conception of health insurance rests on the assumption of the diminishing marginal utility of wealth. Additional increments of wealth bring proportionately less satisfaction when an individual has much wealth than when he or she has less wealth. Consequently, it is the wealthier individuals for whom health insurance provides the most risk reduction and thus has the greatest utility; such individuals simply have more to lose in terms of financial loss than individuals with limited wealth. Therefore, even though, on the average, the economic worth of the benefits is less than the cost of the premium, the protection against risk represents a bargain; the purchase of insurance is rational. This would be less so for low-income persons because each additional increment of income still generates proportionately greater satisfaction than the risk reduction provided by health insurance. This analysis, based on the assumption of diminishing marginal utility of wealth, fails to appreciate that persons with lowest income, and for whom the marginal utility of wealth diminishes little if at all, are the very persons who are most apt to be in poor health and, therefore, apparently in the greatest need of medical care. However, for them to purchase health insurance would not be rational according to the theory, and for the state to provide it for them would distort market forces. (The problem of market distortions is discussed in chapter 6.) In addition, it is for the lowest income groups that advocates of public insurance most frequently demand health insurance coverage. The conception of health insurance as a rational response to uncertainty under conditions of diminishing marginal utility of wealth leaves many issues about health insurance unresolved.[3]

Anthropologists have approached the issue of uncertainty from a different perspective. Bronislaw Malinowski (1954) believed ritualistic behavior was a response to uncertainty. Religion and magic are both forms of ritual. A difference is that "magic is directed towards the attainment of practical aims" whereas religion is directed toward super-empirical ends (Malinowski, 1954:87). According to this formulation, insurance resembles magic since it is directed largely toward the attainment of a practical aim—to better health, physical comfort, and longer life. Malinowski's description of magic as ritual is in some important respects also descriptive of health insurance:

> Magic supplies primitive man with a number of ready-made ritual acts and beliefs, with a definite mental and practical technique which serves to bridge over the dangerous gaps in every important pursuit or critical situation. It enables man to carry out with confidence his important tasks, to maintain his poise and his mental integrity in fits of anger, in the throes of hate, or unrequited love, of despair and anxiety. The function of magic is to revitalize man's

optimism, to enhance his faith in the victory of hope over fear (Malinowski, 1954:90).

The idea of health insurance as ritual is examined in detail in chapter 6.

The widespread demand for health insurance is similar to another form of behavior by people in primitive and underdeveloped countries today. I refer to fertility behavior which results in high birth rates. Birth rates are high in these countries in large part because children are viewed as economic assets. Children provide the economic security of free field labor and the assurance that they will care for their parents when their parents get old (Mamdani, 1972). Couples don't realize that in the long run their standard of living would probably be better with fewer children. The anxiety of having to pay for field labor and of not being cared for in old age overrules rational calculation of the positive long-term consequences of a reduction in fertility. By the same token, the health status of industrial countries would probably be better if people spent less on health insurance and more on programs of environmental and behavioral change. Just as the natives of underdeveloped countries continue to respond to economic insecurity by having more children, we respond to the fear that we will need medical care and to medically induced economic insecurity by purchasing health insurance. In neither case is enough done to reduce the causes of fear and insecurity.

## Conclusion

When the possible macro health and economic effects (namely the health status and economic efficiency of national populations) of health insurance are considered, it is difficult to justify expenditures for health insurance. Little evidence shows that health status rises with increases in health insurance. Since the belief that health insurance increases national efficiency is based on the assumption that improved health increases efficiency, there is little evidence to support the view that health insurance raises national productivity. Economic insecurity is another factor that has been cited as an explanation for health insurance. The general theoretical formulation here is that health insurance reduces insecurity and is purchased to protect against risk. This is consistent with the conception of anthropologists that ritual is a response to anxieties generated by uncertainty. Chapter 6 will explore in detail the role of anxiety in health insurance and the conception of health insurance as a modern-day ritualistic institution.

## Notes

1. A case in point is the reduction in hypertension with free care, as reported in the Rand experiment (Keeler et al., 1985). The authors of one report from this experiment conclude that free care to everyone would be a very expensive way to detect the few persons with hypertension who would not be detected otherwise.

2. However, as the costs have continued to mount and the questionable benefit of much medical care is being recognized, reports in the media (e.g., MacKay, 1984 and Wack and Hornitz, 1985) would suggest that business firms are becoming more concerned with the economic worth of insurance plans for employees.

3. Two issues should be kept distinct when considering the economic risk reduction conception of insurance. One pertains to the cause of health insurance; the other is whether health insurance is consistent with a theoretical argument. As the discussion of economic insecurity and uncertainty indicates, economists view reduction of uncertainty as a causal factor in health insurance. At the same time, they seem mostly concerned with whether the existence of health insurance is consistent with economic behavior as this is pictured in classical and neoclassical economic theory. For example, Arrow argues that because health insurance reduces uncertainty and to most people the reduction of uncertainty has utility, "the government should undertake insurance in those cases where the market, for whatever reason, has failed to emerge" (Arrow, 1963:961). This appears to be more a rationalization for insurance than an explanation of it. It seems concerned with whether health insurance is consistent with the principles of economic theory, which stipulate how the economy of an industrial society *should* operate if it is to realize the most in economic efficiency and productivity. This argument is different from one which is concerned with the causes of health insurance. Observe also that in this argument reference is to the principles by which *industrial* economies operate, or should operate. Some scholars, anthropologists in particular, contend that the principles of classical and neoclassical economic theory are not universal and simply are not valid for nonindustrial economies. They contend that the economic behavior of natives in primitive societies is not consistent with the way Western economists say people behave (see Polnyi, 1944 and 1959; Moore, 1955; and Dalton, 1961).

## References

Aday, Lu Ann, Gretchen V. Fleming, and Ronald M. Andersen. *Access to Medical Care: Who Has It, Who Doesn't*. Chicago: Pluribus Press, Inc., 1984.
Aharoni, Yair. *The No-Risk Society*. NJ: Chatham House Publishers, Inc., 1981.
Arrow, Kenneth J. "Uncertainty and the Welfare Economics of Medical Care." *The American Economic Review* 53 (December 1963):941–973.
Blanchard, Ralph H. *Risk and Insurance and Other Papers*. Lincoln: University of Nebraska Press, 1965.
Bodenheimer, Thomas, Steven Cummings, and Elizabeth Harding. "Capitalizing on Illness: The Health Insurance Industry." *International Journal of Health Services* 4 (Fall 1974):583–598.
Brook, Robert H., John E. Ware, William H. Rogers, Emmett B. Keeler, Allyson R. Davies, Cathy A. Donald, George A. Goldbert, Kathleen N. Lohr, Patricia C. Masthay, and Joseph P. Newhouse. "Does Free Care Improve Adults'

Health? Results from a Randomized Controlled Trial." *The New England Journal of Medicine* 309 (December 8, 1983):1426–1434.

Brown, E. Richard. "Medicare and Medicaid: Band-Aids for the Old and Poor." In Victor W. Sidel and Ruth Sidel (eds.), *Reforming Medicine: Lessons of the Last Quarter Century*, pp. 50–78. New York: Pantheon Books, 1984.

Commons, John R. "A Reconstruction Health Program." *The Survey* 42 (September 6, 1919):798–801, 834.

Cullis, John C., and Peter A. West. *The Economics of Health: An Introduction.* New York: New York University Press, 1979.

Dalton, George. "Economic Theory and Primitive Society." *American Anthropologist* 63 (January 1961):1–25.

Davis, Karen, and Cathy Schoen. *Health and the War on Poverty: A Ten-Year Appraisal.* Washington, DC: The Brookings Institution, 1978.

Douglas, Mary and Aaron Wildavsky. *Risk and Culture: An Essay on the Selection of Technical and Environmental Dangers.* Berkeley and Los Angeles: University of California Press, 1983.

Feldstein, Martin S. *The Rising Cost of Hospital Care.* Washington, DC: Information Resources Press, 1971.

Fisher, Irving. "The Need for Health Insurance." *American Labor Legislation Review* 7 (March 1917):13–24.

Gibson, Robert M., Daniel R. Waldo, and Katherine R. Levit. "National Health Expenditures, 1938," *Health Care Financing Review* 5 (September 1985): 1–31.

Guardino, Richard, and Richard Trubo. *The Great American Insurance Hoax.* Los Angeles: Nash Publishing, 1974.

Harris, Richard. *A Sacred Trust: The Story of Organized Medicine's Multi-Million Dollar Fight Against Public Health Legislation.* New York: The New American Library, Inc., 1966.

Helbing, Charles. "Ten Years of Short-Stay Hospital Utilization and Costs Under Medicare: 1967–1976." *Health Care Financing Research Report.* Washington, DC: Department of Health and Human Services, Health Care Financing Administration, Office of Research, Demonstrations and Statistics, August, 1980.

Hirschfield, Daniel S. *The Lost Reform: The Compaign for Compulsory Health Insurance in the United States from 1932 to 1943.* Cambridge, MA: Harvard University Press, 1970.

Keeler, Emmett B., Robert H. Brook, George A. Goldbert, Caren J. Kambert, and Joseph P. Newhouse. *How Free Care Reduced Hypertension of Participants in the Rand Health Insurance Experiment.* Santa Monica: The Rand Corporation, October 1985.

Kotulak, Ronald. "Songs of Hope in the Fight Against Cancer." *Consumer's Digest* (January/February 1984):19–22.

Kunreuther, Howard. *Disaster Insurance Protection: Public Policy Lessons.* New York: John Wiley & Sons, 1978.

Lees, D.S., and R.G. Rice. "Uncertainty and the Welfare Economics of Medical Care: Comment." *The American Economic Review* 55 (March 1965):140–154.

Leibowitz, Axleen, et al. *The Effect of Cost Sharing on the Use of Medical Services by Children: Interim Results from a Randomized Controlled Trial*. Santa Monica: The Rand Corporation, March 1986.

MacKay, Charles. "CEOs Balance Corporate, Community Needs." *Business and Health* 2 (December 1984):34–37.

MacLeod, Gordon K., and Mark Perlman (eds.). *Health Care Capital: Competition and Control*. Cambridge, MA: Ballinger Publishing Company, 1978.

Malinowski, Bronislaw. *Magic, Science and Religion, and Other Essays*. Garden City, NY: Doubleday & Co., Inc., 1954.

Mamdani, Mahmood. *The Myth of Population Control: Family, Caste, and Class in an Indian Village*. New York: Monthly Review Press, 1972.

Marmor, Theodore R. *The Politics of Medicare*. Chicago: Aldine Publishing Co., 1970.

Merton, Robert K. *Social Theory and Social Structure*, rev. and enlr. ed. Glencoe, IL: The Free Press, 1977.

Moore, Wilbert E. "Labor Attitudes Toward Industrialization in Underdeveloped Countries." *American Economic Review* 45 (May 1955):156–165.

Newhouse, Joseph, et al. "Some Interim Results from a Controlled Trial of Cost Sharing in Health Insurance." *New England Journal of Medicine* 305 (December 1981):1501–1507.

Nixon, Julian H. "The Changing Status of the Negro—Some Implications for Savings and Life Insurance." *The American Behavioral Scientist* 6 (May 1963):80–82.

Organization for Economic Cooperation and Development (OECD). *Studies in Resource Allocation*. No. 4. *Public Expenditures on Health*. Paris: OECD, 1977.

Pauly, M. V. "The Economics of Moral Hazard: Comment." *The American Economic Review* 58 (June 1968):231–237.

Pfeffer, Irving. *Insurance and Economic Theory*. Homewood, IL: Richard D. Irwin, Inc., 1956.

Polanyi, Karl. *The Great Transformation*. New York: Rinehart, 1947.

————. "Anthropology and Economic Theory." In Morton I. Fried (ed.), *Readings in Anthropology*, vol. 2, pp. 161–84. New York: Thomas Y. Crowell, 1959.

Poynter, Noel. *Medicine and Man*. Middlesex, England: Penguin Books, 1973.

Rimlinger, Gaston V. "Welfare Policy and Economic Development: A Comparative Historical Perspective." *Journal of Economic History* 26 (December 1966):556–571.

————. *Welfare Policy and Industrialization in Europe, America, and Russia*. New York: John Wiley & Sons, Inc., 1971.

Rubinow, I. M. "Sickness Insurance." *American Labor Legislation Review* 3 (June 1913):162–171.

————. *Social Insurance*. New York: Henry Holt and Company, 1916.

————. *The Quest for Security*. New York: Henry Holt and Company, 1934.

Rushing, William A. "The Supply of Physicians and Expenditures for Health Services with Implications for the Coming Physician Surplus." *Journal of Health and Social Behavior* 26 (December 1985):297–311.

Sapolsky, Harvey M., Drew Altman, Richard Greene, and Judith D. Moore. "Corporate Attitudes Toward Health Care Costs." *Milbank Memorial Fund Quarterly* 59 (Fall 1981):561–585.

Schwedtman, F.C., and J.A. Emery. *Accident Prevention and Relief.* New York: National Association of Manufacturers, 1911.

Shryock, Richard Harrison. *Medicine in America: Historical Essays.* Baltimore: Johns Hopkins University Press, 1966.

Simons, A.M., and Nathan Sinai. *The Way of Health Insurance.* Chicago: University of Chicago Press, 1932.

Staines, Graham L., and Robert P. Quinn. "American Workers Evaluate the Quality of Their Jobs." *Monthly Labor Review* 102 (January 1979):3–12.

Sumner, William Graham, and Albert G. Keller. *The Science of Society,* vol. 2. New Haven: Yale University Press, 1927.

Thompson, James W. *Organizations in Action.* New York: McGraw-Hill, 1967.

U.S. Department of Health and Human Services. *Health—United States, 1978.* Washington, DC: U.S. Government Printing Office, 1978.

U.S. Department of Health, Education, and Welfare. *Health—United States, 1979.* Washington, DC: U.S. Government Printing Office, 1979.

————. *Health—United States, 1981.* Washington, DC: U.S. Government Printing Office, 1981.

Wack, Robert L., and Larry Horwitz. "An Alliance for Economic Revitalization." *Business And Health* 2 (January—February 1985):34–37.

Wolkstein, Irwin. "The Impact of Legislation of Capital Development for Health Services." In Gordon K. MacLeod and Mark Perlmann (eds.), *Health Care Capital: Competition and Control,* pp. 7–32. Cambridge, MA: Ballinger Publishing Co., 1978.

Valdez, Robert Otto Bwrciaga. *The Effects of Cost Sharing on the Health of Children.* Santa Monica: The Rand Corporation, March 1986.

# 5 CULTURAL FACTORS IN HEALTH INSURANCE

Even if health and economic factors are important in health insurance, they do not operate in a cultural vacuum. Two major cultural factors are involved. They are medical technology and a value system which holds that medical care should be available to persons who need it regardless of economic circumstance.

## Medical Technology

Medical technology has grown greatly the past quarter century or so. Almost miraculous developments, such as hemodialysis, organ transplants, and artificial implants are well known. As Cochrane (1972) and others have cautioned, however, much of the new technology, such as coronary care units (CCUs), computerized axial tomography, and fetal monitoring have not been proven cost effective. During the 1970s it became clear that at least some of these technologies were *not* cost effective, and in fact generated additional costs with no particular gain in effectiveness (decreases in morbidity and mortality). A particularly telling case is the hospital CCUs which proliferated in the late 1960s and the 1970s. Evidence to date shows that CCUs may be no more effective than even home care (Waitzken, 1983). Different writers give different reasons for the widespread adoption of medical technologies before their cost effectiveness has been proven. Waitzken (1983) emphasizes the social, economic, and political structures of a capitalistic society. Others contend that it is the economic incentives and behavior of users and institutional arrangements in which the technology is housed that are at fault; at bottom, this argument emphasizes weak economic restraints in the adoption and use of new medical technology (Altman and Blendon, 1979). Equally plausible is a formulation which emphasized the accumulation of scientific knowledge and social process. Technological innovation is largely a product of the base of scientific knowledge. Then, once new technology is used in one or a few settings, a social process takes over. New technologies and their potential advantages get emphasized in medical circles and in the mass media, and physicians and the public make demands for their purchase and use. For example, physicians may demand that hospitals purchase the new technology (or facility) in order to provide the best care for their patients. They may justify this by pointing out that some few well-known institutions are using that particular technology. As more hospitals adopt the technology, more physicians request that their hospitals purchase it also. In this way the diffusion process speeds up and the new technology becomes widely adopted. All of this before its cost effectiveness has been demonstrated. While economic and other incentives are clearly involved, the diffusion process is basically social. Physicians and hospitals respond to the behavior of others rather than to scientific data in their adoption decisions.[1]

Regardless of exact factors involved, advances in technological development and subsequent use have led to increases in the cost of medical care. This may be seen by way of several examples.

Prior to the development of insulin, diabetics had a short life expectancy. In 1937, several years after the use of insulin on a large scale, only about 0.4% of the population were known to be diabetic (Drury, Harris, and Lipset, 1981:26). Over the years, additional research led to more knowledge about diabetes and more refined diagnostic and treatment procedures. The percentage of the population known to be diabetic had grown to 2.5% by 1981 (U.S. Bureau of the Census, 1984:126). While it is impossible to know how much this has contributed to the expenditures of medical care in general or to the diagnosis and treatment of diabetes in particular, in 1979 diabetics averaged 11 visits to physicians (Drury, Harris, and Lipset, 1981:28) in comparison to an average of 4.7 visits for the total population (U.S. Department of Health and Human Services, 1981:157). Further, the percentage of diabetics who used selected preventive health services in 1979 was significantly higher than for nondiabetics—eye exams (57% versus 50.1%), glaucoma tests (40.5% versus 33%), chest X-rays (59.3% versus 44.1%), and electrocardiograms (51.8% versus 32.0%) (Drury, Harris, and Lipset, 1981:29).

More dramatic examples of how research expenditures may have led to a rise in expenditures for medical care are coronary bypass operations and the treatment of end-stage kidney disease. Since many heart patients and all victims of renal disease are terminally ill and would die without treatment with technology developed in the past quarter century, almost all the expenditure for these people has been due to new technology. The cost of some technologies, such as computer tomography scanners and electronic fetal monitors, have been will publicized.

Increases in costs of new technology has not not limited to large capital items (Moloney and Rogers, 1979). Between 1950 and 1979, the number of laboratory tests available to physicians increased from fewer than 100 to more than 600 (Fineberg, 1979:14). The number of tests performed for specific conditions and the cost of treatments rose accordingly (see Scitovsky, 1979). For example, the average number of laboratory tests per case of uncomplicated appendicitis rose from 4.7 in 1951 to 7.3 in 1964 to 9.3 in 1971; for perforated appendicitis, tests rose from 5.3 to 14.5 to 31.0. Cost also rose. For uncomplicated and perforated appendicitis, costs rose 126% and 144%, respectively, from 1951 to 1964, and 141% and 176% from 1964 to 1971. The average number of tests for other conditions also rose—cancer of the breast (5.9 to 14.8 to 17.5), maternity care (4.8, 11.5, to 13.5), and forearm fractures with general anesthesia (2.0 to 5.4 to 6.4). The cost for treating each of the conditions rose substantially: cancer of the breast (including radiotherapy), 259% (1951 to 1964) and 105% (1964 to 1971); maternity care, 247% and 105%; and forearm fracture, 175% and 114%. Thus expenditures associated with new technology were clearly not confined to those technologies involving large capital outlays and high service fees per usage.[2]

While many other examples could be given, the point is clear enough. Technological innovation in medicine has raised the cost of medical care. And as the costs increased, there was increased need for financial arrangements which assured that the costs of utilizing such technology would be covered. Health insurance has been a response to this need. Hollingsworth states:

> As medical technology became more efficacious—or as the society believes that medical technology becomes more efficacious—and as the cost for health technology mounts, there will be rising public demands that the state increase its responsibilities in providing health services.
>
> There is, over time, an increasing effort to have the state finance the development and distribution of medical technology, for otherwise many citizens would find the consumption of the technology to be prohibitively expensive (Hollingsworth, 1981:269; author's emphasis).

These comments are specifically addressed to the experience of England and Wales, but obviously they also apply to other countries such as the United States where commercial health insurance is more important. Richard Harris observes that in the United States

> ... as medicine became a far more exact and efficacious science than ever before, it became far more expensive for those who needed it. To many experts in the fields of medicine, economics, and sociology, it became increasingly clear that the only way of spreading the cost burden around was to adopt some form of health insurance (Harris, 1966:76).

Actually, another economic response to expensive medical technology preceded the insurance response in the United States. As the complexity and sophistication of medical technology grew, much technology was beyond the means of individual physicians to finance. However, it was not beyond the means of many hospitals with which physicians were affiliated. Hospitals served the physicians' economic needs in the purchase and maintenance of expensive technology and facilities just as insurance served the needs of the public by assuring that the new services would not be denied to people because of their costs.

This is not to say that the development of health insurance was a mechanical response to the development of advanced medical technology. In the first place, health insurance began before medicine was a highly developed discipline with a highly sophisticated technological base. Clearly other factors were involved in the historical origin of health insurance. At the same time, as advances in medical technology occurred, they stimulated the hopes of many in the population, some of whom were disabled or diseased and waiting for newer technological developments which would permit effective treatment for their conditions. Since much new technology was expensive, as the cost of medical care grew, the perceived need for health insurance also grew. Unless the author's experience is unusual, a large proportion of the American public continuously receives in the mail a barrage of solicitations that attempts to strengthen this perception. I refer to solicitations from private insurance companies attempting to sell additional health insurance through the mail (frequently in connection with credit cards and credit accounts with specific firms). In a recent solicitation, which was for essentially a catastrophic plan (coverage of expenses of $1 million with a $25,000 deductible), a brochure raised the question of whether I needed the plan if I already had coverage where I worked. Why do I need the plan?

> Because modern medicine can perform miracles. Kidney transplants are now possible. More cancer victims are surviving. New drugs and lifesaving machines

can help cure yourself and your loved ones. But the cost of medical care keeps climbing. Even higher than the mindboggling rise of inflation itself. Yet, your basic medical plan may only pay up to a $25,000 maximum. And that's it. The end. You've exhausted your coverage.

The message is clear. Technological miracles lead to expensive medical treatments. Insurance will assure you treatment and protect you from the expense. While insurance may indeed encourage the use of expensive technology (e.g., Feldstein, 1971), it is also a response to advances in technology and to anxieties over what it costs and may cost in the future.

No matter that much technology has not been shown to be cost effective. It is *believed* to be effective (or at least people hope it is), and this has an effect on action, even if the action is not a rational response to what may realistically be expected. People respond to the social definition and expectation that medical care and medical technology produce significant benefits. And one response is to purchase health insurance so that expensive medical technology will be available when needed. This has been the typical response in the United States for the past several decades. It is not limited to the United States, of course, but is typical, in varying degrees, of most other industrial countries where chronic illness (e.g., heart disease and cancer) rather than acute illness predominates. To treat these illnesses take complex diagnostic and treatment modalities involving expensive technology and technical personnel. Much insurance designed to cover the high cost of medical care is a response to this state of affairs, as in the 1973 amendment to the Japanese Health Insurance Law which extended the coverage for high cost medical care (Broida and Maeda, 1978). Health insurance is an adaptive institution to technological advance and its accompanying economic costs. It is also a response to cultural (moral) values.

## Moral Imperative of Medical Care as a Right

It is clear that members of advanced countries are not just motivated to assure that they personally have access to advanced medical care; they believe that their fellow citizens should have this assurance as well. The idea that medical care is a basic human right is not altogether unambiguous, however. It is inevitably involved in the notion of "equity" of access to medical care, which may mean different things, depending on the perspective. First, a distinction must be made between the right to health and the right to medical care, since the former is a function of many things (including heredity) besides medical care (and in light of the review in chapter 3, one may wonder to what extent health actually is a function of medical care). Then, depending on the perspective, access to medical care is equitable or consistent with principles of social justice if it is based on merit, a person's contribution to society, forces of a free market, medical need, or similar treatment for similar conditions (see Outka, 1975). According to Outka's analysis, the "need" conception appears to be the most relevant when the basic purpose of medical care is considered. Medical care should be distributed in accordance with medical condition regardless of financial or other circumstances (Outka, 1975:196). This is consistent with Daniel's argument, which states that medical care should be distributed in accordance with needs because it helps to guarantee equality of opportunity, as this is outlined in Rawls' theory of justice (Rawls, 1971); health care institutions, like a number of other institutions (e.g., educational institutions) insure the existence of equal opportunity (Daniels, 1982). However, in light of the seemingly insatiable character of medical needs, a more realistic conception of medical care as a right would mean that similar treatment is provided to people who have similar needs regardless of the economic or other status of the individuals in question (Outka, 1975:196–198). This conception blends the conception of need with a recognition that resources are limited. In other words, the notion of medical care as a right means that people with the same needs will be treated equally but not necessarily optimally (see Gutman, 1981:543).

This seems to be the dominant notion that has evolved in all industrial societies, where medical care is viewed as a right and where it should be distributed equally in accordance with need (see Illich, 1975). Even in the United States, which has lagged behind other industrialized countries in the development of public insurance plans, in the early part of the century there were strong advocates of legislation for universal national health insurance which would be a "remedy for the inequitable distribution of medical services" (Marmor, 1970:9–10). In his 1948 State of the Union address, President Truman recommended the enactment of "a comprehensive insurance system which would remove the money barrier between illness and therapy...which would protect all our people equally... against ill health." His 1952 Commission on the Health Needs of the Nation stated: "Access to the means of attainment and preservation of health is a basic human right" (Marmor, 1970:9–10). The issue is not one of liberals versus conservatives. "The insurance principles of the welfare state reflect a strong bipartisan consensus for which the entire American political order, business and labor, Democrats and Republicans, deserve the credit and blame" (Gilder, 1981:134). This is exemplified in the conclusion of President Reagan's Commission for the Study of Ethical Problems in Medicine and Biomedical and Behavioral Research (1983:22). In words similar to those of Truman's task force, the Commission stated "Society has a moral obligation to ensure that everyone has access to adequate care without being subject to excessive [economic] burdens." The statement is supported in public opinion. Since 1936 public opinion polls have consistently showed that a majority of the American public were in favor of public insurance programs that would pay for medical care, and the percentage favoring insurance for the poor and elderly has been higher (Erskine, 1975). In industrialized societies "...the concern of individuals for the health of others appears to be stronger than for improving other aspects of their welfare" (Arrow, 1963:954). It is an important aspect of the ethic of medicine.

> It is at least claimed that the treatment is dictated by the objective needs of the case and not limited by financial considerations. While the ethical compulsion is surely not as absolute in fact as it is in theory, we can hardly suppose that it has no influence over resource allocation in this area. Charity treatment in one form or another does exist because of this tradition about human rights to adequate medical care.... The belief that the ethic of medicine demands treatment independent of the patient's ability to pay is strongly ingrained (Arrow, 1963: 950, n. 17).

The moral imperative of medical care as a right has not always been as pervasive in society as it is today. The idea was first advocated by liberals and socialists, who viewed it as equal access to medical care. Paul Starr states, "For most of this century...liberals and socialists had a relatively uncomplicated perception of medicine as a political question. There was one fundamental issue: equal access to medical services" (Starr, 1981:435). While the issue has become more complicated, involving questions of organization, regulation, and control, promotion of equal access to medical care is not limited to liberals and socialists. Like many other ideas that were first promoted by liberals and socialists, equal access to medical care is a principle accepted by conservatives and nonsocialists, and indeed by the general population.

The idea is implied in the conclusions of a recent national survey of access to medical care. The investigators—sociologists—found that while inequities or group differences in access to medical care had almost disappeared in the United States, their data showed that almost 10% of the population was still without insurance in 1982. Since health insurance facilitates access to medical care (whether it improves health status is not discussed in the report), the investigators found the 10% figure to be unacceptable (Aday, Fleming, and Andersen, 1984). They expressed further concern that cutbacks in public financing of health insurance through the "cost containment" strategies of the federal government would endanger the gains that had been made since the mid-sixties. Economists Davis and Rowland come to much the same conclusion in their review of data on health insurance coverage. Despite the increase in national costs that insurance generates, the absence of universal coverage "strains our image as a just and humane society when significant portions of the population endure avoidable pain, suffering, and even death because of an inability to pay for health care" (Davis and Rowland, 1983:150). Access to medical care should be equally distributed, and financial status should not be a barrier to such access. Further, some argue that we cannot turn our back on the ill and that every effort should be made to assure that they receive medical care. This is true even if it is recognized that far greater benefits would accrue, for example, from focusing more on prevention and less on cure. Sick people still have a right to receive medical care. "Even if we could deliver on the uncertain promises of prevention, we have not the right to abandon those who are already ill and in need of care that they cannot obtain" (Eisenberg, 1977).

Whether this cultural imperative existed during the early days of public health insurance programs in Europe is questionable. In light of the previous chapter, in its early days health insurance was probably intended more to alleviate the economic problems associated with sickness than to assure that medical care was received. It is probable that in the United States, at least, this cultural force has grown in strength as the national investment in medical research and technological innovations from that research have increased. This is because people believe such developments should be available to everyone. In 1966, just after the passage of the Medicare and Medicaid legislation, Richard Harris wrote:

> There is a growing conviction that we have not matched the great advances in the medical sciences with health care programs which are truly relevant to the needs of our communities—all communities, and all citizens of these communities (Harris, 1966:vii).

Ten years later, in writing about the history of the politics surrounding the National Institutes of Health, Natalie Springarn wrote, using developments from research on heart disease as an example:

> Health disease, like other disease research, had arrived at a fertile, but broad plateau. What's more, the Golden Years which had propelled it to this plateau, had not been golden for everyone. The turbulent sixties highlighted the inability

for many families to gain access to acceptable health care, in remote rural areas as well as inner city slums (Springarn, 1976:31).

Legislation that led to the passage of Medicare and Medicaid in 1965 were responses to this problem.[3]

The implementation of medical care as a right and the removal of inequalities in access to medical care is not just exemplified in public insurance programs. It is found in the private sector as well. "Today the most widely backed extension of the actuarial state—national health insurance—commands the fervent support of the largest U.S. corporations, led by General Motors and U.S. Steel, which currently offer free medical benefits to all their employees, including, in some companies, the retired" (Gilder, 1981:134–135).

The right of the underprivileged to receive medical care also states that the care be no different than that available to other members of society. Thus, Medicaid and Medicare were "intended to enable the poor [and elderly] to obtain their care from 'mainstream' medicine—that is, the same sources from which upper-working-class and middle-class people get their medical care" (Brown, 1984:64). One could argue, of course, that these programs are more the result of political pressure than the force of an ethical imperative. This would be consistent with the view that Medicaid is more vulnerable than Medicare to budget cuts: the elderly represent a more organized and broadly based political force than the poor. Medicaid is certainly more vulnerable for this reason, but one must also recognize that, this being the case, the force for the program had to come from a source other than political pressures for whom the services are targeted. Support for medical care for the underprivileged has been widespread among the American electorate since the thirties (Erskine, 1975).

In sum, contrary to the way people view many goods and services, people do not view medical care purely from the standpoint of their own self-interest. They believe medical care should be available to others when it is needed. As noted in the previous chapter, some have argued that this enhances health and thus raises the economic productivity of the population. In the economist's terminology this would be a positive "externality" of medical care. Another externality sometimes cited is the decrease in the spread of infectious disease; in this way each individual benefits when others have convenient access to medical care. Therefore, a collective plan which assures that everyone has access to medical care and which pays for medical care is sometimes justified because of the collective benefits that accrue from the diffusion of medical care throughout the population. The problem with this idea is that there is no evidence that increased medical care has, in fact, led to improvements in productivity, and infectious diseases have been largely controlled by changes in public health and in the socioeconomic environment, and these have very little to do with curative medicine (McKeown, 1975). More generally, there is the question about the effectiveness of medical care contributing to the health of large populations. Indeed, as we saw in the last chapter, this has been recognized by others who have examined national health insurance. The search for an economic explanation for the belief that medical care is a right is probably as futile as the search for an economic explanation for freedom of speech. Certainly it is hard to explain in terms of the above-mentioned externalities.

The idea that medical care is a right probably has a number of specific sources, but the fact is, it is a cultural imperative of industrial society. Income and other differences can be tolerated much easier than differences in medical care. Just as everyone is equal in the eyes of God, so everyone is (or should be) equal in medical care. This imperative is unrelenting. Its power is reflected in the works of such persons as Richard Carlson (1975), who believes that medical care has become irrelevant, and Howard Waitzkin (1983), who believes that health is far more a function of the socioeconomic environment than of medical care: both argue that medical personnel and technology should be more evenly distributed across regions, ethnic groups, and socioeconomic classes. Even the most ideo-logically conservative persons, those who might argue against hot school breakfast and lunch programs for children because they believe that feeding children is the responsibility of parents, seem unwilling to argue that medical care for children is solely the responsibility of parents. Medical care, or at least access to medical care, is not something that should distinguish between sectors of the population. Indeed this is one of the most common social defenses of health insurance, particularly of public insurance. For example, the Organization for Economic Cooperation and Development (OECD) report of 1977 states that "the reduction of inequality of access to and use of medical treatment" is one of the two arguments used to justify public expenditures on health (OECD, 1977: 43).

The equalization of medical care by shifting the burden, through insurance, to a large number of policyholders and to society as a whole is a general trend in industrial societies; it is not limited to medical care.

Ever since the enactment of the Poor Laws of Elizabethan England, govern-ments have felt compelled to add a "distributional corrective" to soften the burdens that market forces bring to people....By the twentieth century, social reforms were no longer expressions of *noblesse oblige* but demands—backed by political power—of the more recently enfranchised for greater equality in income opportunity, and, quite often, results. Poverty and disease are no longer accepted simply as unfortunate manifestations of the natural order of things (Aharoni, 1981:135).

In this development, "the new social order...sees equitable solutions as requiring that risks borne by individuals or business be shifted to society" and it "is legitimized by calls for equity, justice and fair play." If equity cannot be achieved, it may impose barriers to the development of new products. "In extreme cases, such as the development of life-prolonging devices (an artificial heart or organ transplant), the impossibility of equitable distribution hinders the development of new techniques" (Aharoni, 1981:8).[4] While the socialization of risk to achieve equity and social justice in society is not limited to medical care, this may be the area that is considered the most important. The OECD report states that equality of access to health care *"may be judged as important as actually redistributing income"* (OECD, 1977:86; emphasis in original). Even countries, such as the United States, where medical care is still predominantly controlled by the private sector and most insurance coverage is in the commercial rather than governmental sector, the dominant view is still that medical care should conform to the principal of equity and social justice. Medical care is a basic human right, and if people or groups of people are denied this right, it is a concern for society as a whole. If the problem is not rectified through private initiative, it should be redressed by public policy, as was done with the Medicare and Medicaid programs.

In general, industrialized societies have achieved this objective rather well. The OECD report observes that "public financing of health services has been found to be reasonably successful in ensuring equality of access to health care." Consequently, today "in most OECD Member countries, children, the old, the disabled, widows and low income earners usually now have access to most types of medical care at no charge or at token charges only" (OECD, 1977:43). In the United States, evidence indicates that public insurance has greatly reduced class and ethnic differences (particularly the differences between blacks and whites) in access to medical services (see Aday, Fleming, and Andersen, 1984). Industrial societies have clearly gone a long way toward implementing the moral imperative that access to medical care is a basic human right and of redistributing medical care across work and ethnic groups and the class structure on an equal basis. This has been accomplished with health insurance.

Implicit in the defense of health insurance on the grounds that it equalizes access to medical care, or at least reduces the differences between groups and subpopulations, is the assumption that equal access would make groups and subpopulations more equal in health status. In light of the nonexistent or weak relationship that national expenditures on health services and health insurance plans have to indices of health status, such an assumption is to be questioned.

In fact, two studies of England, which examine the relationship over time between social class and mortality rates, indicate no reduction in class differences. One study examines whether declines in inequality of access to medical care in the distribution of resources from 1891 to 1971 in England and Wales led to a decline in class differences in mortality rates. Findings show that the proportional differences between classes in mortality actually *increased* despite the decline in access and resources (Hollingsworth, 1981). The author concludes, therefore, that "increasing equality of access, of distribution of resources, of utilization of services has not brought about equality in levels of health across social classes" (Hollingsworth, 1981:268). The other study, the so-called Black Report, was referred to in chapter 3. Findings showed no evidence of a decline in class differences in mortality rates since 1948, the year the National Health Service began, though there was an overall decline for all classes (Gray, 1982). Turning to the United States, racial differences in utilization of medical care have declined since the introduction of federal insurance in 1965, but the infant mortality rate for blacks was about twice as high as for whites in 1982 just as it was in 1965 (U.S. Department of Health and Human Services, 1983).[5]

A qualification to the possible ineffectiveness of insurance programs in reducing group differences in health status pertains to programs that have unquestioned dramatic life-saving effects. If an effective treatment is found for a terminable condition, the assurance that all victims will receive the same treatment regardless of economic circumstances will clearly reduce group differences in survival rates. For example, comparison of patients with end-stage renal disease (ESRD) who were receiving hemodialysis in 1967 to those receiving it in 1978 (several years after this treatment for ESRD victims qualified for Medicare reimbursement) shows that the sexual, racial, educational, age, marital status, employment status, and income status composition of patients clearly shifted to a more equitable distribution (Evans, Blagg, and Bryan, 1981). The analysis by Fox and Swazy (1974:240–279) indicates that selection of patients for treatment prior to Medicare coverage was influenced by considerations of social class and imputed social worth. At the same time, considering the comparative small number of renal disease victims, a change to uniform treatment could have had no significant effect on differences in mortality rates between socioeconomic and demographic categories in the overall population.

Furthermore, it is not altogether clear that a reduction of class and other group differences in health status is always the objective of those who urge more insurance coverage for underprivileged and needy groups. Just as the seeking of medical care seems to be an end in itself sometimes, the equalizaton of class and group differences in *access* to medical care may be viewed as an end in itself. Indeed, some even acknowledge that inequities in access may not reduce differences in health status, but still believe that efforts should be made to remove inequities anyway. Gray quotes the Black Report as follows: "Inequality in the availability and use of health services in relation to need is in itself socially unjust and requires alleviation. This remains true *whatever the proportional contribution which the health services make to health* though the priority to social policy may well properly depend on that proportionality" (Gray, 1982:360; emphasis supplied). The lack of evidence showing that public insurance programs reduce differences between classes in mortality rates and health status has not reduced the conviction of persons who advocate public insurance programs to equalize medical care. Many advocates think such programs should be implemented by society even if there is no apparent tangible health benefit from those programs.

## Conclusion

The roles of medical technology and cultural values as forces in health insurance programs undoubtedly changed over time as the perceived importance of medical care changed. Technology and the very high potential costs of medical care are more important today than they were in the early period of health insurance, whereas economic subsistence and sickness pay during periods of medical crisis were probably more important in an earlier period. And it was probably not until countries had developed to an advanced stage of industrialization and when very definite benefits of medical technology could be demonstrated, at least for certain diseases and injuries, that the cultural imperative that medical care should be available to all regardless of ability to pay developed into a strong moral force.

In this and the previous chapter, the role of several factors as causes of health insurance have been examined. Despite the differences among them, implicit in much of the discussion of all is a common thread, namely, that health insurance serves to alleviate anxiety and insecurity. In the next chapter we will examine health insurance from this perspective in detail.

## Notes

1. The same general process has been described in the prescription of new drugs by physicians at the community level (Coleman, Katz, and Menzel, 1966).

2. Two recent studies indicate that the costs due to the so-called "little-ticket" (low cost per usage) technologies may have leveled off in the 1970s (Scitovsky, 1985; Showstack, Stone, and Schroeder, 1986). Steep rises continued, however, for expensive procedures (sometimes called "big-ticket" technologies), particularly surgery, such as treatment for myocardial infarction, respiratory distress, breast cancer, and maternity care (because of an increase in deliveries by Caesarian section).

3. Medicare and Medicaid were only two such programs, though they were the only insurance programs in the strict sense.

4. Aharoni's reference to artificial hearts is apparently to the federal government's termination of support for the artificial heart program. As is well known, research and development activities on the artificial heart have been assumed by the Humana Institute International, a component of the Humana Corporation, the for-profit hospital chain.

5. Findings that health insurance may not reduce group differences in illness are consistent with the results of other programs designed to reduce inequalities in the population (e.g., Haveman, 1977).

## References

Aday, Lu Ann, Gretchen V. Fleming, and Ronald M. Andersen. *Access to Medical Care: Who Has It, Who Doesn't.* Chicago: Pluribus Press, Inc., 1984.

Aharoni, Yair. *The No-Risk Society.* Chatham, NJ: Chatham House Publishers, Inc., 1981.

Altman, Stuart H., and Robert Blendon (eds.). *Medical Technology: The Culprit Behind Health Care Costs?* Washington, DC: U.S. Government Printing Office, 1979.

Arrow, Kenneth J. "Uncertainty and the Welfare Economics of Medical Care," *The American Economic Review* 53 (December 1963):941–973.

Broida, Joel H., and Nobuo Maeda. "Japan's High-Cost Illness Insurance Program: A Study of Its First Three Years, 1974–1976." *Public Health Reports* 93 (No.2, 1978):153–160.

Brown, E. Richard. "Medicare and Medicaid: Band-Aids for the Old and Poor." In Victor W. Sidel and Ruth Sidel (eds.), *Reforming Medicine: Lessons of the Last Quarter Century,* p. 50–78. New York: Pantheon Books, 1984.

Carlson, Rick J. *The End of Medicine.* New York: John Wiley & Sons, 1975.

Cochrane, A. L. *Efficiency and Effectiveness: Random Reflections on Health Services.* London: Nuffield Hospitals Trust, 1972.

Coleman, James S., Elihu Katz, and Herbert Menzel. *Medical Innovation: A Diffusion Study.* Indianapolis: The Bobs-Merrill Company, Inc., 1966.

Daniels, Norman, "Equity of Access to Health Care: Some Conceptual and Ethical Issues," *Milbank Memorial Fund Quarterly* 61 (Spring 1983):149–176.

Davis, Karen, and Diane Rowland. "Uninsured and Undeserved: Inequities in

Health Care in the United States," *Milbank Memorial Fund Quarterly* 61 (Spring 1983):149–176.

Drury, Thomas F., Maureen Harris, and Lois Lipsett. "Prevalence and Management of Diabetes." In U.S. Department of Health and Human Services, *Health: United States, 1981*, p. 25–31. Washington, DC: U.S. Government Printing Office, 1981.

Eisenberg, Leon. "The Perils of Prevention: A Cautionary Note." *New England Journal of Medicine* 297 (December 1977):1230–1232.

Erskine, Hazel. "The Polls: Health Insurance." *Public Opinion Quarterly* 39 (Spring 1975):128–143.

Evans, Roger W., Christopher R. Blagg, and Fred A. Bryan, Jr. "Implications for Health Care Policy: A Social and Demographic Profile of Hemodialysis Patients in the United States." *Journal of American Medical Association* 245 (February 6, 1981):487–491.

Feldstein, Martin S. *The Rising Cost of Hospital Care*. Washington, DC: Learning Resource Press, 1971.

Fineberg, Harvey V. "Clinical Chemistries: The High Cost of Low-Cost Diagnostic Tests." In Stuart H. Altman and Robert Blendon (eds.), *Medical Technology: The Culprit Behind Health Care Costs?*, p. 144–165. Washington, DC: U.S. Government Printing Office.

Fox, Renee C., and John P. Swazey. *The Courage to Fail*. Chicago: University of Chicago Press, 1974.

Gilder, George. *Wealth and Poverty*. New York: Bantom Books, 1981.

Gray, Alastair McIntosh. "Inequalities in Health. The Black Report: A Summary and Comment." *International Journal of Health Services* 12 (No.3, 1983): 349–380.

Gutman, Amy. "For and Against Equal Access to Health Care." *Milbank Memorial Fund Quarterly* 59 (1981):541–560.

Harris, Richard. *A Sacred Trust: The Story of Organized Medicine's Multi-Million Dollar Fight Against Public Health Legislation*. New York: The New American Library, Inc., 1966.

Haveman, Robert (ed.). *A Decade of Antipoverty Programs: Achievements, Failures, Lessons*. New York: Academic Press, 1977.

Hollingsworth, J. Rogers. "Inequality in Levels of Health in England and Wales, 1891–1971." *Journal of Health and Social Behavior* 22 (September 1981): 268–283.

Illich, Ivan. *Medical Nemesis: The Expropriation of Health*. New York: Random House, 1976.

Marmor, Theodore R. *The Politics of Medicare*. Chicago: Aldine Publishing Co., 1970.

McKeown, Thomas. *The Role of Medicine: Dream, Mirage, or Nemesis*. Nuffield, England: Nuffield Provincial Hospitals Trust, 1976.

Moloney, Thomas W., and David E. Rogers. "Medical Technology—A Different View of the Contentious Debate Over Costs." *New England Journal of Medicine* 301 (December 1979):1413–1419.

Organization for Economic Cooperation and Development (OECD). *Studies in Resource Allocation*. No.4, *Public Expenditures on Health*. Paris: OECD, 1977.

Outka, Gene. "Social Justice and Equal Access to Health Care." *Perspectives in Biology and Medicine* 18 (Winter 1975):185–203.

President's Commission for the Study of Ethical Problems in Medicine and Bio-medical and Behavioral Research. *Securing Access to Medical Care: The Ethical Implications of Differences in the Availability of Health Services*, Vol. I: *Report*. Washington, DC: U.S. Government Printing Office, 1983.

Rawls, John. *A Theory of Justice*. Cambridge, MA: Harvard University Press, 1971.

Scitovsky, Anne A. "Changes in the Use of Ancillary Services for 'Common' Illness." In Stuart A. Altman and Robert Blendon (eds.), *Medical Technology: The Culprit Behind Health Care Costs?*, pp. 39–56. Washington, DC: U.S. Government Printing Office, 1979.

———. "Changes in the Costs of Treatment of Selected Illnesses, 1971–1981." *Medical Care* 23 (December 1985):1345–1357.

Showstack, Jonathan A., Mary Hughes Stone, and Steven A. Schroeder. "The Role of Changing Clinical Practices in the Rising Costs of Hospital Care." *New England Journal of Medicine* 313 (November 7, 1985):1201–1207.

Springarn, Natalie Davis. *Heartbeat: The Politics of Health Research*. Washington–New York: Robert B. Luce, Inc., 1976.

Starr, Paul. "The Politics of Therapeutic Nihilism." In Peter Conrad and Rochelle Kern (eds.), *The Sociology of Health and Illness: Critical Perspectives*, pp.434–448. New York: St. Martins Press, 1981. Originally published in *Working Papers for a New Society*. Washington, DC: Center for the Study of Public Policy, 1976.

U.S. Bureau of the Census. *Statistical Abstract of the United States*, 104th ed. Washington, DC: U.S. Government Printing Office, 1984.

U.S. Department of Health and Human Services. *Health—United States, 1981*. Washington, DC: U.S. Government Printing Office, 1981.

———. *Health—United States, 1983*. Washington, DC: U.S. Government Printing Office, 1983.

Waitzkin, Howard. "A Marxist View of Health and Health Care." In David Mechanic (ed.), *Handbook of Health, Health Care, and the Health Professions*, pp.657–682. New York: The Free Press, 1983.

# 6 HEALTH INSURANCE AND INSTITUTIONALIZING MARGINAL UTILITY DECISIONS

The most common interpretation of health insurance emphasizes the reduction of economic risk. As noted in the previous chapter, however, risk reduction fails to account for the fact that people want health insurance for others and not just for themselves. Further, it does not explain why people want health insurance despite the questionable medical and economic benefits it apparently provides; other factors besides medical and economic outcomes must be involved. And some economists question the economic utility of health insurance because of moral hazards and administrative costs. In addition, health insurance has significant social consequences for society that are simply beyond the purview of frameworks that emphasize the reduction of economic risk. In this and the next chapter an alternative interpretation of health insurance will be presented in which social consequences are central. The interpretation will be in the tradition of functional theory in anthropology and sociology. In this framework a clear distinction is made between the causes and the consequences of social institutions. The causes of any social institution involve historical, social, economic, and political events and processes. Some of these were described with respect to health insurance in the previous two chapters. However, the focus of the functional framework is the motives, attitudes, and perceptions that underlie social institutions: in this particular case, health insurance. It therefore emphasizes psychological factors which support the existence of a social institution. From this perspective, health insurance is viewed as having significant features in

117

common with certain institutions in simple societies that anthropologists study. It is viewed as a form of modern-day ritual. Then in the next chapter, the social consequences of health insurance for society will also be viewed as similar to those of ritual in simple societies. The focus of the interpretation, then, is on the psychological causes of health insurance at the individual or micro level and the social consequences at the societal or macro level.

This is not to say that economic factors are to be ignored. The purchase of health insurance is, after all, a form of economic behavior. Indeed, the idea of utility maximization and marginal utility in economic theory serves as a point of departure for the interpretation presented.

## Health Insurance and Marginal Utility

Optimally, according to economic theory, when individuals make purchasing decisions, they buy "at the margins." This means that the satisfaction expected from the good or service being purchased is compared to the satisfaction that is foregone from not purchasing other goods and services. The theory assumes that the buyer has perfect knowledge of the goods and services and that he or she rationally weighs alternative ways of spending his or her money. Thus, in medical care, individuals would compare the benefits they forego with the health benefits they expect when they spend money for health services. If the expected utility is greater than the utility expected from alternative goods and services, the individual will choose to purchase medical care.

Most economists recognize that decisions about medical care deviate from this conception in a number of respects. People rarely have adequate knowledge on which to make rational decisions about medical care, and this is particularly true for hospitalization and technologically based treatment; they must rely on physicians to make decisions for them. Also, quality of medical care is more difficult to assess than most products; patients frequently do not know if an incomplete recovery is due to less than adequate treatment, and conversely, patients don't usually know the probability that the lack of provider intervention would either make no difference, make them well, or make them worse. In addition, the subsequent cost of medical care may not be known, and because of the potential complications, physicians will frequently not know this either. Knowledge about the quality of care, the outcome to expect, and the economic consequences is most limited. This obviously makes rational reflection difficult. Furthermore, because restrictions are put on providers' or suppliers' entry in the market, the patient is limited in alternative sources of care he or she may seek. Of course, one may choose between physicians, but "shopping around" can be expensive, it may delay treatment and therefore cause the condition to worsen, and it tends to be discouraged by the norms regulating peer relationships between physicians. Thus, even if one makes a calculated choice between medical expenditures and other products (a choice that, I will note below, is most difficult and in certain respects undesirable), comparison of the same product (medical care) provided by different suppliers may be difficult to make. Decisions to seek medical care deviate from the economic model of the rational buyer in a number of respects.

Nevertheless, economists use this model in their analysis of health insurance. It is used by those who believe that insurance produces, on the average, more satisfaction or utility than dissatisfaction or disutility. In this instance it is viewed as an adaption to conditions of uncertainty, as we saw in chapter 4. Others criticize health insurance from the perspective of this model. This criticisms will be reviewed below. Then the limitations of this criticism from a *social* perspective will be presented.

The criticism emphasizes the causal role of health insurance in the rising cost of medical care. With health insurance, as with insurance in general, responsibility for the economic consequences of individual decisions is shifted to a larger group with whom one pools his resources (premiums). Consequently, "the movement is away from a reliance on the rational individual as decision maker and a bearer of the consequences of his choice..." (Aharoni, 1981:1). Since one does not suffer the full economic burden of his or her behavior, one is less constrained by market forces. A problem in most forms of insurance, therefore, "is that the insured may modify their behavior: They may even attempt to cause the events against which they are insured to happen" (Aharoni, 1981:1). This is the moral hazard problem which leads to higher prices. More generally, the problems may be viewed as a distortion of marginal utility functions. This will be discussed with specific references to the effect of health insurance on hospital care as outlined by Martin S. Feldstein.

According to Feldstein, "the growth of private and public insurance coverage has no doubt been the single greatest cause of rising hospital costs" (Feldstein, 1971:27). He believes that "the essence of the hospital-cost inflation problem" is that "*increased insurance has induced hospitals to improve their product and provide much more* expensive and sophisticated care" (Feldstein, 1977:43; author's emphasis). Since hospitals can be assured that expensive treatment will be paid by insurance, budgetary restraints are relaxed and greater investments are made in expensive medical technology. This occurs despite the lack of any particular desire on the part of the public for more expensive care. Indeed, "the effect of prepaying health care through insurance, both private and government, is to encourage hospitals to produce a more expensive product than consumers actually wish to purchase...to produce more expensive care than the public really *wants*" (Feldstein, 1971:76; emphasis supplied). If it weren't for third-party payers, hospitals would weigh their decisions more before investing in expensive technology and would not invest so much money in such technology. The supply side of the market is therefore distorted. Similarly, if patients did not know that hospital payments (or a large proportion thereof) would be paid by a third party, they (or presumably physicians) would seek fewer services, and this would give people more money to spend on alternative goods and services. Thus, health insurance distorts demand also. Consequently, "the result of... extensive insurance has been to extend the provision of hospital care far beyond the point where an extra dollar's worth of cost is justified by the benefits that it produces" (Feldstein, 1978:226). Without insurance, people would purchase more nonmedical goods and services from which they would derive more utility and they would derive more utility from the medical care they did purchase. With insurance, marginal utility decisions are distorted. People act irrationally by purchasing something that provides little if any benefit and, indeed, something they don't even *want*. In general, then, health insurance distorts the market because it encourages providers to supply more care and more expensive care, and purchasers to purchase more care and more expensive care than would be the case if payment came directly from the patient's pocketbook. Such expenditure is considered irrational because it does not produce as many benefits as its cost justifies; more benefit could be obtained by purchasing alternative products.

Evidence does indeed show that people who are fully insured utilize more services than persons who are at risk for part of the cost of medical care. (For a review of studies prior to 1978, see United States Department of Health, Education, and Welfare, 1978:13–14; and Newhouse, et al., 1981). Presumably persons at most economic risk (with no health insurance) are more apt to purchase services more consistent with their medical needs and, hence, services that produce benefits that justify their costs.[1] This is not inconsistent with the evidence reviewed in chapters 3 and 4 concerning the effect of medical care and health insurance on health status. It is something else to say, however, that people do not *want* the medical care they receive. Carlson and McKeown, both of whom also question the benefit of curative medical care, recognize that their view is not shared by the public. Carlson states, "The public's value preferences [for medical care] are real" and that "only when those value preferences change will medicine change" (Carlson, 1975:29), and McKeown acknowledge that "the provision of acute [including hospital] care...is a response to what the patient usually considers to be his more urgent need" (McKeown, 1976:179). Thus, even if the health benefits of medical care are most limited and additional increments of care yields no health benefit at all, people still want medical care, as the review of the evidence in chapter 3 indicates. This is not to say that people are not concerned about the cost of medical care. Data from the 1982 National Survey of Access to Medical Care reveals that out-of-pocket costs were the most frequently cited source of dissatisfaction with medical care, with 40% expressing that they were less than "completely satisfied" with this (there was no difference between the poor and nonpoor in this regard). In another study conducted by Louis Harris (1979:17–18), respondents were asked, "If there was *one* change you could make in health and the health care system in the United States, what would it be?" Twenty-five percent mentioned costs. And 35% disagreed with the statement that hospitals "give good value for the money" (Harris, 1979:72). Still, 48% agreed that hospitals do give good value, 82% believed that hospital care provided by physicians was "pretty good" to "excellent," and 79% believed the same for nursing care; and of those persons hospitalized within the past year, 87% were "somewhat" to "very satisfied" with the care they received (Harris, 1979:71, 72). While most people (82%) said they believe "we should be able to get the same quality of hospital care we now get at a lower price" (Harris, 1979:71), it is not improbable that the percentage would be as high or higher for most other goods and services. For persons who were hospitalized, 42% expressed "a great deal" of confidence in the "people in charge of running hospitals." This is higher than any other institution (29% expressed confidence in schools and 16% in law firms) (Harris, 1979:8). Fifty-seven percent believed that the quality of care in hospitals today is better than it was 10 years ago (Harris, 1979:23). A review of studies of patient satisfaction with medical care (Aday et al., 1980) concludes that all ethnic, age, residential, regional, and other demographic and social categories express high levels of satisfaction with medical care.

In terms of stated preferences, there is simply no evidence that people believe they get less benefit and satisfaction from expenditures for medical care than from other products. At the same time, the tangible health benefits appear to be most limited. Hence, health insurance would appear not to be rational. The question, however, is not whether it is rational but why people want insurance protection so that medical care is available when it is thought to be needed. A major reason is to avoid having to make marginal utility decisions when purchasing medical care.

## Institutionalizing Decisions to Purchase Medical Care

It is possible to avoid such decisions if they are institutionalized, as with health insurance. Then decisions are based on requirements as stated in insurance policies, and these are frequently the result of decisions by persons other than the recipients of care (e.g., by legislators, employee representatives, and representatives of employing organizations, often in negotiation with representatives of insurance companies). Marginal utility functions may indeed by "distorted" because of this. But greater overall satisfaction may actually be the result. People may rather have the "distortion" than to have to make marginal utility decisions themselves, in which they would pay for the costs of medical care directly and be constrained to compare the costs and benefits of medical care with the costs and benefits of alternative products.[2]

One advantage of not having to make such decisions pertains to the unpredictable nature of illness and injury. Although changes in illness patterns make the need for medical care relatively less unexpected today than in the past, need for medical care still "is not a matter of choice, like the purchase of a new car, [and sometimes it does come] unexpectedly, out of the blue..." (Poynter, 1973:157). The conception of health insurance as adaptation to uncertainty emphasizes this idea. When people purchase health insurance, they may calculate that the premium is worth the cost because of the reduction of economic risk that a medical crisis might entail. Whether it is really worth the cost and a rational decision is, as we know, something on which economists do not agree. The point to note here, however, is that a decision about insurance is made prior to the crisis itself. Then the time when medical care is *needed*, the necessity to make a decision is lessened if there is insurance coverage, and in some instances decisions are altogether removed from the realm of choice. Since the cost of treatment is covered, people may not even think of foregoing treatment. Indeed, this may be the tendency even when people are *not* covered by insurance. When people think they need medical care, they are less apt to compare its costs and possible benefits with other products than is normally the case in economic transactions.

> It is frequently said...that medical care is pricing itself out of the market, a misleading phrase inasmuch as medical care is not a commodity which we

choose to buy or not as we please but as we must. However plausible economists may present this situation, it is, when stripped of all verbage, one in which patients are at a disadvantage in that they can have no means of judging the true economic cost of their treatment, and if they exercise "consumer resistance" by deferring to a consultation, their disease may be beyond treatment (Poynter, 1973:12–13).

In a sudden medical crisis, calculating the cost and benefit of medical care may be virtually impossible because of the crush of events alone. Consideration of alternative ways to spend money is out of the question because no alternative to medical treatment is thinkable at the time. In 1934, before health insurance was so widespread, I. M. Rubinow (1934: 195) stated:

> Medical aid is a service of a peculiarly urgent character. There is not much weighing or measuring of the quantity of service needed or desired. Normally the consumer does not want it at all. In fact, he does not even want to want it (if that does not sound too Irish); but when he wants it he wants it badly. He wants as much of it as the situation may demand and more, and at the time he is willing to pay the highest possible price he can pay, whether he can afford it or not. [He may be] willing to sacrifice his savings of the past and mortgage his future. He is even willing sometimes to contract for a price which he knows he will never be able to pay. In other words, the conditions for price-making are quite different from [conditions for the ordinary economic products]. Medical aid deals with health and life. When needed, it has infinite use value.

When medical care is needed or thought to be needed, people often do not weight alternative uses of their money; the need is too pressing and considered too urgent. To be forced to choose between medical care and alternatives in one's expenditure would be unbearable in many instances. Since health insurance insulates people from having to make such a choice, it eliminates or at least reduces the agony and stress that could be involved in even having to consider losing something that has "infinite use value." Health insurance makes it easier for people to do what they think is best for their physical welfare when they think it may be in jeopardy.

In addition, as is all too often the case, medical treatment may have long-term adverse consequences. Health insurance is beneficial in this respect also. If decisions about medical care were not institutionalized, or largely so, the individual makes an autonomous choice. This "implies first that the chooser knows the real alternatives which are open to him," which we have seen may not exactly be the case, but in addition, the choice is made "according to the value criteria or a utility function which [the individual] will not later regret" (Boulding, 1973:24). However, at the time medical care is needed, possible long-term adverse consequences may not be considered because of the press of events. Long-term physical and financial tragedies may be such that, in *hindsight*, the individual may wish he/she had given more weight to such consequences at the time the decision was made. The individual may regret the decision he or she made to purchase medical care that resulted in a dire economic or physical fate. Health insurance moderates the *long*-term regret that might be a result of a deliberate choice. If treatment is chosen that leads to a tragic result, the individual must accept the fact that he or she was at least partly responsible. In many instances the agony would be great. Although health insurance does not make the objective consequences any less tragic or regrettable, it may make them easier to live with simply because the consequences are not the result of the victim's calculated decision. The decision was largely institutionalized. By alleviating the personal agony involved, health insurance has significant long-term psychological utility.[3]

Some proposals emphasize more cost-sharing by patients in insurance plans (e.g., greater use of co-payment and deductibles) (e.g., Feldstein, 1977; Enthovan, 1980). In essence, such plans are designed to generate or increase the agony of persons when they need, or think they need, medical services in order to reduce expenditures for medical care. As Ginzberg states, advocates of such programs "want consumers to feel the pain of parting with their limited dollars at the moment of purchase, as a means of moderating demand for more numerous and more expensive services" (Ginzberg, 1980:114). This may indeed lower the consumption of medical care, but it would have significant adverse consequences as well. Furthermore, to what extent such a strategy is acceptable to the American public (or to the citizens of other industrial countries) is most debatable. Prepaid health insurance may raise the cost of medical care, but people apparently prefer this to having to weight out-of-pocket expenditures for medical care versus other goods and services.

### Health Insurance as Ritual

In writing about insurance in general, Pfeffer and Klock (1974:249) state that it is the "underlying anxieties and uncertainties [rather than rational calculation that] create the product demand." Although "there is no easy way to quantify the factors that cause people to act in a given way with respect to anxieties and uncertainties" (Pfeffer and Klock, 1974:246), this does not make them any less significant to individual policyholders. Health insurance has significant benefits because it absorbs much of the anxiety, fear, and uncertainty that would be involved in decisions and outcomes connected with medical treatment. The tendency to institutionalize decision-making under conditions of uncertainty is not limited to medical care. As Douglas and Wildavsky observe, decisions involving risk in general tend not to be made by "private ratiocination" but occur in such a way that "the social process slides the decision making and prior editing of choices onto social institutions" (Douglas and Wildavsky, 1983:85). Health insurance is a form of such "sliding." The routinization of purchasing decisions about medical care by institutions is the result of underlying anxieties, and it has psychological benefits accordingly.

As has been noted, when only the health benefits are considered, one may logically conclude that the purchase of health insurance is irrational; the cost paid is usually greater than the benefits received. Clearly improvement in the health status of the population over the years has not been proportional to the additional expenditure for health services. Anthropologists and sociologists have long observed, however, that just because institutionalized behavior is irrational does not necessarily mean that it is undesirable. Behavior that results in the distortion of economic utility functions may still have significant noneconomic utility. The ritual of the Trobriand Islanders before they enter their canoes to fish in the dangerous sea (Malinowski, 1954) or the rain ritual performed by members of other preliterate societies are clearly not rational in the sense that they accomplish what they are intended to. One may say of the rain ritual, for example, that marginal utility functions, in the general sense, are distorted since the value received in terms of the objectives sought—higher crop yields—is less than it would be if the same behavior were devoted to the cultivation of crops. At the same time, ritual, which is an institutionalized response to anxiety and fear (Homans, 1950:322–30), may serve to reduce the perceived uncertainty of important outcomes—e.g., the uncertainty of a good crop because of the unpredictability of the weather. It may give a sense of confidence and security about the future. It is repeated, not because it leads to higher crop yields but because it relieves anxiety, gives confidence, and reduces uncertainty. And it will abate only when the conditions causing anxiety, insecurity, and uncertainty change. The same is true of health insurance.

There are important differences between health insurance and the rituals of preliterate societies, of course. Social relations among insurance policyholders are based on pooled interdependence whereas participants in preliterate rituals are more apt to be bound by ties of reciprocal interdependence and to be engaged in intense face-to-face interaction. Nevertheless, there are important similarities to be noted.

Like the rain ritual, health insurance appears not to lead to the intended outcome. Certainly in many instances medical care which health insurance makes available contributes little if anything to physical health, and in some instances it may actually lead to physical harm (we don't know the frequency of iatrogenic effects, though some claim they are frighteningly high—e.g., Mendelsohn, 1979), and of course the rain ritual does not make it rain. Furthermore, in both instances other types of behavior would be more effective in achieving the intended results. Efforts would be better spent in the interest of crop yields if the time devoted to ritual were devoted to the cultivation of crops, and changing eating and personal habits as well as joining collective action to create a more hygienic environment would, on average, yield more health benefit than does health insurance. However, such actions would have less effect on a person's sense of security.

In a sense, such a perspective is really not inconsistent with the perspective that argues that since health insurance raises the threshold where marginal choices are made, it distorts economic markets. At the same time, it is a radical departure from that perspective since behavior is not viewed as necessarily undersirable because of the distortion. In the remainder of this chapter we will elaborate on differences between the two perspectives. The discussion will be organized in terms of microsocial benefits of health insurance, that is, the benefits at the individual level; these are reductions in medical, economic, and moral or social anxieties. Then in the next chapter we will examine macrosocial benefits or the positive social consequences for society.

## Medical and Economic Anxiety

In normal circumstances, having to choose between the purchase of medical care and some other product would be difficult. This itself is not unique to medical care; it is often difficult for individuals to choose between the various market products in accordance with their expected utility. There are special circumstances with respect to medical care and health insurance, however.

Medical care itself is often accompanied (and sometimes prompted) by fear and anxiety. This may be due in part to uncertainty, but it may occur even when the diagnosis and treatment is certain, as in a terminal illness. Fear and anxiety inhibit decision-making and make rational calculation of marginal utility difficult. Consequently, the influence of price in guiding purchasing decisions decreases when anxiety plays a role in the decision.

Since health insurance may reduce anxiety to a manageable level (one doesn't have to worry about the economic outcome as well as the medical outcome), it may actually reduce market distortions. Anxiety makes it inevitable that some distortion will exist when one seeks medical care. By lowering anxiety about the cost of medical care (economic anxiety), health insurance permits a more carefully considered decision to be made. A more measured response to perceived need is likely.

This is not to say that the removal of health insurance would not cause people (including physicians) to conserve on medical care, but, rather, that its removal would intensify the anxieties that already exist. Considering the anxiety and fear associated with medical care (and remember some believe that the alleviation of medical anxiety and enhanced peace of mind is the primary function of medical care), the increase in anxiety would be substantial. And contrary to Feldstein's claim that the care provided is more sophisticated and expensive than people actually want, there is the opposite argument that the physician needs a strong technical base and therefore sophisticated and expensive care, in order to give patients the peace of mind they seek (see p. 32).

The argument that there should be less extensive health insurance in order to reduce the expenditures for medical care implicitly focuses on the moral hazard problem. It is thus focused at that point in time when medical care is actually purchased. It argues, essentially, that people should have to make more marginal decisions with respect to medical care at the time it is needed, or thought to be, by reducing their insurance coverage. As noted, this would compound the medical anxiety (e.g., anxiety that care won't be available). In addition, it would introduce the problem of comparing the anticipated benefits from medical care with benefits from alternative expenditures. The assumption that such comparisons should be made is that the comparative benefits can be expressed in terms of the same metric or value; that is, that they can both be measured in monetary units. The ability of people to make such comparisons is questionable. The difficulty can be seen with respect to cost-benefit analysis, which some economists advocate in making decisions about public expenditures on medical care (see Rushing, 1984).

Cost-benefit analysis does in the public sector what the forces of supply and demand sometimes do in the private sector. In the private sector, purchasing and investment decisions are made on the basis of what the purchase or investment would cost the purchaser or investor and what the anticipated return would be. Decisions are made in accordance with the working of market forces. However, some decisions are made in accordance with public policy rather than by forces of the market. In such instances, cost-benefit analysis may assist the policymaker to choose among alternative investments (or "purchases"). In general, policymakers want to invest in those projects that promise to provide the largest surplus of benefits over costs. Cost-benefit analysis requires that costs and benefits be quantifiable in terms of a common metric which allows costs and benefits to be compared. Both must be measured in monetary terms. In this way, the link between the program and the outcome, or between inputs and outputs, is known; the outcomes (benefits) of a program are measured in terms which may be compared with the inputs (costs) of the program. When the anticipated monetary benefits of a program are greater than the monetary costs, the program yields a net benefit. Under this circumstance, the program is worth doing—it is cost beneficial. (However, it may be worth doing less than some alternative program if the net benefits of alternatives were greater.)

A problem occurs in public policies about health because it may not be possible to give medical benefits unequivocal monetary expression. While there are some who contend that the problem is not insurmountable, most authorities would agree with the Office of Technology Assessment (1980) that cost-benefit analysis is not appropriate for evaluating medical technology and other medical programs. Most people refuse or are unable to evaluate public health policies in which explicit monetary values are put on health, life, and freedom from pain. This is reflected in choices of policymakers. An official from the Environmental Protection Agency (EPA) states: "At congressional hearings the political figures won't answer if you ask them to set a limit on the amount that should be spent to save a human life. They take the stance that if there is a risk, then we should do what is necessary to minimize it" (quoted in Douglas and Wildavsky, 1983: 12). The issue of how much health or how many lives saved we get from the cost of a program and whether such outcomes are worth the expenditures are difficult for people to address directly and explicitly. Once public health insurance programs are introduced, as we saw in chapter 4, questions about their actual health benefits have seldom been asked.[4]

The same is true for insurance programs in private industry. Since business firms purchase many billions of dollars worth of health insurance for their employees, some argue that American industry could be a potent force in reducing upward pressures on medical costs (see Council on Wage and Price Stability, 1976). The assumption is that once management finds that its expenditures for health insurance are too great for the return it gets in the form of increased worker health and productivity, it will reduce the insurance coverage. The difficulty here is measuring the benefits business firms receive from health insurance. Presumably business firms pay more attention to the relationship between inputs (cost of materials, of labor fringe benefits, etc.) and outputs (productivity, profits) than most types of organizations. But as noted in chapter 4, a study of 69 Fortune 500 firms indicates that this is not the way decisions about health insurance are usually made (Sapolsky, Altman, Greene, and Moore, 1981). They are made on the basis of what other firms do.

Observe that it may be easier for governments and employers to ascertain the relationship between the economic costs and the medical outputs of health insurance (or other medical programs) than it is for individuals. This is because governments and employers can express outputs as averages and rates, thus eliminating the extreme variation between individuals. However, if the summary value of outcomes of public policy programs cannot be assessed in terms of their costs and if business firms are unable to measure the average effect of health insurance on the health status and productivity of workers, it is *at least* as difficult for individuals to compare medical treatment with alternative uses of their money in their private lives.

Some believe people are able and willing to make such comparisons, and certainly there may be some instances in which some comparisons are appropriate. But most people would agree that the hoped-for results of much medical treatment (health and life) are on a different scale of value from most of the things we purchase. As I. M. Rubinow observed a half a century ago (see above), medical care (or at least the hoped-for results of medical care) has "infinite use value." The difficulty of comparing the hoped for outcomes of medical care with most economic commodities is well reflected in the following statement:

> Expectations of a long life is the most tangible end product of western European civilization.... Besides this gift the material things of our civilization are insignificant. Who would exchange 30 years of life for all the automobiles, radios, television sets, telephones, or even all the bathtubs in the United States? (Osborn, 1951:xi).

To the extent that health insurance is perceived as aiding us to achieve the goal of better health and longer life, the cost of health insurance cannot be compared with outcomes that are measured in monetary units:

> ...in dollars and cents, insurance must actually cost more than the total loss amounts to. But can human happiness or misery be measured so easily by the simple addition of dollars and cents?... The payment of a small insurance premium may cause at most a small amount of discomfort, the effect if multiplied ten thousand times still weighs very much less on the scale of human happiness than ten cases of actual distress (Rubinow, 1916:9).

Thus, although a few people contend that the problem of measuring health benefits in monetary units is solvable in the cost-benefit analysis of medical policy programs (Abt, 1977), probably almost everyone would agree that the assessment is most difficult if not impossible at the individual level. Positive medical outcomes do not just have "infinite use value." They are also uncertain (e.g., the probability that an individual will completely recover from an operation is usually not known to the patient). A patient may therefore be in a position of doing nothing versus spending a large sum of money for an uncertain but highly valued outcome, and in many instances, the most important human outcome at that. Furthermore, the eventual economic costs are uncertain. At best, comparisons of costs and benefits are ambiguous; to have to make such comparisons about matters of life, illness, pain, or impairment would evoke anxiety of a high order. Such comparisons would mean that individuals would deliberately choose between expenditures for their physical comfort, health, or life, for which it is most difficult to give a monetary value, and expenditures for something else. Health insurance eliminates or reduces the necessity to make these choices that everyone will admit would be agonizing to make; hence, the advantage of "sliding" the decision over into the institutional realm.

To summarize, a focus on the distortion of marginal economic utility functions that health insurance creates in the purchase of medical care distracts attention away from some important consequences that health insurance has for individuals. One such consequence pertains to economic anxiety; a major reason health insurance came into existence was to "ensure that patients could receive care without worrying about the cost" (Carels, Neuhauser, and Stason, 1980:xi). "The spread of third-party coverage through private insurance and public programs has freed more patients and physicians from the need to worry about the cost at the time of care" (Aaron and Schwartz, 1984:117). This may have raised the demand and, thus, the cost of medical care, but as Ginzberg (1983:1222) observes, "All nations have determined that prepayment (or entitlement for the entire population) is the only effective way to protect the public against the high costs of hospitalization." Simply stated, if people had to make marginal decisions, they would have to worry about the possibility of such high costs. In many instances the adverse psychological effect of having to make such a decision may be as bad as the uncertainty of the outcome of medical treatment. And since health insurance alleviates such worry about costs, it probably reduces the fear and anxiety associated with medical care itself (medical anxiety). There is a paradox here. Insurance may contribute to a lack of rationality in purchasing decisions; weakened price restraints may lead to more expenditures for medical care than are needed. B.. anxiety impedes rational calculation and insurance reduces anxiety. Consequently, at the time medical care is needed, or thought to be, when decisions become institutionalized by health insurance they are probably at least as rational as marginal decisions precisely *because* they have been institutionalized.

As much of the above discussion reveals, the distinction between medical and economic anxiety is difficult to make in concrete cases. There are no empirical data to show that health insurance has specific consequences with respect to these two conditions. However, several threads of evidence do indicate that health insurance does reduce the level of anxiety and fear in general. In national surveys, fear of illness for self or family, as volunteered in response to an open-ended question, decreased from 65% to 52% to 44% from 1959 to 1964 to 1971 (Cantril and Roll, 1971:19). Significantly, the decline occurred during periods which correspond roughly to periods in which the percentage of health care expenditures paid by third-party payment increased substantially. The percentages for 1955, 1965, and 1970 are 42%, 48%, and 60% (Gibson, Waldo, and Levit, 1983:8). As a result of Medicare, insurance for the elderly increased more than for the general population. Significantly, a more direct measure of anxiety indicates that anxiety decreased for the aged, relative to the rest of the population. In 1957, on a psychological scale of anxiety, 23% of persons over 64 scored "high" and this declined to 17% in 1976, whereas the percent either increased or remained fairly constant for other age groups. For example, for persons in their forties it increased from 14% to 18% (Veroff, Douvan, and Kulka, 1981:354). While the bench mark date in this study is not the year Medicare began, which is 1965, other evidence indicates that anxiety of older persons did begin to decline at this time. Many contend that "the suicide rate can be considered an index of social and psychological adjustment" (Seiden and Freitas, 1980:198). Therefore, a decrease in the suicide rate would be evidence of a reduction of anxiety and, hence, better social and psychological adjustment. Therefore, if the suicide rate has decreased for the elderly more than for the nonelderly since the passage of Medicare, it would suggest that health insurance has decreased anxiety, or at least fear and depression, among the elderly. Statistics show that the suicide rate among the elderly decreased from 12.4% between 1966 and 1975. In comparison, there was an *in*crease of 16.5% for all ages during the same time period (Seiden and Freitas, 1980:198). In accounting for this, Seiden and Freitas state that "an informed observer would have to consider the improvements in Social Security benefits [and] Medicare..." (Seiden and Freitas, 1980:198).

Although the effects of Medicare in reducing anxieties about health and life obviously cannot be separated from those associated with the financial consequences of medical care among the elderly, the evidence would certainly indicate that Medicare does contribute to a greater sense of well-being. Of course, health insurance may contribute to higher costs of medical care, which may increase the level of anxiety. However, evidence indicates that those who have insurance coverage are more satisfied with medical care than those who do not. In the 1982 National Survey of Access to Medical Care, findings show that in comparison to all other groups (as defined by ethnicity, age, residence, region) "the group that was least satisfied with medical care in almost every respect is the uninsured" (Aday, Fleming, and Andersen, 1984:40).

Thus, a perspective that emphasizes market distortions and the irrational or inefficient allocation of resources in the analysis of health insurance is too narrow. That perspective implies that it would be better for society if people took more risks and chances in the market and relied less on health insurance to cover medical expenses. The problems of moral hazards and spiraling costs of medical care would be reduced. The average person would be better off financially. Because health insurance reduces the necessity of making marginal decisions when peole think they may need medical care, they pay more than they would pay if choices had to be made, or in the case of providers, fewer tests would be conducted and less treatment performed. Thus, although health insurance may alleviate much anxiety, insecurity, agony, and personal catastrophe, it does so at the price of inflation. But matters go the other way as well. The objective medical benefits may be small in comparison to what they cost, but the price of health insurance buys more than medical care itself. It buys less fear and anxiety and more economical and mecial security.

## The Sacred, The Profane, and Moral Anxiety

In the previous chapter we observed that medical care has become a fundamental human right in the minds of many persons and is, thus, a moral imperative. People believe it should be available for others and not just for themselves. At the same time, we have observed that, except for programs which have dramatic and immediate life-saving results, health insurance appears to have had little effect in equalizing health status between sectors of the population. This, however, has not deterred advocates of public insurance programs. A reason is that unless medical care is made available to others on the basis of need, it creates moral problems for people.

The moral imperative of medical care is particularly significant for two sectors of the population. One is the poor (including many of the elderly) who do not have the economic wherewithal to pay for much medical care, who are more apt than the well-to-do to be sick, and for whom the cost of medical care even for minor conditions may involve hardship. The other sector consists of persons who have medical conditions that involve expenditures that are beyond the reach of any but the very well-to-do. Unless there were insurance coverage for such persons, medical care could not be distributed equitably. This is because no matter how expensive, some individuals will be able to purchase medical care that they believe or at least hope will be life-saving and life-enhancing in nature. But once a select few receive such care, even if only a small proportion of these are helped substantially, demands are made that it be available to all who may need the care. People believe it is unfair and immoral to limit care to those who can afford to pay for it. This is clearly exemplified in the End-Stage Renal Disease (ESRD) legislation in connection with Medicare.

In 1963, a conference was held to consider the treatment of patients with chronic kidney disease. A conclusion was as follows:

> At this moment there are only a certain number of people who are able to be helped through the technique of hemodialysis. In the immediate future, also, just a small number of people will be able to be treated.... The implementation of a full-scale program will take a number of years. Therefore, we in this country will be faced with the moral problem of having at hand a method of saving life which is not available to all who need it (quote, cited in Rettig [1976:203], is a conclusion of a workshop held in 1963, "Suggestions Regarding Activation and Operation of Community Hemodialysis Centers for the Treatment of Chronic Uremia," in American Medical Association and National Kidney Disease Foundation, Proceedings. Conference to Consider the Treatment of Patients with Chronic Kidney Disease with Uremia 20–28).

Subsequently, the issue became a matter of congressional attention. The issue was whether the cost of hemodialysis and kidney transplants should be provided by the federal government and covered through the Medicare program. One senator stated that although "two proven life-saving therapies for terminal patients" are now available, only persons who can afford to pay for them receive them. "How do we explain that the difference between life and death is a matter of dollars? How do we explain that those who are wealthy have a greater chance to enjoy a longer life that those who are not?" He argued that the U.S. Congress should "begin to set our national priorities straight by undertaking a national effort to bring kidney disease treatment within the reach of all those in need" and not just those who have the ability to pay (Rettig, 1976: 223–234). Another senator stated:

> ...in this country with so much affluence, to think that there are people who will die this year merely because we do not have enough of these machines and do not have enough dollars, so that we do have to make the choice of who will live and who will die, when we already know we have a good treatment that can succeed and keep these people alive, while we are working out other improvements in transplants, finding cures, and everything else necessary. This should not happen in this country (Rettig, 1976:224).

As most people are now aware, legislation for the ESRD program was passed and was incorporated in the Medicare program.

Part of the problem here was purely economic. Some believe that the cost of medical care should not be an undue economic burden; the right to medical care includes the right not to suffer greatly or to die because of its costs. Poynter states, for example, that "if a great number of people in any community are so placed that they become impoverished, and even destitute, through sickness, then any self-respecting community has to do something about it" (Poynter, 1973:31). Clearly, end-stage renal disease would create tremendous financial burdens for most victims if they had to pay for the treatment themselves. But more is involved than economics. While the high cost of treatment was a major factor in the government-subsidizing treatment, "the federal government appears to have been more concerned with ridding itself of the moral dilemma of indirectly deciding who would live and who would die in a country of almost unlimited resources. The easiest way to eradicate this problem was to treat everyone equally by making everyone eligible for the same benefits" (Evans, Blagg, and Bryan, 1981:487). In other words, it was morally unsettling to others (in this specific instance, members of Congress) if choices had to be made as to who got care and who did not. Institutionalizing decisions with health insurance removes the necessity of making such a choice. Since the ESRD program has significant benefits for persons other than the victims, it has important *social* utility as well as utility for the victims themselves.

All instances of medical need are not as severe as this terminal illness, of course, but less severe needs may also involve moral concern. This is true despite the lack of compelling evidence that health insurance has tangible health benefits. For example, Paul Starr (1981) recognizes that much evidence shows weak or nonexistent correlations between resources devoted to medical care and mortality rates and that equalizing medical care does little to equalize health status.[5] He contends nevertheless that equal utilization of medical care has "psychological and moral significance' (Starr, 1981:440). More explicitly, Ramsey states that having to choose between medical and alternative goods and services is "almost, if not altogether, incorrigible to moral reasoning" (Ramsey, 1970:24). When people have to make such decisions and the result is economic hardship or the necessity to forego medical care, we are frequently outraged and upset. As with medical and economic anxiety, moral (social) anxiety—worry, fear, and concern for the welfare of others—is reduced if decisions about seeking medical care are institutionalized by health insurance.[6] Then we don't need to worry as much and be concerned about persons in need (e.g., the elderly) doing without medical care when it is thought to be needed, or of having to do without necessities because of medical expense.

The social significance of medical care in this respect may be understood from the perspective of Emile Durkheim's distinction between the sacred and the profane. In his study of primitive religion, Durkheim argued that societies distinguish two realms of life—the sacred and the profane (Durkheim, 1961). The sacred may include visible objects (natural and man-made) as well as invisible objects and ideas (e.g., God). The crucial difference is in the attitude that members of society have toward them. Objects toward which people feel a sense of awe and veneration are sacred. They may also induce fear and anxiety. The world of the profane is best exemplified by things toward which people have utilitarian attitudes, such as objects involved in economic transactions. An economic value can be given to profane objects and activities but not to sacred objects and activities. The two orders are mutually exclusive, according to Durkheim, and cannot be mixed. People cannot treat sacred objects as profane objects and vice versa.

Medical care in industrial societies contradicts the proposition that the two orders are mutually exclusive. Medical services are provided in exchange for money (though in a small proportion of cases there is no charge). To this extent medical care is profane and utilitarian activity. At the same time, the reverence, awe, and God-like qualities which society imposes on medicine and physicians have been commented upon by more than a few people. Illness and death also receive the attention of officials and members of religious bodies. Because of illness and death, medical care may also induce fear and anxiety as well as reduce those states. Furthermore, since medical care is considered a fundamental right and not just another form of ordinary economic activity, it is not viewed solely in utilitarian terms. It is directed to matters—life and health—that are held to be as sacred as other rights; the availability of medical care should not depend on economic factors. The special place medical care is given by society may be seen by comparing it to other things on which people purchase insurance, such as automobiles, real estate, and credit. It is true that most forms of insurance are regulated by the state, but only in the case of medical care does the state provide a guarantee. (In most industrial countries the state provides universal insurance coverage, and in the United States it is provided for the elderly, the poor, and certain specific groups, such as veterans.) In terms of the attitude and behavior of people with respect to medical care, medical care is certainly imbued with what Durkheim considered sacred qualities. The distinction here is related to the argument that cost-benefit analysis is not appropriate to medical care because it is difficult to put monetary values on life extension, health, and freedom from pain. Of course, if the distribution of death, morbidity, and pain in the population were known, certain economic values could be estimated for earnings lost. Still this would not capture the social cost to society of people saying that they do not experience a sense of duty, of obligation, or responsibility for the medical well-being of persons unknown to them. "What implied money values would [one] place on human lives saved and lost, on sickness induced and prevented?" (Titmuss, 1971:222). In Durkheim's terms, to put economic values on such matters would be profane. If the laws of the market dominated in medical care and decisions about medical care were based altogether on marginal utility, people would get only the medical care they could afford to buy or which they were willing to pay for by doing without other things they might want or need. Viewed from this perspective, there is a conflict between the view that the receipt of medical care should be based on marginal utility decisions and the view that it should be based on need. Medical care is considered an ethical and moral matter, not just an economic matter. It should be distributed in accordance with human need and not economic demand.

At the same time, it *is* purchased in the market for a price. In some instances the price is set by market forces, and in other cases it is based on what is "reasonable and customary" or by a fee schedule, or paid through a capitation plan. Regardless of how the price is set and paid, medical care is activity that is normally performed in exchange for money. In this sense, it is the object of a utilitarian attitude and treated as profane activity. Medical care is thus treated with a mixture of sacred and profane attitudes. Sometimes this is referred to as the "conflicting traditions of the profession" of medicine.

> From the Middle Ages was inherited a semiclerical status—physicians should be more concerned with service than with profits. Hence arose the obligation to

give freely to the poor, a generosity which was rarely expected of merchants. But modern capitalism had involved physicians in a competition for income which could not be ignored and which they tried to reconcile with the service ideal in ethical codes. . . . The public, although it recognized medical charges as an obligation, tacitly assumed that these would not be pressed. Was not the physician the friend of the family, and was not this relationship above mercenary considerations? Professionally speaking, the practitioner thus lived a double life—half benefactor, half businessman—with all the difficulties this entailed. The basic problem remains today. . .(Shryock, 1966:161–162).

The ambivalence between the sacred and profane in medical care is reflected in the public's apparent approval of physicians' high incomes but indignation when they hear about people going without medical care for economic reasons. Such events are newsworthy. It is also seen in the attitudes people have about the geographical distribution of medical personnel and facilities. In a market-driven economy, workers locate where they can sell their labor, and this is often where labor will command the highest wage. Similarly, physicians and other health care personnel are distributed in accordance with, among other things, the ability of various groups to pay for their services. The many programs that the federal and state governments have introduced to bring about a more even distribution of medical services (see Rushing, 1975) is testament that there is a strong force in society which does not think medical care should be distributed solely in accordance with market principles. The distribution of life, health, and freedom of pain should not be distributed by the forces of the market.

The mixture of attitudes, sacred and profane, that we as a society have for medical care, or at least the hoped-for results of medical care, characterize different people in different ways. This is seen with respect to attitudes toward health insurance. Some free-market economists argue that private insurance is all right but public insurance is not (Friedman and Friedman, 1980:103–106). That is, medical care should be treated as an economic commodity like other commodities, even if other free-market economists observe that private insurance as well as public insurance inflates the price of medical care. Other people, however, reject this utilitarian attitude or "profanation" of medical care. In arguing in favor of nonprofit hospital insurance plans, C. Rufus Rorem (1940:92–93), on behalf of the American Hospital Association, stated:

The [nonprofit hospital plan] deal with a service which has long been recognized as a community responsibility. Hospital care must be provided for all persons regardless of their ability to pay. Such responsibility cannot and should not be assumed by a private insurance company [that is, the forces of a free market], the first concern of which should be the financial interests of the policyholders and stockholders....

We have seen that people have difficulty putting a monetary value on medical care and the hoped-for results of medical care. There are a variety of reasons for this, such as the emotional nature of illness and uncertain nature of the outcome of medical care. In addition, however, sacred qualities make medical care something other than *just* a form of economic activity. This is not to say that people view medical care as noneconomic in the same sense that they view freedom of speech and religious expression as noneconomic, though the moral fervor with which some people espouse the principle that medical care should be universally available in response to need is sometimes as strong as that found among those who defend freedom of speech and religion. Medical care occupies an ambivalent position in society with respect to its sacred and profane qualities. While its economic aspect is recognized—providers should be paid, and some are paid very well indeed—most people believe that individuals in need should not have to make marginal decisions when it comes to medical care. Medical care is special. It is a moral matter. We want it for others when they need it as well as for ourselves. Its denial is not just a matter of people doing without in the same sense that people are denied new automobiles and new clothes because their economic resources are limited. Its denial to others evokes a sense of outrage and moral revulsion in us. Health insurance helps to prevent these moral concerns. Even to cut back on public expenditures from the currently high level may be upsetting even if the benefits from such expenditures are hard to document. The Organization for Economic Cooperation and Development (OECD) study put it this way:

> Aspects of medicine appear to be pursued for their "own sake" with little regard for their cost effectiveness. In a sense, this is understandable because the issue is literally one of life and death for the people most closely concerned. In the circumstances it is hard, and *can even appear unworthy*, to suggest that different forms of expenditure would be more desirable (OECD, 1977:83; emphasis supplied).

Even if it doesn't make a difference in mortality and morbidity statistics, how does one put a monetary value on an additional two or three years of life that a cancer victim gains because of the (very costly) treatment he or she has received? The fact is, one can't, as we observed above. In addition, one shouldn't even try. It would be unworthy.

The tendency not to view medical care as ordinary economic activity is even reflected in the private economy, and is illustrated by the provision of charity care for persons who are unable to pay. It is more general than this, however, as the following comment by a member of a cost-conscious health delivery organization (Health Maintenance Organization) illustrates.

> We [this organization] have a long history of taking care of the medical needs of people. It is very difficult to justify withholding something on the basis of...costs. *What people want is what is important.* (Office of Technology Assistance, 1980:136; emphasis supplied.)

The idea that an economic value should not be put on life and health has been espoused by spokesmen for the EPA and the Occupational Safety and Health Administration (OSHA), among others, and the Supreme Court has agreed. On June 18, 1981, the Court upheld a regulation by OSHA which limited the exposure of textile employees to cotton dust, which may contribute to brown lung disease. The Court said that Congress, in passing OSHA regulations, has decided that health is "above all other considerations," and that the economic expense of protecting employees' health is "part of the cost of doing business." This clearly puts health and life, which many believe are enhanced by medical care, on a different scale of value from ordinary economic commodities. Life and health must be protected regardless of cost.

The special attitude we have toward medical care is revealed in the fact that the costs of medical care are often downplayed by those who espouse medical care as a right. As Rettig states, "The policy decision [to extend medical benefits] is normally framed broadly in terms of benefits and costs of saving lives, with the former typically overstated and the latter understated, and cost control is generally a later and subordinate concern. The likelihood that cost control considerations will enter into the initial policy is not high" (Rettig, 1979:109). This is not to say that costs are of no concern. However, people hold medical care in special regard. While it may not be as sacred as freedom of speech and religion, it is certainly considered as more than just another commodity that is bought and sold in the marketplace.

Again an alternative is suggested to the view that greater satisfaction will occur if people are forced to make marginal utility decisions when they purchase medical care. This is that marginal utility decisions are in conflict with the way people view medical care, for others as well as for themselves. This is why even cost-effective analysis and not just cost-benefit analysis is so difficult in medical care. In cost-effective analysis, the benefits and costs of two or more programs are compared, and the metric for measuring outcomes is different from the metric for measuring inputs, which is in monetary units. In medicine, outcomes are measured in terms of such things as relief of pain, reduction in morbidity, and increases in life expectancy, whereas inputs are measured in dollars. Even when a new program or procedure improves outcomes only slightly but has much higher costs than other programs or procedures, the innovation can still be defended as worth the additional cost. Almost any program can be defended, no matter how expensive, in comparision to no program at all. Unless the additional utilization and expenditures associated with the program yields *no* benefit at all, the economically efficient utilization of medical care and medical efficacy are in conflict (Schwartz, and Jostrow, 1978). "The public will almost certainly complain angrily about limits imposed on the use of *potentially* beneficial tests and treatment simply *because they are expensive*" (Schwartz and Jostrow, 1978:1464). Another way of putting this is to say that treating medical care as just an economic commodity that is made available in response to marginal utility functions is in conflict with the prevalent belief that medical care is also moral activity and the expectation that it should be made available when needed regardless of what it costs. When this is not the case, we experience moral anxiety—e.g., worry about others not receiving medical care when it is needed. Since health insurance reduces this anxiety, it has important social benefit. It has significant social utility even though its economic utility may be "distorted."

## Conclusion

To recapitulate, health insurance alleviates anxiety from several sources. The most common view is that it reduces economic anxiety. In this respect health insurance works like other forms of insurance: it protects against financial burdens and disasters. Also, by guaranteeing that medical care will not be denied because of economic reasons, health insurance also alleviates medical anxiety, thus reducing fear of illness or death and contributing to peace of mind. In addition, health insurance protects against moral anxiety. With near universal health insurance, members of society do not have to be concerned about other members of society being denied what is increasingly perceived to be a fundamental human right. Such concern is exemplified by the almost daily heart-rending publicity and subsequent public and congressional responses to individuals and families who suffer from impairments who are unable to pay for the necessary but very expensive treatment. In the United States, Medicare and Medicaid reduce the concern of the *non*elderly and *non*poor that the elderly and the poor will be denied medical care, or that neither will suffer greatly from the economic consequences of receiving medical treatment. Health insurance alleviates moral anxiety by institutionalizing many of the medical decisions that individuals and families, as well as providers, would have to make in terms of marginal utility.

The difference between purchasing health insurance and other products may be seen as follows. Boulding states that "economists study primarily that segment of the social system that is dominated by exchange, and a system of exchange introduces the possibility of a 'measuring rod'—which may be money or some other convenient commodity—by which heterogeneous aggregates of goods may be reduced to a common measure. This advantage is clearly a real one" (Boulding, 1967:5). An advantage of the insurance premium to pay for medical care is not that it allows people a common measure against which they can compare the costs and benefits of other products. Rather, the advantage is that it absorbs much of the uncertainty, ambiguity, conflict, and distress that are inherent in illness and medical care. If medical care were purchased exclusively or largely at the margins, this complex of attitudes would intensify. Health insurance thus helps to moderate the strength of these attitudes. It also serves to alleviate tension and conflict between groups in society, a subject to which we now turn.

## Notes

1. Because of the moral hazard problem, even those economists who view health insurance as producing utility because it reduces risk seem not to disagree with this conclusion (e.g., Arrow, 1968; Cullis and West, 1979:69–70).

2. Institutionalization of decisions is clearly a matter of degree and would vary depending on the level of the deductible and co-payment. To keep the argument simple, this paragraph assumes 100% coverage ("free care").

3. In contemporary economic theory the problem would be viewed differently. According to Weisskopf, in neoclassical theory, whose "founder" is considered to be Alfred Marshall, a decision "that causes regret later is considered as an irrational failure. Allocation of time and energy of resources and income should be based on a lifelong, permanent, lasting scale of preferences, values, goals and meanings" (Weisskopf, 1971:85). As noted, many major medical decisions must be made quickly and in the crush of events. The individual may not have the time or knowledge to make well-thought-out decisions, in which case the decisions are outside the purview of economic theory. And if it is well-thought-out and calculated but with tragic consequences, it may be considered an "irrational failure." Thus, even when the individual does act in a way that economic theory states one should act by purchasing medical care at the margin, an "irrational failure" may be the result.

4. The phenomenon here is reflected in the expenditure of great effort, much time, and thousands and sometimes millions of dollars on rescue missions to save lives of very few persons (sometimes just one). Whether this is a rational allocation of resources is seldom if ever asked.

5. Even so, by citing statistics which show a decline in mortality rates in the post-1965 era, Starr in his major work seems to suggest that government programs for medical care have been partly responsible for reductions in the death rate and improvements in health, though he acknowledges that other programs (e.g., food stamps program) may have been responsible (see Starr, 1982:410).

6. At one level, the term "moral anxiety" is used in the same way it is used in Freud's writings. It is the result of actions and thoughts that deviate from one's conscience, which is the psychological counterpart of cultural beliefs in society, such as the belief that medical care should be available when it is needed as a fundamental human right. However, there is no implication of deeper psychological and biological aspects as is the case in Freud's writings.

## References

Aaron, Henry J., and William B. Schwartz. *The Painful Prescription: Rationing Hospital Care*. Washington, DC: The Brookings Institution, 1984.

Abt, Clark C. "The Issue of Social Costs in Cost-Benefit Analysis of Surgery." In J.P. Bunker, B. Barnes, and F. Mosteller (eds.), *Costs, Risks, and Benefits of Surgery*, pp. 40–55. New York: Oxford University Press, 1977.

Aday, Lu Ann, Gretchen V. Fleming, and Ronald M. Andersen. *Access to Medical Care in the United States: Who Has It, Who Doesn't*. Chicago: Pluribus Press, Inc. 1984.

Aday, Lu Ann, et al. *Health Care in the U.S.: Equitable for Whom?* Beverly Hills, CA: Sage Publications, 1980.

Aharoni, Yair. *The No-Risk Society*. Chatham, NJ: Chatham House Publishers, Inc., 1981.

Arrow, Kenneth J. "Uncertainty and the Welfare Economics of Medical Care." *The American Economic Review* 53 (January 1963):941–973.

————. "The Economics of Moral Hazard: Further Comment." *American Economic Review* 58 (September 1968):154–158.

Boulding, Kenneth E. "The Boundaries of Social Policy." *Social Work* 12 (1967):3–11.

————. "The Concept of Need for Health Services." In John B. McKinlay (ed.), *Economic Aspects of Health Care: A Selection of Articles from the Milbank Memorial Fund Quarterly*, pp. 3–22. New York: Prodist, 1973.

Cantril, Albert H., and Charles W. Roll, Jr. *Hopes and Fears of the American People*. New York: Universe Books, 1971.

Carels, Edward J., Duncan Neuhauser, and William B. Stason. *The Physicians and Cost Control*. Cambridge, MA: Oegelschlager, Bunn, and Hain, Publishers, Inc. 1980.

Carlson, Rick J. *The End of Medicine*. New York: John Wiley & Sons, 1975.

Cullis, John C., and Peter A. West. *The Economics of Health: An Introduction*. New York: New York University Press, 1979.

Council on Wage and Price Stability. "Employee Health Care Benefits: Labor Management Innovations in Controlling Cost." *Federal Register* 41 (September 17):40298–40326.

Douglas, Mary, and Aaron Wildavsky. *Risk and Culture: An Essay on the Selection of Technological and Environmental Dangers*. Berkeley and Los Angeles: University of California Press, 1983.

Durkheim, Emile. *The Elementary Forms of the Religious Life*, translated by Joseph Ward Swain. New York: Collier Books, 1961.

Enthovan, Alain C. *Health Plan: The Only Practical Solution to the Soaring Cost of Medical Care*. Reading, MA: Addison-Wesley, 1980.

Evans, Roger W., Christopher R. Blagg, and Fred A. Bryan, Jr. "Implications for Health Care Policy: A Social and Demographic Profile of Hemodialysis Patients in the United States." *Journal of American Medical Association* 245 (February 6, 1981):487–491.

Feldstein, Martin S. *The Rising Cost of Hospital Care*. Washington, DC: Information Resource Press, 1971.

—————. "The High Cost of Hospitals—and What to Do about It." *The Public Interest* 48 (Summer 1977):40–54.

—————. "Discussion of Inducement and Impediments for Private Corporate Investment in the Delivery of Health Services." In Gordon K. MacLeod and Mark Perlman (eds.), *Health Care Capital: Competition and Control*, pp. 225–227 Cambridge, MA: Ballinger Publishing Company, 1978.

Friedman, Milton, and Rose Friedman. *Free to Choose*. New York: Avon Books, 1980.

Gibson, Robert M., Daniel R. Waldo, and Katharine R. Levit. "National Health Expenditures, 1982." *Health Care Financing Review* 5 (September 1983):1–31.

Ginzberg, Eli. "The Competitive Solution: Two Views." *New England Journal of Medicine* 303 (November 6, 1980):1112–1115.

—————. "Cost Containment—Imaginary and Real." *New England Journal of Medicine* 308 (May 19, 1983):1220–1224.

—————. "The Monetarization of Medical Care." *New England Journal of Medicine* 310 (May 3, 1984): 1162–1165.

Harris, Louis, and Associates. *Hospital Care in America*. Conducted for Hospital Affiliates International, Inc., Nashville, TN, April 1978.

Homans, George C. *The Human Group*. New York: Harcourt, Brace, 1950.

Law, Sylvia A. "Blue Cross—What Went Wrong?" In Peter Conrad and Rochelle Kern (eds.), *The Sociology of Health and Illness: Critical Perspectives*, pp. 280–303. New York: St. Martin's Press, 1981.

Malinowski, Bronislaw. *Magic, Science and Religion, and Other Essays*. Garden City, NY: Doubleday & Co., Inc., 1954.

McKeown, Thomas. *The Role of Medicine: Dream, Mirage or Nemesis?* Nuffield, England: Nuffield Provincial Hospitals Trust, 1976.

Mendelsohn, Robert S. *Confessions of a Medical Heretic*. New York: Warner Books, 1979.

Newhouse, Joseph P., Willard G. Manning, Carl N. Morris, Larry L. Orr, Naihua Duan, Emmet B. Keeler, Arleen Leibowitz, Kent H. Marquis, M. Susan Marquis, Charles E. Phelps and Robert H. Brook. "Some Interim Results from a Controlled Trial of Cost Sharing in Health Insurance." *The New England*

*Journal of Medicine* 305 (December 17, 1981):1501–1507.

Organization for Economic Cooperation and Development. *Studies in Resource Allocation* No. 4. *Public Expenditures on Health*. Paris: Organization for Economic Cooperation and Development, 1977.

Office of Technology Assistance. *The Implications of Cost-Effectiveness of Medical Technology*. Washington, DC: United States Government Printing Office, 1980.

Osborn, Frederick. *Preface to Eugenics*. New York: Harper and Brothers, 1951.

Pfeffer, Irving, and David R. Klock. *Perspectives on Insurance*. Englewood Cliffs, NJ: Prentice-Hall Inc., 1974.

Polanyi, Karl. *The Great Transformation*. New York: Rinehart, 1944.

Poynter, Noel. *Man and Medicine*. Middlesex, England: Penguin Books, 1973.

Ramsey, Paul. *The Patient as Person*. New Haven, CT: Yale University Press. 1970.

Rettig, Richard A. "The Policy Debate on Patient Care Financing for Victims of End-Stage Renal Disease." *Law and Contemporary Problems* 40 (December 1976):196–230.

————. "End-Stage Renal Disease and the 'Cost' of Medical Technology." In Stuart H. Altman and Robert Blendon (eds.), *Medical Technology: The Culprit Behind Health Care Costs*, pp. 88–115. Washington, DC: U.S. Government Printing Office, 1979.

Rorem, C. Rufus. *Non-Profit Hospital Service Plans*. Chicago: Commission on Hospital Services, 1940.

Rubinow, I.M. *Social Insurance*. New York: Henry Holt and Company, 1916.

————. *The Quest for Security*. New York: Henry Holt and Company, 1934.

Rushing, William A. "Social Factors in the Rise of Hospital Costs." *Research in the Sociology of Health Care* 3 (Fall 1984):27–114.

————. *Community, Physicians, and Inequality: A Sociological Study of the Maldistribution of Physicians*. Lexington, MA: D.C. Heath and Company, 1975.

Sapolsky, Harvey M., Drew Altman, Richard Greene, and Judith D. Moore. "Corporate Attitudes toward Health Care Costs." *Milbank Memorial Fund Quarterly* 59 (Fall 1981):561–585.

Schwartz, William B., and P.L. Jostrow. "Medical Efficacy Versus Economic Efficiency: A Conflict in Values." *New England Journal of Medicine* 299 (1979):1462–1464.

Seiden, Richard, and Raymond P. Freitas. "Shifting Patterns of Deadly Violence." *Suicide and Life Threatening Behavior* 10 (Winter 1980):195–209.

Shrylock, Richard Harrison. *Medicine in America: Historical Essays*. Baltimore: Johns Hopkins University Press.

Staines, Graham L., and Robert P. Quinn. "American Workers Evaluate the Quality of Their Jobs." *Monthly Labor Review* 102 (January 1979):3–12.

Starr, Paul. "The Politics of Therapeutic Nihilism." In Peter Conrad and Rochelle Kern (eds.), *The Sociology of Health and Illness: Critical Perspectives*, pp. 434–448. New York: St. Martins Press, 1981.

————. *The Social Transformation of American Medicine*. New York: Basic Books, 1982.

Titmuss, Richard M. *The Gift Relationship from Human Blood to Social Policy*. New York: Vintage Books, 1971.

U.S. Department of Health, Education, and Welfare. *Health—the United States: 1978*. Washington, DC. U.S. Government Printing Office, 1978.

Veroff, Joseph, Elizabeth Douvan, and Richard A. Kulka. *The Inner American: A Self Portrait from 1957 to 1976*. New York: Basic Books, Inc., Publishers, 1981.

Weisskopf, Walter A. *Alienation and Economics*. New York: E.P. Dutton & Co., 1971.

# 7 HEALTH INSURANCE, SOCIAL INTEGRATION, AND SOCIAL COHESION

Although irrational economic behavior may lead to economic inefficiencies, anthropologists and sociologists have long observed that such behavior may have significant psychological and social utility. In the previous chapter, we saw that even if health insurance is irrational from an economic perspective, it may have positive consequences for individuals not unlike those associated with ritual in preliterate societies. Some functional theorists argue, however, that ritual performs a more important service than simply to alleviate anxiety. (Indeed, some argue that rather than anxiety leading to ritualized behavior, it is the failure to perform ritualized behavior that leads to anxiety.) (See Radcliffe-Brown, 1938:46.) Although a rain dance does not lead to the objective that is intended (e.g., to produce rain and, thus, a good crop yield), it may have significant social benefits nevertheless. It brings people together to share in common group activity and thus enhances social integration. In doing so it also promotes a sense of group identity or social cohesion. Health insurance may also promote social integration and cohesion, though for different reasons.

In the first place, since health insurance often makes it unnecessary for individuals—victims, relatives, or providers—to make decisions that would deny people medical care when it is perceived to be needed, health insurance protects people from being excluded from a valued sector of life. Also, with medical care people may be enabled to participate in more of the normal activities of society. Health insurance therefore facilitates people sharing in common activities, thus promoting social integration. Since it assumes that medical care is not denied to persons for economic reasons, it also alleviates discontent and alienation, thus promoting social cohesion.

The view that insurance may promote the social integration of society has been noted by others. It is particularly explicit in Spencer L. Kimball's analysis of insurance law in Wisconsin.[1] Below we will see how health insurance promotes social integration, stability, and cohesion in certain areas, namely, provider-patient relations, hospitals, the class structure, employee-employer relations, the age structure, and the kinship unit. Observations on medical care, health insurance, and social policy will provide a general perspective.

## Medical Care, Health Insurance, and Social Policy

The terms social integration and social cohesion are widely used in sociology but have different meanings. By social integration I will mean participation in activities with others, and by cohesion I will mean a minimum of individual discontent, individual isolation, and alienation, and in consequence, a low level of conflict in social relations. Both connote a social condition which differs from that pictured in classical and neo-classical economic theory in which individuals are viewed in isolation of their group context and where relations (exchange relations) are promoted by differences rather than similarities and are in a state of flux depending on changes in prices and marginal utility. Whereas social integration and cohesion connote stability, economic theory implies change. Consequently, the differences that distinguish modern economics and sociology is "perhaps best illustrated by considering the question of what it is that holds societies together or allows them to collapse. The stability of a society is perhaps as central as any concern in sociology" (Olson, 1968:106). Health insurance promotes integration and cohesion in society and encourages individuals to identify with a collective unit rather than being alienated from it. It thus promotes stability and order. This occurs despite the fact that it may encourage waste and inefficiencies and less than optimal economic outcomes for much of the population (e.g., deviations from optimum marginal utility).

The economist's distinction between collective and noncollective goods provides a good starting point for the analysis of health insurance as an integrating and cohesion-producing institution. Olson defines a collective good "as a good such that nonpurchasers cannot feasibly be excluded from its consumption" (1968:108). Examples of collective goods are national defense and the benefits provided by law enforcement and the system of justice. Noncollective goods are goods that nonpurchasers can be prohibited from consuming; if an individual buys an automobile or loaf of bread, others are usually prohibited from consuming them. Olson argues that in general a society will be more likely to cohere "if people are socialized to have diverse wants with respect to private goods and similar wants with respect to collective goods" (Olson, 1968:108). (A good is anything that people value.) This means that "where individuals have objectives that they can consume or enjoy without others having to participate in this consumption, they will tend to cohere better if they have different tastes and productive capabilities, because this will maximize the gains from exchange among them; on the other hand, where individuals have objectives such that if they are achieved for some they are automatically also achieved for others, the greater the similarity in their tastes and situations the easier it will be for them to agree on a common policy" (Olson, 1968:108–109).

A question is whether medical care is a collective or noncollective good. Obviously, the same precise services that one patient receives cannot be "consumed" by another. At the same time, to the extent that the services received by one promotes the health of others, as in the treatment of infectious diseases, medical care would qualify as a collective good. We have seen, however, that the role of medical care in producing such positive externalities appears to be far less than some suppose. From this perspective, medical care fits the definition of a collective good in only a very limited respect.

The distinction between collective and noncollective goods is related to the distinction between need and economic demand, and to moral anxiety and the moral imperative of medical care as a fundamental human right. Demand is related to differences in income; hence the greater one's ability to purchase medical care, the more one is apt to get it. Need, on the other hand, is not necessarily related to the ability to pay. Need is an equalitarian concept, demand is a libertarian concept, and, as Boulding notes, "liberty is seldom equally divided" (Boulding, 1966:18). If medical care is distributed by the demand, that is, by market forces, it will not be distributed equally in accordance with needs. Need is unifying, demand is divisive. If medical care is distributed solely in accordance with demand, it creates morally indefensible divisions. "One of the main concerns of society for the need for medical care...is the fact that [income] of a sizable proportion of the population...is not large enough to provide a demand for the minimum medical care which a society, or a profession, identifies as need" (Boulding, 1973:18). When the medical needs of others are met, then something of value is also achieved for persons who did not actually purchase and consume the services themselves. People have been socialized to have similar wants with respect to medical care—people want medical care to be based on need rather than on economic demand. In this sense, it should be common activity and not distinguish between people. When this does not occur, as when people are denied medical care because of their economic circumstances, medical care is being treated as a non-collective good. This is inconsistent with the view that medical care is a right, and it causes moral anxiety accordingly. Discontent, alienation, and even outrage may ensue. Cohesion deteriorates accordingly. To the extent that insurance assures that medical care will be made available on the basis of need, it raises the level of cohesion in society. Because of the ethical imperative involved, the denial of medical care may result in alienation and weakened identification with the collective unit (e.g., the United States) among those for whom medical care is readily available as well as among those who have been denied medical care.

This implies that social policy, as distinct from economic policy, focuses on social integration and cohesion rather than on economic efficiencies and demand. Kenneth E. Boulding (1967:7) states:

> If there is one common thread that unites all aspects of social policy and distinguishes them from merely economic policy, it is the thread of what has . . . been called the "integrative system." This includes those aspects of social life that are characterized not so much by exchange in which a quid is got for a quo as by unilateral transfers that are justified by some kind of appeal of status legitimacy, identity, . . . community, [or need].

In the present instance, for example, universal compulsory health insurance would be, and often is, justified because medical care is considered to be a fundamental right. People should receive medical care when they need it. In such instances, most who pay premiums (taxes) do not get benefits that are equal to what they pay; it is not a good economic bargain. This, however, is a "bad deal" only when viewed exclusively in terms of economic self-interest for it provides for a fundamental human right; moreover, many of those who were seriously in need of medical care (e.g., the diabetic, the person who needs an artificial hip) would be more disabled than they would be without the care. Their functional activities would be less, and they would be confined to the margins of society rather than being participants in aspects of the mainstream of society (e.g., work, family, voluntary associations).

In chapter 3 we observed that medical care may help decrease functioning status as well as raise it (because it increases residual disability). If this is true, medical care would have less effect on integrating the chronically ill into society than the above paragraph implies. Observe also, however, that we *know* what the fate will be of many chronically ill persons if they do not get medical care. To withhold care from such persons because on the average it will produce as much or more residual disability than it reduces would evoke the anger and outrage of many people. In a more positive view, in those instances where medical care does not lead to improved social functioning of the chronically ill, there is the good feeling of loved ones, and usually the victim himself or herself, that all was done that could be done. This serves to enhance an individual's feelings of allegiance and identity to the collective unit that provided the "free" care. Therefore, even if there were no objective benefits from medical care in raising the function status of populations, there may be substantial social benefit. While there is no such thing as "free medical care" any more than there is a "free lunch," the return on the economic cost of what is considered free care goes beyond the economic. The issue here is related, of course, to reducing moral anxiety and the idea that medical care is a fundamental human right. While pooled interdependence which characterizes insurance programs may erode the spontaneous personal helping responses, typical in reciprocal interdependence, to come to the aid of one's fellows out of a sense of duty, loyalty, and morality, it does not eliminate the belief that assistance should be provided individuals and families during certain crises. Furthermore, such aid should not be provided on the basis of a strict *quid pro quo* since this could lead to economic ruin for individuals and families. It would also result in more discontent, individual isolation, and alienation from society.

From this perpective, social policy does not rest solely with government actions. Similarities in the social consequences of private and public health insurance are far more significant than differences in underlying motives associated with the development of each. Boulding's statement that "by and large it is an objective of social policy to build identity of a person around some community with which he is associated" (Boulding, 1967:7) could apply to the employee who receives health insurance which his company provides as a fringe benefit. Considering the cynicism that is so widespread today, it may be going a bit far to contend that this evokes feelings of appreciation so strong that the individual's identification with an employing organization is complete. The point is, however, that feelings of appreciation are felt, if only temporarily, and some degree of identification is established or reinforced (see quote below from Sapolsky, Altman, Greene and Moore, 1981:7–26). Observe further that the health insurance fringe benefit is not really an economic bargain to the average worker;

the average worker will pay more than he or she receives in benefits. Additional comments by Boulding are relevant in this respect.

> It sounds a little cynical to say that the object of this [building identity around a collective unit] is to make the individual content with rather poor terms of trade and to persuade him to give up a lot and not get very much in return. There may be very good reasons, however, why unfavorable terms of trade at the psychological level are necessary. In the world of physical commodities terms of trade are usually favorable because exchange in this area is so efficient and is almost always a gain to both parties. The actual cost of the transaction is small in terms of the satisfaction gained by both parties (Boulding, 1967:7).

In the present context (that is, health insurance), terms of trade are un-favorable and there is much inefficiency in the exchanges that are made. However, payers do not usually realize that they are not getting a good economic bargain and they are satisfied with the assurance of coverage, and certainly the beneficiaries are relieved by the benefits they receive.

Recall that the network of social relations established by health insurance is one of pooled interdependence. The relations between policyholders stem from their dependence on the same pool of funds. They pay a small premium in return for the assurance that they will receive a large return when in need. However, while large benefits may be received, the beneficiaries are not asked to make a return gift, other policyholders do not expect one, and there is no moral expectation for the beneficiary to give one. Since the benefits may (and often are) many times greater than the premiums the beneficiary has paid, the benefits operate almost like a grant or unilateral transfer. In this connection, observe Boulding's statement that in contrast to exchange or bilateral transfer, which is the distinguishing mark of the economic, "the 'grant' or unilateral transfer—whether money, time, satisfaction, energy, or even life itself—[is] the distinguishing mark of the social.... This means that...social policy has to concern itself pro-foundly with questions of identity and alienation, for alienation destroys the grant system.·.... Social policy, therefore, is centered in those institu-tions that create integration and discourage alienation, and its success would be measured by the degree to which individual are persuaded to make unilateral transfers in the interest of some larger group or com-munity" (Boulding, 1967:7–8). The benefit paid by health insurance is to a certain extent a form of unilateral transfer: it is not exchange where each party's benefits are proportional to his or her payment; each party assumes that he or she will benefit in time of need; and people on the average give more than they receive. Furthermore, because of the nature of pooled interdependence, those whose benefits are disproportionately high are usually not known to other payers; they are strangers, as it were. Titmuss' summary of social policy is applicable to health insurance (private and public.)

> Considered individually as examples of stranger relationships, more people are expected to contribute—to give—to serve the interests of other people. There is in all these transactions an unspoken assumption of some form of gift-reciprocity; that those who give as members of a society to strangers will themselves (or their families) eventually benefit as members of society. More often than not, however, such donors are in a captive situation; the transaction cannot, therefore, be considered to be spontaneously altruistic in its most attainable form. There is, nevertheless, a vague and general presumption of a return gift at some future date, but a gift that may not be deliberately sought or desired by the individual concerned—as with voluntary blood donors. Few people when well wish to be ill; few people desire operations, blood transfusions, inpatient treatment or social care from social workers. More and more instruments of social policy are in action requiring...these acts of "voluntaryism" which carry with them no wish to return acts or return gifts (Titmuss, 1971:215).

Health insurance benefits are unilateral transfers that require no reciprocal act by the beneficiary or the assumption that the "givers" (those who pay premiums or taxes) will someday be beneficiaries. And because this builds allegiance and cohesion, health insurance must be assesssed in accordance with its *social* consequences, not just the economic costs and the medical benefits it produces.

When viewed from this perspective, private insurance plays a role in social policy despite the fact that the insurer's aim is to make a profit. In discussing policy regulating blood transfusions (whether it should be considered a gift and treated as a donation or an economic commodity and bought and sold in the market), Titmuss makes the following comments about medical care policy in general.

> We speak here, of course, of those areas of personal behavior and relationship which lie outside the reciprocal rights and obligations of family and kinship in modern society. We are thus chiefly concerned—as much social policy is—with "stranger" relationships, with processes, institutions and structures which encourage or discourage the intensity and extensiveness of anonymous helpfulness in society; with "ultra obligations" which derive from their own character and are not contractual in nature. In the ultimate analysis it is these concerns and their expression which distinguish social policy from economic policy... (Titmuss, 1971:212).

While the inclusion of commercial transactions, such as we have in private insurance, would appear to be beyond the spirit of Titmuss' thesis, reflection indicates that the above statement holds for private insurance as well as public insurance. As with public insurance, relations in private insurance are characterized by pooled interdependence and, as a result, we enter an area of "stranger relationships." Also, with unilateral transfers (payments to beneficiaries) we have "anonymous helpfulness" and "personal behavior and relationships which [are] outside the reciprocal rights and obligations of family and kinship." The fact that individuals purchase private insurance with the intention of helping themselves rather than others does not refute the fact that such purchases may have helpful consequences for others. Of course, there are differences between public and private insurance. The beneficiaries of private insurance do not have the sense of appreciation that beneficiaries of public insurance may have for the government and political figures (and society more generally if they understand the source of funds for government insurance). But the unilateral transfer of private insurance may nevertheless give the beneficiary a general sense of thankfulness and lower feelings of discontent and bitterness, which in turn helps to promote positive relations with others (e.g., friends, neighbors, and family). Private health insurance may play an important role in social policy because it has significant social results.

Economists have also noted the similarity between private and public health insurance. For example, Feldstein emphasizes the similarity in his argument that both tend to have adverse economic consequences (Feldstein, 1978). The difference between that analysis and the one presented here is that in the present analysis both types of insurance are viewed as producing positive social consequences. These consequences for specific relations will now be examined.

## Provider-Patient Relations

In the ordinary buyer-seller relationship, two parties come together and each gives up something that the other wants. In most instances, the buyer exchanges money for a commodity (good or service) that the seller has. Economists assume that the buyer has knowledge of the commodity he is buying and is able to judge, in terms of his own preferences, whether the commodity he is buying is worth the price. The cost of the commodity to the buyer is the most valuable alternative to which he or she could otherwise use the same amount of money (which includes saving it); this is the opportunity cost. If the buyer considers the commodity overpriced—if he or she could get the same commodity elsewhere at a lower price or purchase an alternative commodity in which the opportunity cost is less, the buyer goes to another seller who offers the same commodity or another commodity in which the buyer believes the opportunity costs are lower (or utility is higher).

As applied to medical care, there are several problems with this formulation of provider-patient relations, as economists have recognized. One is that the buyer, in this case the patient, usually knows very little about the commodity (the service) and is unable to make an informed judgment as to whether the service is in his best interest in terms of his own preferences. He is dependent on the physician to make such decisions for him, or at least to make strong recommendations with respect to these decisions. Consequently, the behavior expected of the physician toward the patient is different from that of the usual seller toward the buyer. The relationship is based in large part on the expectation that the physician will act in the patient's best interest rather than in terms of his own financial interest (Parsons, 1951:428–479). While the expectation rarely if ever exists in pure form, most will nevertheless agree that society's expectations of physicians with respect to patients is far different from society's expectations of the usual seller toward buyers.[2]

This social bond between patient and physician, and between patient and other providers of health care (e.g., hospitals), is undermined if decisions must be made on the basis of the patient's ability to pay as well as, or instead of, his apparent objective medical needs. It is underminded even if the physician prescribes treatment that is designed to save the patient money if this savings yields lower quality care than would have otherwise been provided. Arrow (1963:966) states, "The safest course [for the physician] to take to avoid not being a true agent is to give the socially prescribed 'best' treatment of the day. Compromise in quality, even for the purpose of saving the patient money, is to risk an imputation of failure to live up to the social bond" that society expects between physician and patient. Victor Fuchs refers to this as the "technological imperative" in medicine, that is, to use all the most advanced and sophisticated technology available that may be of possible benefit to a patient regardless of cost (Fuchs, 1968).

The method by which services are paid is apt to influence the patient's trust of the physician and his relationship with him. If payment is out-of-pocket, the patient may be in the undesirable or frightening position of trying to bargain with the physician about the price of the service he or she thinks she needs, or for a service that he or she can afford. In so doing, the belief that the physician will make the decision that is in the best interest of the patient's health or life is brought into question; trust is undermined. The patient cannot be sure when the physician is responding to the physician's economic interest or to the patient's medical needs. Health insurance helps to eliminate the potential for such mistrust. And, of course, the greater the trust, the greater the cohesion between physician and patient. Except for reasons of personal style and incompetence of the physician or lack of compliance by the patient, neither patient nor physician is apt to become aliented from or disaffected with the other. What is true of the physician-patient relationship is also true of other provider-patient relationships in the medical sector. This is particularly reflected in the indignation that is often expressed when hospitals do not provide the needed service for patients because the patient does not have the ability to pay for it. Such indignation is a reflection of discontent and alienation.

The method of payment that is most apt to generate cohesion in the patient-provider relationship is third-party cost-plus reimbursement. Because third parties pay what the providers say the services cost, plus a percentage for profit, overhead, and the like, there are weak financial restraints on types of treatments the providers administer. This is the best way to assure patients that treatment that is in their best interest will be provided. But this type of financial arrangement is also the most expensive. As in other matters, the economic utility and social utility are in conflict. This is true even if health insurance, either based on costs or some other payment, does not lead to better care. It is difficult to assess the quality of care, and very little evidence indicates that variation in outcomes of care is closely associated with variation in types of treatment. But it is *expectations* on which the trust of physician and cohesion between provider and patient are built. And the expectation is that providers will work for the patients' interests, and this is more apt to occur when the financial restraints on the type of treatment provided are weak. While this causes substantial deviation from the ideal relationship from an economic perspective, it contributes to the attainment of the ideal from a social perspective.[3] It is more apt to assure that decisions will be based on medical grounds rather than financial grounds.

It is possible that the high level of third-party reimbursement for medical services contributes to a paradox in American medicine. People are generally well satisfied with the care they personally receive but believe that there is a general crisis in American medicine and that the care received by others is not as good as the care that they themselves receive (Anderson, Fleming, Champney, 1982). People are made aware through the media of the problems of medical care, particularly the spiraling costs of medical care. However, in their private lives health insurance insulates them from much of the economic adversity as well as personal agony if decisions about medical care were made by them with no institutional supports. By providing such supports, health insurance very probably contributes to greater satisfaction with physicians who provide the care and, thus, to more cohesive provider-patient relationships.

As a corollary to provider-patient relations, there are relations among the providers themselves, particularly in hospitals. Liberal insurance reimbursement policies assure the financial well being of many hospitals, and this provides physicians greater discretion to act in accordance with the patient's medical needs rather than hospital financial needs. As insurance coverage decreases, hospital income may decrease and physicians may come under pressure to make decisions more in keeping with the financial needs of the institution (e.g., to discharge patients sooner, to order fewer clinical tests). This may increase conflict between physicians and the hospital administration. Reductions in hospital revenue may also require that the number of personnel be reduced. This increases job insecurities which, in turn, increases the potential for conflictual relations between personnel and hospital administration and may endanger harmony among personnel themselves. In extreme cases, hospital solvency may be threatened, thus jeopardizing the relation between the hospital and the community as a whole.

## Class Structure

Since medical care is viewed predominantly as a service which is not to be distributed in accordance with the ability to pay, its uneven distribution among economic classes is apt to provoke tension, discord, and conflict. Thus, Medicaid, which assures care for indigent persons, reduces a source of potential tension between the very poor (and those concerned about the poor) and other sectors of society. Also, private insurance alleviates or removes potential conflict between the very well-to-do who could afford to purchase the best in medical care without insurance and other members of society who could not. The role of health insurance in alleviating tensions between classes was recognized in the early study by Simons and Sinai (1932). Their analysis deserves quoting in some detail.

As noted in chapter 4, Simons and Sinai argued that health insurance is the result of low wages. They elaborated as follows:

> Social insurance is always a result of low wages. In all industrialized countries the wages of large sections of the population are so low that adequate individual protection against [such] crises [as unemployment, bankruptcy, industrial accidents and poverty due to old age and sickness] is impossible. Income is so

close to the subsistence point that the practice of the necessary thrift to provide for such emergencies would simply substitute continuous deprivation for the acute suffering of the crisis period, and would probably, by lowering the vitality of the worker, reduce his earning power (Simons and Sinai, 1932:16).

Reference here is to more than just health insurance, of course, but health insurance is central, and it is the focus of Simons' and Simai's analysis. And the consequences of health insurance "is something almost wholly apart from the question of medical and health care. If it were not for the cash benefits in times of sickness, none of these questions [about health insurance] would arise." (Simons and Sinai, 1983:132.)

With the coming of industrialization came discontent among the industrial working class. Politicians in western Europe were not unconcerned with this. This is particularly true of Germany's Bismarck. Rothfels (1938) observes that Bismarck was continually concerned about the disintegrating effects of industrialization, particularly of the industrial working class. In "sarcastic words he attacked the doctrine of the blessings arising from unlimited capitalistic competition," and in one of his earlier speeches stated that while economic freedom may produce cheaper goods, "this cheapness is inseparably bound up with the misery and complaints of workers. . .and I believe that our cheap clothes will finally be very uncomfortable on our backs when those who make them despair of being able to make an honest living thereby" (Rothfels, 1938:87). Bismarck was not just concerned about the misery of the workers, he was most concerned about the potential consequences of that misery. In a speech as a member of the Prussian Diet in 1849, he stated: "Factories make a few individuals wealthy but they generate the mass of proletarians, of ill-fed workers whose insecurity of existence makes them dangerous to the state. . ." (quoted in Rimlinger, 1971:100). It is significant, therefore, that the first compulsory health insurance plan was introduced by Bismarck in 1883. Health insurance was part of a more general program of insurance.

> As industrialization advanced, democratic and other radical ideas filtered down to the lower classes. The intensification of social problems made imperative a reinterpretation of the rights and responsibilities of the working man. Liberals and conservatives became engaged in a lengthy debate on how to resolve this social question. . . . The most significant of [the resulting] policies was the introduction of social insurance (Rimlinger, 1971:93).

To Bismarck class tensions were not the only disintegrative aspects of industrialization; he saw industrialization as having disruptive effects on the traditional social order in general. His aim, therefore, was to reintegrate the whole of Germany, not just to reduce discontent among the working class. "The tactical planning of winning over workers does not cover the whole of Bismarcks' intentions.... The insurance legislation which charged young people with imposts for sake of the older ones, the present generation for the sake of the future one, was to some extent the symbol of his belief in the State of 'Permanent Identity'" (Rothfels, 1938:301). And he saw no quick solution to this problem, as his remarks in the Reichstage in 1881 indicate: "I do not believe that our children and grandchildren will completely solve the social question" (Rothfels, 1938:302). Nevertheless, he believed that social insurance was an answer to one aspect of this question, and it was the centerpiece of his efforts to alleviate discontent among the proletarian industrial class.

Others also observed the significance of social insurance for alleviating class tensions.

> The Social Democrats were frightened by Bismarck's hope that social insurance would cripple their movement, and, for several years, opposed its growth. It was denounced by them as a "palliative" that would soothe working-class revolt (Simons and Sinai, 1932:47).

Since an increase in the strength of the Socialist movement depended on the discontent of the lower and working class, the significance of public health insurance for the alleviation of class tensions is obvious.

> Before the coming of social insurance, and in its early stages, in Germany the socialists and much of the trade-union movement were hostile or indifferent to insurance.... Today in Germany and Great Britain and most other European countries these politicians say little abouit increased wages or socialization of industry, but much about increasing the amount and scope of social insurance. So it is that social insurance has come to be known as *"revolution insurance"* in many European countries (Simons and Sinai, 1932:165–66, emphasis supplied).

It was not the workers' material well being that many politicians, such as Bismarck, had in mind, but workers' discontent and behavior. "The effect [of social insurance] on the worker's attitude, not on his welfare, was upper-most in Bismarck's mind" (Rimlinger, 1971:118). In other words, health insurance, along with other insurance programs (e.g., old-age pensions, unemployment insurance), was a form of *social*, that is, behavior control, rather than a form of relief for the lower classes.[4] By alleviating discontent among the lower and working class, it reduced expressions of violent, riotous, and other forms of disruptive behavior. This was recognized by some of Bismarck's political opponents; and their opposition to his programs "was mainly to the manner in which [Bismarck] was trying to use social insurance as a tool of social and political control" (Rimlinger, 1971:115).

By reducing class tensions, health insurance promotes greater cohesion in society. It also promotes cohesion by creating loyalty, identity, and allegiance with the entire nation rather than with the working class. "With the rise of the labor movement, especially since it was largely under the banner of Marxism, the question of worker loyalty became a crucial issue and could not help but become a major influence in the deliberation concerning the nature of the social insurance system" (Rimlinger, 1971:111). Bismarck wanted workers to identify with the state rather than with the working class; and if they were dependent on the state rather than their unions for benefits, they would have a stronger sense of unity with the state.[5] Social insurance was, therefore,

> ...a conscious attempt at cementing the social fabric of the industrial order with the interest of the state instead of the welfare of the worker as the prime objective.... [Social insurance was] a form of indirect social planning that aims at the social reintegration of the workingman... (Rimlinger, 1971:93).

While Bismarck may have thought national social insurance would promote national unity and cohesion, it is questionable if this was the objective of many proponents of national programs, or even if it was recognized as a possible consequence. As noted in chapter 4, reducing the workers' economic insecurity appeared to be the primary objective. However, greater national unity and cohesion appear to have been a consequence. In any case, Lloyd George of England as well as Bismarck rationalized their insurance programs in these terms.

> In the late nineteenth century, Marx raised the possibility that Britain's imperial position had converted the British working class into a privilege group. In the wars for European hegemony fought since 1866, the European working classes have generally sided with their national elites against other nation states. Indeed, part of the rationale for the development of national welfare institutions by Bismarck and David Lloyd George was the necessity of increasing national cohesion in the interest of the more efficacious conduct of imperialist rivalry (Birnbaum, 1971:112).

All of this would suggest, therefore, that during the early development of health insurance in Europe, the social consequences of health insurance were far more important than the health benefits. When compulsory insurance programs were first being developed, medicine had very little to offer most people during illness, so it would seem clear that little real health benefit could have been the result. Still, some may have believed that health insurance would have such benefit; this, after all, was an apparent assumption of those who believed that economic productivity and national efficiency (e.g., military preparedness) would be achieved. This seems clear from David Lloyd George's statement, "You cannot maintain an A-1 empire with a C-3 population" (Gilbert, 1970:15). (This also indicates that it was not the health benefit per se that was the ultimate goal.) It is most questionable, however, if workers were much concerned about the overall quality of the population. Their concerns were no doubt focused on the assurance that medical care would be available during periods of physical trauma and severe illness in hopes that such care would alleviate their discomfort and provide cures. More particularly, they were focused on income assistance during such periods. Whether health insurance did in fact have significant benefits in these respects was less important than the workers' belief that it did. Insofar as class conflict and national cohesion were concerned, it was the workers' attitude regardless of their material welfare that was so important in worker discontent, as Bismarck recognized. One scholar of Bismarck's policy has stated:

> In its practical objectives, Bismarck's social policy is determined by neither religious nor by provident care considerations; it has to do with neither the soul nor the welfare of the individual or the sum of individuals; rather, it is conceived in principle as state directed, and it aims at the good of the community unified in the state (das Wohl der staatlich geeinten Gemeinschaft).[6]

Whether the social consequences were worth the price depends upon one's political persuasions, of course. Marxists certainly did not consider it a worthy policy. Of course, the dissolution of the Socialist movement, which some say was an objective of proponents of social insurance, or at least an objective of Bismarck, was not achieved, contrary to the fact that "many observers consider[ed] it possible" in 1932 (Simons and Sinai, 1932:47). However, social insurance does appear to have had the pallative effect that the German Social Democrats and labor union leaders feared, even though the exact form of the subsequent German program was not the paternalistic form that Bismarck wanted (Light, Liebfried, and Tennstedt, 1986:78).

Rimlinger observes that "American visitors [of Germany] felt...that welfare measures [including health insurance] reduced the aggressiveness of trade unions."[7] Although Rimlinger believes that the development of welfare measures and health insurance was linked to the belief that they would result in higher productivity of the population (see chapter 4), he also observed that they may have also contributed "to a containment of revolutionary fervor and the rise of Revisionism" (Rimlinger, 1966:566). He states that Bismarck's program "was without doubt an important factor in the mollification of revolutionary ardor in the early part of this century"

(Rimlinger, 1971:130). And as for its effects on worker's health and income status versus class discontent, Simons and Sinai remarked that whether health insurance "affords a more certain protection against revolution than against poverty and sickness, the curtain that covers the future still conceals" (Simon and Sinai, 1932:166). We have already seen that the historical increase in the health status of populations is due very little to medical care. At the same time worker discontent has declined. Health insurance may well have contributed more to a reduction of class tensions than to differences between classes in health status.

Since government health insurance in this country did not really begin until 1965, the experience in the United States with government health insurance and its potential effect on class tensions is much more limited than in Europe. In light of the vehemence with which some proponents of Medicaid fought for the program and the complaints voiced about recent cutbacks in this program (e.g., Davis and Rowland, 1982; Aday, Fleming, and Andersen, 1984), Medicaid has certainly reduced the level of discontent among the poor and persons who view themselves as representing the interest of the poor. Recall also that survey data since 1936 indicate a majority of the population to be in favor of health insurance for the poor. The issue here is related to the moral imperative that medical care is a fundamental human right. As noted, pooled interdependence may contribute to the erosion of spontaneous efforts to aid one's fellows out of a sense of duty, loyalty, and morality, but it does not eliminate the belief that for certain types of crises individuals and families deserve assistance when they are unable for economic reasons to deal with their problems themselves. Whether Medicaid has led to a stronger sense of national unity in the United States as programs apparently did in Europe it is difficult to say. However, it probably does ease the difficulties and insecurities in life for many of the very poor. Consequently, it probably reduces the discontent of the poor and of persons who are most concerned about this sector of society.

In some respects the history of national health insurance legislation in the United States is certainly similar to the European experience. Legislative efforts to introduce national health insurance were made since the early part of the twentieth century. In reviewing the history of these efforts, Hirschfield characterizes the pre-1920 period as follows:

In simple terms, members of the middle class were afraid that unless they did something significant to correct economically caused health problems among the poor, their own security and social position would be threatened. The middle class could buy decent medical care through private purchases; the poor could not. Therefore, some mechanism for helping the poor solve their personal medical problems was needed—a way which would correct the new imbalance in the medical care system but which would not destroy traditional individualistic values. Social insurance for illness appeared to be a way in which this problem could be solved (Hirschfield, 1970:11).

Our entry into World War I and the negative reaction to "German style" health insurance weakened the thrust toward national health insurance. In addition, as in Europe, the movement was opposed by organized labor.

One significant group in [the] alliance [against compulsory health insurance in the pre-World War I period] consisted of America's most important labor leaders. These men...feared that the enactment of social insurance measures would weaken the nation's labor unions. They felt that if compulsory health insurance were passed there would be less need for workers to join and support unions and less reason for employers to be willing to raise worker's wages (Hirschfield, 1970:20).

In a similar vein, Krauss states:

[In the] pre-World War I period, academic economists, social workers, sociologists, and other intellectual leaders were the only block interested in a German-style national health insurance system. Samuel Gompers, a leader of American organized labor, and most of this followers fought *against* the idea ...for they feared that health and pension benefits offered by management would detract from union loyalty (Krauss, 1977:26; author's emphasis. See also Rimlinger, 1971:80–85).

The presence of class conflict and the fear among labor leaders that health insurance would alleviate class tensions is clearly reflected in the remarks of a leader of the Sailor's Union of the Pacific:

Sometimes it is better to let the wounded die, sometimes it is better to let the old die than sacrifice the fire of fighting and the ability to win battles.... This appeal for old-age pensions...for sickness insurance...for unemployment insurance —what is it?... It is nothing more than sentiment that stands in the way of real fighting (Weintraub, 1969:184).

The role of health insurance in alleviating tensions between the working class and the rest of society holds for private insurance plans as well as programs financed by the public. A national survey by Staines and Quinn (1979) shows that almost 80% of the workforce gets health insurance as a fringe benefit of their employment. This is an aspect of "welfare capitalism" (Brandes, 1976). But this also creates division within the working class. Quattrachiocchi (1981:422) sees inequities in health insurance coverage from the fact that in 1978 only 40% of the rural poor and 50% of urban poor qualified for Medicare. He also notes that because of private insurance, only 4.1 million families who spend more than 15% of their income on medical care earned less than $4,000 a year, and just 0.2% of families who earned $20,000 or more had out-of-pocket expense equal to 15% or more of their income. Furthermore, because private insurance plans tend to raise the cost of medical care, the benefits enjoyed by the stable working class further impoverishes the less well-off by raising the costs of their medical care. In addition, the beneficiaries of private insurance programs enjoy tax benefits since the employer's contribution is not counted as income. The development of health insurance as a form of welfare capitalism encourages voluntarism rather than government intervention in providing for health insurance coverage. However, the poor and marginally poor

> ...are often poorly equipped to take on this role. For high-wage workers, employee benefits may be an attractive alternative to government programs. These workers are able to achieve a degree of comprehensiveness without cutting too deeply into their wages. Their jobs tend to be relatively stable and there is a less pressing need for the various programs that form a financial safety net for the worker and his or her family. But for the low-wage workers, the situaton is reversed. Programs tend to be meager even though the need for protection may be great. By tying insurance programs to the workplace, the most vulnerable groups have the least protection (Root, 1981:106).

The objective differences within the working and lower classes appear to be reflected to some extent in subjective attitudes within more fortunate members of the workforce. Because fringe benefit programs such as health insurance have been so successful in easing discontent among the stable working class (and incidentally, among workers who are the most apt to be organized), members of this sector are apt to oppose programs for the low-paid workers and those who do not or who are unable to work. "As protected workers' standards of living continue to rise [partially through increases in health insurance benefits] the rebellion against so-called poverty programs also rises" (Quattrociocchi, 1981:431). This suggests that the tension and discontent that Marxian theory states is inherent in the working class is dissipated and turned inward. Health insurance would appear to be another element that characterizes the dual labor market of skilled workers with stable employment and unskilled, marginal workers in which employment is unstable (Doeringer and Piore, 1975). Some argue that race has been imposed on the dual labor market, producing what is called the "split-labor market" (Geschwender, 1978). Just as racial prejudice among the stable working group helps to deflect worker discontent onto the marginal and unstable workers, many of whom are black, so health insurance for the more stable workers may help to redirect worker discontent against low-paid marginal workers who are recipients of Medicaid and other forms of welfare. At the same time, poverty programs, such as Medicaid, help to ease the discontent of the lower-paid workers against society in general. The overall result is less class conflict and more cohesion in society.

The growth of health insurance as it relates to the class structure has not been an isolated movement, of course. It is part of a series of benefits covered by a variety of insurance programs. Furthermore, while the easing of class tensions is no doubt important, moral considerations are also involved, if in no other way than as rationalization for the programs. Aharoni (1981:1) states, "The expanding role of the government started from moral and equity considerations: The recognition that an unfettered market might lead to what was considered socially unacceptable income and wealth distribution." While the historical analysis remains to be done, the following sequence is suggested as the process through which public insurance programs have grown. They were precipitated by class tensions, and were extensions of poor laws and programs of relief, which, according to some analysts (e.g., Pivan and Cloward, 1977), were also introduced to maintain social control. In due course, and in some instances simultaneously, such programs were defended in terms of equity and moral considerations, as when medical care is proclaimed a fundamental right. Less frequently they were defended in terms of interests of economic productivity and the economic well-being of the society. In time, more affluent sectors of the population recognized the apparent benefits of many of these programs and wanted programs extended into areas that applied to them; the stable working class, for example, did not want health insurance limited to the low-income workers. Further, many government regulations and subsidies perform for the middle and upper classes the same economic functions that many welfare programs perform for the poor. And the same is true for many private insurance programs. Therefore, as the value of programs originally designed for the lower-paid workers became known, or at least *perceived* to be of significant value, programs moved outward in society and upward in the class structure. Programs that eased tensions within the class structure functioned also to ease tensions and discontent within other sectors of the population. The modern welfare state may be more appropriately labeled the insurance society. Much of the discontent, tension, conflict, and alienation inherent in modern industrial society is absorbed by the institution of insurance, private and public. This includes, in particular, health insurance.

## Private Industry, Health Insurance, and Employee Morale

Health insurance in industrial countries has been largely associated with state and compulsory universal insurance systems, but, as noted, private insurance has also grown, particularly in the United States. Its growth in the United States was particularly rapid from 1950 to 1965, growing from 9.1% to 24.4% of all payments for health services. During this period, the proportion paid by the federal government was stable, constituting 10.4% and 10.1% of payments in 1950 and 1965, respectively. In 1970, five years after the passage of Medicare, federal payments had grown to 22.3%, which was still less than payments from the private sector (24.0%); in 1980 it was still about the same as the private sector (28.6% versus 26.6%). However, when local and state government payments are included, the govenment share grew almost threefold, from 9.1% to 26.6% (Gibson, Waldo, and Levit, 1983:8). Thus, both public and private health insurance have grown since 1950, and there was parity between federal and private insurance in 1950 and in 1980. The major rise in health insurance in the United States began first in the private sector with the public sector following several years later.

It is the private sector that provides the bulk of the health insurance for American workers. As noted above, the study by Staines and Quinn (1979) shows that almost 80% of American workers have some form of health insurance. Data are not available to show how much the fringe benefits of health insurance have grown over time, though, as just noted, the proportion of all expenditures paid by private insurance increased threefold from 1950 to 1980. All of this was not in connection with employment in the private sector, of course (much of it was in government agencies, public school systems, state universities, etc.). However, analysis of the way health insurance is perceived by management in private industry will be instructive.

In discussing the survey of the 69 Fortune 500 business firms (Sapolsky, Altman, Greene, and Moore, 1981) in chapter 4, we observed that workers' health and productivity were not the primary basis for management's decisions about health insurance benefits for workers. Comments by the authors indicate that while comparisons with similar firms influence the exact level of benefits provided, the provisions of health insurance is generally dictated by worker satisfaction and morale. "Benefits are provided because many workers want them.... For some of the firms we interviewed the key benefit issue is whether or not the employees are satisfied, not why the benefits costs are high" (Sapolsky, Altman, Greene, and Moore, 1981:582). Furthermore, when an employee's costs exceed the limit of insurance coverage, "top executives are occasionally so sensitive to the morale aspects of the health benefit and human needs it embodies that they are willing to break company rules in order to provide extra care and financial support for employees and their families" (Sapolsky, Altman, Greene, and Moore, 1981:582).

Such policy by management is consistent with worker attitudes as revealed in the Staines and Quinn (1979) survey, which shows that 84% of American workers who have health insurance consider this their most important fringe benefit, and 47% would be willing to trade increases in pay for more health benefits. It is understandable, therefore, that management would give little thought to reducing health benefits despite the lack of evidence for its beneficial effect on firm performance.[8] To deny or reduce such benefits would create tensions and dissatisfactions among employees.

> Major corporations are under no illusions that they can do much individually to alter their health benefit costs. The benefits have long since been given to employees and cannot now be called back without risking more employee dissatisfaction than most of these firms appear willing to tolerate (Sapolsky, Altman, Greene, and Moore, 1981:587).

Such benefits are used in an explicit effort to establish workers' identity with the firm much as Bismarck tried to establish the proletariate's identity with the state. For example, attempts are made

> ...to make certain that employees in time of need identify the benefit they receive with the corporation, rather than that they meet restricted access to these benefits [by having insurance companies process claims]. Thus, some firms use their own staff to process claims instead of that of their insurers so as to heighten the firms' identification with the benefits (Sapolsky, Altman, Greene, and Moore, 1981:576).

In summary, the function of private health insurance provided to workers by business firms, and probably by other organizations as well, is to alleviate employee dissatisfaction and to promote morale rather than to enhance productivity. While the primary function of health insurance for industrial workers in its beginning in Europe may have been to alleviate class tension between the proletarians and the capitalists, managers, and the state, today it has significant consequences for the alleviation of organizational tension and promotion of organizational morale; its effects are not limited to the alleviation of class tension, as such. Health insurance promotes the morale of employees in various professional and income positions in the same workplace.

## Generations, Kinship Units, and the Family

The sector of the population with the greatest risk of severe illness and in need of medical care is the elderly. Assurance of medical care for this sector of the population through Medicare performs integrating functions in several respects. First, the fact that medical care is available allows a number of older persons to function at levels and participate in institutionalized activities in ways that they could not do without medical care. This makes their day-to-day existence less marginal, and accordingly they are more involved with normal activities of society. It also probably gives them a greater sense that others care about them, and their feelings of alienation and isolation are undoubtedly lower as a result. In addition, since younger sectors of the population have more assurance that their elders will be provided with needed medical care, there is less reason for worry and concern by persons who are disposed to worry about the medical needs of others. This may give them a stronger sense of identity with society than would be the case if the needs of the elderly were neglected, or left solely to the elderly and their younger relatives to be responsible for. In addition, in a political democracy the inability of the elderly, who constitute a significant proportion of the population, to obtain medical care creates the potential for conflict between the elderly and the rest of the population. Failure to assure medical care through health insurance may therefore become a political issue which creates cleavage between the elderly and the younger sectors of the population. Health insurance for the elderly reduces such cleavage and moderates conflict across generations.

Since few of the elderly are productive members of the population, almost all being out of the labor force, health insurance for this sector cannot be justified on economic grounds. Indeed, from a purely economic point of view, medical care for this group is the hardest of any group to justify. Of course, a disproportionate share of medical expenditures is also spent on young children, who are also nonproductive elements of the population. However, expenditures for this sector can be justified on economic grounds as investments in human capital. No such argument can be made for the elderly. It would seem, therefore, that the primary benefits to be derived from health insurance for the elderly is the promotion of social integration and cohesion, as outlined in the paragraph above.

There is evidence that Medicare has indeed had these effects for the elderly. Since Emile Durkheim's study of *Suicide* almost a century ago (Durkheim, 1949), statistics have uniformly shown that the suicide rate is higher for the socially isolated. As noted in the previous chapter, the suicide rate for persons 65 and over decreased substantially (12.4%) after the passage of Medicare despite the overall increase (16.5%) for the total population. Since the insurance coverage for the elderly increased at a far greater rate than the coverage for the total population, data clearly support the thesis that health insurance is a factor in the decrease of suicide. And since social integration and cohesion are major factors in suicide, by inference data support the thesis that health insurance promotes the integration and cohesion of the older sector of the population in society.

Health insurance for the elderly does more than reduce conflict between broad age sectors of the population. It also reduces conflict and the potential for conflict within kinship units and has positive effects on our kinship relations as a result. In the absence of health insurance for the elderly, the elderly must pay for medical care themselves or depend on their relatives to do so. Considering the high cost of medical care, particularly for many of the chronic conditions of the elderly, the financial burden for the aged's medical care would often fall to younger relatives. Indeed, as noted in chapter 4, this is one of the appeals made by supporters in the political debate over Medicare. Either for moral or legal reasons, people often come to the aid of a disabled relative, particularly if the relative is elderly. As the supporters of Medicare noted, when many of the elderly needed medical care, they had to depend on their children for financial assistance. Political supporters of Medical care stressed this point to gain support from persons who might be burdened with the financial responsibility of paying the cost of medical care for an older relative (Marmor 1970:17). The appeal was economic, but the consequence was social. There are several respects in which this is so.

If an aged relative needs medical care but neither he or she nor younger members of the kinship unit have the money to provide it, interpersonal discord may develop because the younger members have a feeling of helplessness with respect to their elders, and the elders have a sense of being denied and rejected. Also, when nothing can even be done just to try to ease the pain and illness of people, it is particularly unpleasant and painful to others. Since people tend to avoid unpleasant and distressing situations, when the pain and illness of older members of a kinship unit go untreated, younger members may withdraw from the members who are older. This would further the elders' sense of isolation. In addition, the younger members' helplessness may give them a sense of guilt which may cause even more friction and discord between younger people and older sick relatives. In general, therefore, untreated illness among the elderly is apt to produce alienation and a deterioration of harmony across generational lines among members of the same kinship unit.

In other instances, younger members of kinship units may pay for the medical care received by older members. This, however, may deny younger members goods and services they would like for themselves. Such denial is apt to produce resentment of the older members by the younger. The latter may experience a severe conflict between their own economic welfare and comfort and the medical and/or economic welfare of their older relative. However, with Medicare, or other forms of health insurance which provide the financial expense for medical care, the feeling of conflict is avoided. Of course, the cost of health insurance for most kinship units may be hard to justify on economic grounds. However, the contribution to the social cohesion and to the avoidance of interpersonal conflict in a few kinship units may be very great.

In addition, benefits of cohesion are derived even when no illness occurs. As persons grow older the probability of illness increases and, hence, the probability of medical expense increases; and sometimes the expense may be of catastrophic proportions. Therefore, as members of kinship units grow older, they are apt to be viewed as potential economic burdens and *perceived* as economic threats. For younger members to view older members this way can only damage interpersonal relations between the young and the old and produce feelings of alienation between them. Since health insurance removes or reduces the worry about the medical expense of older members, it promotes kinship cohesion across generations.

Health insurance for the elderly may also prevent conflict and tension between members of the nuclear unit. Without such coverage, when illness does strike an older relative, spouses may quarrel about the extent of their economic responsibility. Further, health insurance reduces the potential for conflict between older siblings who might otherwise disagree over how the cost of care for a parent is to be apportioned between them. In many instances siblings will not be equally able to assume the financial burden so that an equal apportioning of expenses may create discord for the less financially well off, whereas a disproportionate division may create resentment among those who are better off and thus expected to assume a larger share of the burden. Medical expense for the older relative that is not covered by health insurance may weaken relations between parents and children within the nuclear unit and between adult siblings in separate units.

Problems are compounded by the fact that so many marriages end in divorce, almost one in two. Without health insurance, the medical expenses of an older relative would in many instances be borne by families headed by a single adult. This would only make the economic burden worse. The situation may be little better in the case of remarriage. Persons may feel little responsibility for the parent-in-law by virtue of their second (or third or fourth) marriage. In another view, decisions concerning remarriage may depend very much on the extent to which the parent of the prospective spouse has adequate health insurance coverage. In the absence of such coverage, social reintegration in marriage and psychological satisfactions that are promoted by cohesive relations with a marital partner are lessened.

The role of health insurance in resolving conflict and promoting social cohesion within the nuclear unit is not limited to Medicare and insurance for the aged. Insurance for others also has this effect. This is particularly true when the primary breadwinner of the household is ill.

> For the breadwinner living in a country where medical care is regarded as a "consumer good," to be bought and paid at the time of consumption, his illness alone can have disastrous effects on the way of life and future expectations of the family (Poynter, 1973:142).

Of course, such effects may not be limited to illness to the breadwinner; they may also occur when the illness of other members of the household creates strain and burdens for other members. Without adequate insurance coverage, interpersonal damage may result because other members of the nuclear unit must do without because of the medical expense of a sick member. Studies of hemophiliacs in the United States where hemophiliacs do not have state insurance coverage indicate that "the financial aspect alone can cause family problems and disruption." The burden is not just on other members since the patients themselves "often relate guilt feelings because of the financial burden they cause their families" (Titmuss, 1971:207).[9] In addition, hemophiliacs are "continually reminded by... market forces that for their survival from one bleeding episode to the next they are dependent on blood supplies from strangers. They are 'bad risks'; non-insurable by the private market in the United States; not acceptable by profit-making hospitals" (Titmuss, 1971:207). Life-sustaining medical care or, in this case, blood is not viewed as a right and something owed by society (or by an insurance company) to the victim in question. Aside from the financial impact and the family discord this may cause, this may also have damaging psychological effects on the victim and give a sense of rejection. Such problems are less probable if the cost of blood were covered by third-party reimbursement.[10] The general situation is not limited to hemophiliacs, of course, but applies to all persons who because of their poor health are "bad risks" for commercial carriers or whose medical expense creates a burden for other family members.

Reference here has been to the difference between countries with national health insurance programs for medical care (or aspects of it, such as blood transfusions) and nations where such programs do not exist.

However, even where medical care is considered a "consumer good," similar functions are performed by private insurance. While there are significant economic differences between privately financed and publicly financed health insurance, the interpersonal consequences of health insurance do not depend so much on whether the insurance is private or public but whether it exists and is dependable.

## Social Policy and Social Exchange

The role of health insurance in kinship cohesion has important implications for the conception of social policy as outlined earlier in this chapter and to theories of social exchange. It was noted that social policy operated much like a grant, such that there is no particular relation between what one pays and what one receives. As noted, this is the way insurance operates, though to the extent that insurance is based on actuarial experience, as is sometimes the case with private insurance, the relationship between payment and benefits is closer. Social exchange theories (Thibaut and Kelley, 1959; Homans, 1961; Blau, 1964; see also Heath, 1976), which are based largely on classical economic theory, view relations among individuals and groups as forms of exchange, though the things exchanged need not be economical commodities but may also be visitation, friendship, moral support, and, especially, social status and approval. As with economic relations, social relations are a function of the rewards and costs of the different parties involved. The anthropologist Marshall Sahlins (1965) views social exchange somewhat differently and his conception is especially relevant to health insurance as it operates with respect to kinship relations. Sahlins views exchange as a continuum. At one extreme is negative reciprocity, in which individuals attempt to obtain something for nothing, as in blackmail and armed robbery; self-interest is dominant. Toward the middle of the continuum we have balanced reciprocity in which each party receives the equivalent, in terms of utility, that the other gives up. This includes relations in which the thing returned is the exact equivalent of that received, such as the lending and repayment of a monetary sum, but includes types of exchange which are addressed by social exchange theories as well. The receiver feels obligated to return something of equivalent utility by a definite time to the giver and is expected by the giver to do so. At the other extreme is generalized reciprocity. What a person contributes to, gives up, or otherwise provides another is based on the other's need, not on expectations as to what the other will give in return. Meeting another person's need may establish a counter obligation, of course, but the expectation that the recipient will reciprocate is indefinite as to the precise obligation or when the return will be forthcoming; the obligation is diffuse, and a return is contingent on the recipient's ability and resources.

Sahlins believes that the form of exchange, or the point on the exchange continuum, is determined by the "span of social distance" between the parties involved. Negative reciprocity is characterized by individuals acting in their own self-interest whereas generalized reciprocity is characterized by the respective needs of the interactants, and is thus the "solitary extreme" (Sahlins, 1965:147). Since kinship is a crucial determinant of social distance, exchange between close relatives approaches that of generalized reciprocity. Thus, according to Sahlin's framework, generalized exchange is expected with respect to relations between relatives. Children providing for the health needs of older parents would be an example. No particular tally is made by the children as to what the parent owes them in return—and in many instances the parents will be unable to give anything other than expressions of gratitude in return. While such expressions will in most instances be appreciated, in many instances the magnitude of the economic burden would be such that such expression would not be considered "fair compensation" for the deprivations incurred. Helping one's parents in this way would frequently not be a form of balanced exchange; it would be a form of generalized exchange instead. It is something society expects of children and which children may expect of themselves; it is morally imposed.

At the same time, meeting such obligations can create economic hardship and deprivation. This in turn may generate resentment and bitterness, particularly if the relations between younger and older relatives are weak, as they are in most industrialized societies. It is here that the role of social policy and insurance in decreasing alienation and promoting social cohesion is so important. Medicare helps to preserve relations between older and younger members of kinship units.

Observe, however, that social institutions do not just exist and have consequences; they also require normative definitions, moral appeals, rationalizations, and justifications that are accepted by members of society, usually on the grounds that they are good for society. For example, we have seen that health insurance has been defended on the grounds that it promotes the nation's health, military preparedness, and economic productivity. The rationalizations need not be true; as long as they are accepted, myths may have as strong a hold on members of society as beliefs that are based in reality. However, when rationalizations are too inconsistent with underlying social relations, support for the institution may be undermined. In the case of Medicare (and Social Security), rationalizations of the program must be consistent with the underlying social relations between generations. For example, as long as the payroll tax was not viewed by younger generations as a major burden, retirement benefits for the elderly could be justified in terms of balanced exchange ("earned" right). However, when the tax increases rapidly, as it has in recent years and may continue to do so in the future, it is increasingly difficult to defend the program in terms of balanced exchange. Rationalizations and appeals for support must increasingly be patterned on the notion of generalized exchange. Paradoxically, however, such justifications and rationalizations may find less structural support in social relations because extended kin relations have grown weaker relative to the cost of the payroll tax. We will return to the problems of exchange and structural support for Medicare and Social Security in the next two chapters.

## Conclusion

A central premise of the structure-function framework is that the consequences of social institutions help to promote social integration and cohesion in society. This is not to say that such consequences are always envisioned and recognized. Private insurance companies are concerned with how health insurance promotes the company's cash flow and profit, not with social cohesion. And public insurance stems from decisions by policy-makers made in response to public pressure and moral concerns that medical care be responsive to medical need and not just economic demand. The positive effects of insurance in promoting social integration and cohesion may be far from most policy makers' minds, though in the case of some insightful politicians, such as Bismarck, and apparently some executives of business firms in the United States, some of the social effects of health insurance do appear to be recognized.

Such effects are not possible if medical care were treated solely as an economic commodity. Health insurance, including private insurance, works in such a way that exchanges deviate from that envisioned in economic theory. In this theory individuals give in return for something of equal value; one buys and one sells at a price that each considers proportionate to what is given up. Such exchange takes the form of reciprocal interdependence in a formal sense, and some have extended the principle to social exchange itself; a quid is given for a quo, whether the quids and quos are money, commodities, social status, or social approval. However, because of pooled interdependence which characterizes insurance, it is the collective that provides benefits for the individual. Each individual contributes his premium to protect himself or herself, but on the average he or she receives far less than he or she gives up. This is not true exchange as envisioned in economic theory or the derivatives of that theory that are designed to describe social exchange. This is because a few receive a disproportionate share of the benefits. The well take care of the sick, and the implication is that if you are sick, you deserve a higher rate of return. Or alternatively, if you suffer, society believes it should try to alleviate your plight. Clearly, more is involved here than the aversion of economic risks. The social integration and cohesion of society is also involved.

Such a result is clearly different from that which economic theory views as the ideal. In classical economic theory, going back to Adam Smith, it is when there is perfect competition, when producers are motivated to maximize profits, and when consumers buy at the margins, that the sum of individual outcomes is socially the most desirable. Feldstein states:

> I believe that one of the most important things we teach in economics is that the competitive market and the profit motive are generally the best way to allocate resources.... Economists [understand] that individuals who act out of self-interest can thereby achieve the allocation of resources that is *socially* most desirable.... In their search for profits, companies are forced by competition to produce the goods and services that consumers want (and are willing to pay for) and to produce them at the lowerest possible cost. Since we generally assume that individuals are the best judges of their own best interest, firms that seek profits are induced to provide the goods that consumers should have.... A crucial step in the argument for relying on profit-seeking firms in general is that that is the best way of making the provision of goods and services correspond to the preference of consumers as indicated by their willingness to pay (Feldstein, 1978:225–226; author's emphasis).

However, because of the way so much of health care is paid for, "consumers' demand for hospital care is greatly distorted," and the sum of individual outcomes is not the best social outcome. We should observe, however, that questions about the best social outcome are questions of values. The social outcomes of social integration and cohesion may be considered just as desirable as lower prices which stem from individuals being at risk.

Another problem in saying that health insurance leads to a socially incorrect or undesirable outcome (because of moral hazards and the reduction of competition) is that there is no evidence that we would be better off as a society if we spent less on health care and more on something else, say, automobiles, energy, alcohol, or even defense, which we would probably do if it were not for third-party reimbursement for health services. Many critics of health insurance take an atomistic view of society in which costs and benefits are assessed in terms of individual utility. Consequently, the sum total of independent individual decisions amounts to a social decision; and in the case of medical care, health insurance leads to a decision that is "incorrect" or undesirable. This is because the amount that is spent is higher than the amount that would be spent if individuals were are risk and responsible for a higher proportion of the costs of their medical care as out-of-pocket expense. The integrative and cohesive consequences, which are certainly *social* outcomes of important significance, are not considered.

These consequences as well as those outlined in the previous chapter are not medical in nature, of course. It was noted in chapter 4 that historically the question of whether public insurance programs do in fact promote health in the population, or sectors of the populations such as the low-income sector, is rarely asked after the program has been introduced. Supporters usually assume that the program does improve the health of the general population or certain subpopulations, and sometimes cite utilization statistics as evidence of this. However, the relationship of insurance to health status is seldom shown, and certainly the evidence in this respect is far from compelling. In the face of evidence which shows little or no effect, as in the Black Report which shows little effect of the National Health Service on class differences in health status in England, the evidence may simply be given little attention and its impact on public policy may be minimal (Gray, 1982). The faith of supporters of public health insurance programs seems unshakable. A major reason for this may stem from the nonmedical benefits of these programs, namely the alleviation of moral concerns about medical care not being distributed in accordance with needs. Also, some may perceive more or less clearly that these programs reduce divisiveness in society and promote social integration and cohesion. These benefits are not without an economic cost, however, a topic to which we now turn.

## Notes

1. Kimball observes that in addition to performing certain obvious economic functions in society, insurance also contributes "to building a more tightly structured society which [has] assumed responsibility for the welfare of its members" (Kimball, 1960:306). He views insurance as contributing to the integration of society and to social order. "The attitude closely connected with the growth of insurance law...was the twentieth century's insistence upon an ordered and secure existence" (Kimball, 1960:303–304).

2. The formulation here is not limited to physicians but characterizes professional-client relations (lawyer-client, teacher-student) in general, and distinguishes them from ordinary economic relations which are typically between business persons and customers. The formulation, and the distinction between business-customer relations, is only an approximation, of

course, with some professional-client relationships characterized largely by the interests of the provider more than the formulation indicates. Nevertheless, the expectations of society are that the professional more than the businessman will have the interest of the buyer foremost in his or her thinking and decisions. Profiteering by businessmen (e.g., used car salesmen) is acceptable; profiteering by physicians, lawyers, and teachers is not, and is reflected in the reaction of others when it is known to exist.

3. One might claim that the apparent increase in malpractice suits against physicians as insurance coverage has increased would not support this conclusion. In her review of the evidence, however, Mumford (1983:175–181) reports that proportionate increases in malpractice suits is far less than is commonly believed. Furthermore, modern malpractice suits may be due more to technological development than to anything else. With modern technology physicians are able to treat more life-threatening conditions and invade sensitive areas than in the past. Consequently, they are more apt today to make tragic mistakes as well as perform miraculous cures than in the past. Also, an increase in malpractice claims may be due more to widespread and higher insurance carried by physicians than to weak patient-provider relations. With an increase in physicians' malpractice insurance, patients and lawyers have more incentive to bring legal action for malpractice (the so-called "deep pockets theory" of liability ligitation).

4. This is exemplified in the fact that under Bismarck's plan workers had to be 70 years old before they were eligible for retirement pay when the life expectancy for Germany at the time was much lower than this; few workers lived to draw old-age pensions. The fact that this apparently was viewed as an important positive step by workers also illustrates how matters such as old age and illness are not viewed objectively or rationally.

5. This is said to have been one reason why he wanted the insurance premium paid by the employer and the state rather than by the workers. It would make the workers more dependent on business firms and the state.

6. From Hans Rothfels (1935:53). Quote is from Rimlinger (1971:116).

7. The visitors were F. S. Schwedtman and J. A. Emery (1911), who went to Germany to study the German system on behalf of the National Association of Manufacturers.

8. Media accounts during the early 1980s suggest that because of the continuing cost spiral, private industry is becoming more concerned with the cost of employee health insurance. In some instances this has led to closer comparisons of different insurance plans, such as that between traditional insurance plans and a health maintenance organization (HMO). (Federal law requires that firms that have at least 25 workers for whom health insurance is provided give workers the alternative of an HMO if such an alternative is available and cheaper.)

9. Quoted by Titmuss from Taylor's study of hemophiliacs in the United States (Taylor, 1969).

10. The conclusion is supported by different findings for studies of hemophiliacs in the United States (Taylor, 1969), where blood is commercialized, and studies of hemophiliacs in the United Kingdom (Bronks, Blackburn and Path, 1968), where it is not commercialized (see Titmuss, 1971).

# References

Aday, Lu Ann, Gretchen V. Fleming, and Ronald Andersen. *Access to Medical Care in the U.S.: Who Has It, Who Doesn't*. Chicago: Pluribus Press, Inc., 1984.

Aharoni, Yair. *The No-Risk Society*. Chatham, NJ: Chatham House Publishers, Inc., 1981.

Andersen, Ronald M., Gretchen V. Fleming, and Timothy F. Champney. "Exploring a Paradox: Belief in a Crisis and General Satisfaction with Medical Care." *Milbank Memorial Fund Quarterly* 60 (Fall 1982):329–354.

Arrow, Kenneth J. "Uncertainty and the Welfare Economics of Medical Care." *The American Economic Review* 53 (December 1963):941–973.

Birnbaum, Norman. *Toward a Critical Sociology*. New York: Oxford University Press, 1971.

Blau, Peter. *Power and Exchange in Social Life*. New York: John Wiley and Sons, 1964.

Boulding, Kenneth E. "The Concept of Need for Health Services." In John B. McKinlay (ed.), *Economic Aspects of Health Care: A Selection of Articles from the Milbank Memorial Fund Quarterly*, pp. 3–22. New York: Prodist, 1973.

Brandes, Stuart D. *American Welfare Capitalism, 1880–1949*. Chicago: University of Chicago Press, 1976.

Bronks, I.G., E.K. Blackburn, and F.C. Path. "A Socio-Medical Study of Haemophilia and Related States." *British Journal of Preventive and Social Medicine* 22 (April 1968):68–72.

Davis, Karen, and Diane Rowland. "Uninsured and Undeserved: Inequities in Health Care in the United States." *Milbank Memorial Fund Quarterly* 61 (Spring 1983):149–176.

Doeringer, Peter B., and Michael J. Piore. "Unemployment and the Dual Labor Market." *The Public Interest* 38 (Winter 1975):67–79.

Durkheim, Emile. *Suicide*. Glencoe, IL: Free Press, 1951.

Feldstein, Martin S. "Discussion of Inducement and Impediments for Private Corporate Investment in the Delivery of Health Services." In Gordon K. MacLeod and Mark Perlman (eds.), *Health Care Capital: Competition and Control*, pp. 225–227. Cambridge, MA: Ballinger Publishing Company, 1978.

Fuchs, Victor R. "The Growing Demand for Medical Care." *New England Journal of Medicine* 279 (July 25, 1968):190–195.

Geschwender, James A. *Racial Stratification in America*. Davenport, Iowa: William C. Brown Company, Publishers, 1978.

Gibson, Robert M., Daniel R. Waldo, and Katharine R. Levit. "National Health Expenditures, 1982." *Health Care Financing Review* 5 (Fall 1983):1–31.

Gilbert, Bentley B. *British Social Policy, 1914–1939*. London: Batsford, 1970.

Gray, Alastair McIntosh. "Inequalities in Health. The Black Report: A Summary and Comment." *International Journal of Health Services* 12 (No. 3, 1982):249–380.

Heath, Anthony. *Rational Choice and Social Exchange*. Cambridge, England: Cambridge University Press, 1976.

Hirschfield, Daniel S. *The Lost Reform: The Campaign for Compulsory Health Insurance in the United States from 1932 to 1943*. Cambridge, MA: Harvard University Press, 1970.

Homans, George C. *Social Behavior: Its Elementary Forms*. New York: Harcourt, Brace and World, Inc., 1961.

Kimball, Spencer L. *Insurance and Public Policy: A Study in the Legal Implementation of Social and Economic Public Policy Based on Wisconsin Records, 1835–1959.* Madison: The University of Wisconsin Press, 1960.

Krauss, Elliott A. *Power and Illness: The Political Sociology of Health and Medical Care.* New York: Elsevier North-Holland, Inc., 1977.

Light, Donald W., Stephan Liebfried, and Florian Tennstodt. "Social Medicine vs Professional Doninance: The German Experience." *American Journal of Public Health* 76 (January 1986):78–83.

Marmor, Theodore R. *The Politics of Medicare.* Chicago: Aldine Publishing Co., 1970.

Mumford, Emily. *Medical Sociology: Patients, Providers and Policies.* New York: Random House, 1983.

Olson, Mancur, Jr. "Economics, Sociology, and the Best of All Possible Worlds." *The Public Interest* 12 (Summer 1968):96–118.

Parsons, Talcott. *The Social System.* Glencoe, IL: The Free Press, 1951.

Piven, Frances Fox, and Richard A. Cloward. *Regulating the Poor: The Functions of Public Welfare.* New York: Vintage Books, 1971.

Poynter, Noel. *Medicine and Man.* Middlesex, England: Penguin Books, Ltd., 1973.

Quattrociocchi, Susan M. "Fringe Benefits as Private Social Policy." In John M. Tropman, Milan J. Kluhy, and Roger M. Lind (eds.), *New Strategic Perspectives on Social Policy*, pp. 422–433. New York: Pergamon Press, 1981.

Radcliff-Brown, A. R. *Taboo.* Cambridge, England: Cambridge University Press, 1939.

Rimlinger, Gaston V. "Welfare Policy and Economic Development: A Comparative Historical Perspective." *Journal of Economic History* 26 (December 1966): 557–571.

——————. *Welfare Policy and Industrialization in Europe, America and Russia.* New York: John Wiley & Sons, Inc., 1971.

Root, Lawrence S. "Employee Benefits and Income Security: Private Social Policy and Public Interest." In John Tropman, Milan J. Kluhy, and Roger M. Lind (eds.), *New Strategic Perspectives in Social Policy*, pp. 97–109. New York: Pergamon Press, 1981.

Rothfels, Hans. "Prinzipienfrage der Bismarckschen Szialpolitik." *Koenigberger Historische Forschunger* 7 (1935):49–54.

——————. "Bismarck's Social Policy and the Problem of State Socialism in Germany, Part I and Part II." *Sociological Review* 30 (January and July 1938):81–90, 288–302.

Sahlins, Marshall D. *The Relevance of Models for Social Anthropology.* London: Frederick A. Praeger, Publisher, 1965.

Sapolsky, Harvey M., Drew Altman, Richard Greene, and Judith D. Moore. "Corporate Attitudes toward Health Care Costs." *Milbank Memorial Fund Quarterly* 59 (Fall 1981):561–585.

Schwedtman, F. C., and J. A. Emery. *Accident Prevention and Relief.* New York: National Association of Manufacturers, 1911. Cited in Gaston V. Rimlinger,

"Welfare Policy and Economic Development: A Comparative Historical Perspective." *Journal of Economic History* 26 (December 1966):556–571.

Simons, A.M., and Nathan Sinai. *The Way of Health Insurance.* Chicago: University of Chicago Press, 1932.

Staines, Graham L., and Robert P. Quinn. "American Workers Evaluate the Quality of Their Jobs." *Monthly Labor Review* 102 (January 1979):3–12.

Taylor, C. "Hemophiliac Center at Work." *Rehabilitation Record*, Rehabilitation Services Administration 10 (March–April 1969):1–6. Washington, DC: Department of Health, Education and Welfare.

Thibaut, John W., and Harold H. Kelley. *The Social Psychology of Groups.* New York: John W. Wiley and Sons, 1959.

Titmuss, Richard M. *The Gift Relationship: From Human Blood to Social Policy.* New York: Vintage Books, 1971.

Weintraub, Hyman. *Andrew Furuseth.* Berkeley and Los Angeles: University of California Press, 1959. Cited in Gaston V. Rimlinger, *Welfare Policy and Industrialization in Europe, America, and Russia.* New York: John Wiley & Sons, 1971.

# 8 ECONOMIC COSTS VERSUS SOCIAL BENEFITS OF HEALTH INSURANCE

Since so little evidence shows that health insurance leads to better physical health, the argument that health insurance costs more money than it is worth would appear to be a compelling argument for reducing health insurance coverage. However, this ignores that the benefits of health insurance include more than medical benefits.

First, nonmedical benefits include reduction in anxiety—moral, medical, and economic. It is true that some of these anxieties are medically induced as when hopes are raised by new developments in medical technology. Since the outcome of medical intervention in such instances may be uncertain, anxiety may be heightened. Of course, the anxiety associated with medical care is difficult to express quantitatively. But whether medically induced or measurable in precise terms, anxieties are associated with illness and medical care. Health insurance alleviates those anxieties to a substantial degree.

Second, health insurance promotes social integration and cohesion in general and in specific sectors of society in particular. As with anxieties and fears, social integration and especially cohesion are not easy to measure. But it takes very little reflection to realize that a significant number of people are going to be excluded from institutional participation and alienated from society if medical care is denied to persons who need it. It also takes little reflection to realize that when illness creates serious economic burdens, it is apt to create tension and conflict between members of family units. Since health insurance reduces these problems, its nonmedical benefits are substantial.

181

Although precise measures of the social benefits of health insurance are difficult to come by, the same is true of medical benefits; even mortality statistics of populations are not without serious measurement deficiencies and errors. This aside, difficulty of measurement does not mean that the thing for which measurement is attempted is unimportant. The theoretical or substantive significance of something must be assessed in terms of the logic of an argument and its consistency with existing facts. Only at that point do problems of measurement come into the picture.

But problems of measurement aside, one may argue, after all, that the function of medical care is to improve certain "objective" medical conditions, such as lowering mortality and morbidity and raising the functioning status of individuals and populations. One may argue further that problems of anxiety are overblown precisely because curative medical care cannot contribute to raising longevity, reducing morbidity, and improving the functioning status of individuals and populations as much as the public commonly believes; there may be less reason to fear the unavailability of medical care than most people think. This may be true. The fact is, however, that people value medical care, and put much confidence and hope in its ability to cure illness, alleviate pain, and reduce disability. The *social* reality of medical care is most important, and may be more important than the medical reality.

A reduction of health insurance coverage would thus raise the level of anxiety and lower the level of social integration and cohesion in society. Significant reductions in expenditures for health insurance would result in significant increases in social costs. To a substantial degree, then, the economic consequences and social consequences of medical care are in conflict; the positive consequences of one tend to increase as the positive consequences of the other decrease. It does not follow, therefore, that we would be better off as a society if we spent less money on medical care by reducing health insurance coverage even if it is true that additional expenditures do not improve health. Also, since people express a high degree of satisfaction with medical care and the current methods of financing, they apparently would rather pay higher prices for the nonmedical benefits they receive from health insurance than to pay less as a result of less extensive insurance coverage in which health benefits were more in line with expenditures. The conflict between economic and social outcomes of health insurance and medical care is reflected in several ways.

There is a conflict between life-enhancing values and economic values. Life-enhancing values—the desire for better health and longer life— are continuously stimulated as new medical technology and treatments are developed, providing hope where none existed before. The implementation of these values has become increasingly costly as the cost of new medical technology and treatment continues to rise. Also, health insurance implements the social value that medical care should be available to all regardless of ability to pay, and it reduces anxiety and promotes social integration and cohesion in society. At the same time, it distorts marginal utility functions and reduces rationality in the marketplace, thus raising the cost of medical care. The social utilities of health insurance are not without an economic cost. This requires detailed discussion.

Observe, first, that the conflict is more than just a conflict between individuals and groups. It is a conflict between the economic well-being and the social well-being of society. The problem is aggravated because the social benefits cannot be expressed very precisely (if at all) in monetary terms. (How much is a warm affectionate relation between an older and younger member of a kinship unit worth in monetary units, and how much is the aggregate of such relations worth to society?) The conflict is thus a *qualitative* conflict and cannot be expressed in quantitative monetary terms.

Some may be inclined to view the conflict as one between individual and social interests, of self-centered economic interests versus the welfare of society. It is more than this since the conflict is experienced by the same individuals. Individuals are torn between their *own* economic self-interest and their moral concern for the welfare of others. As noted in chapter 6, surveys show that the cost of medical care is the most frequently mentioned criticism of medical care. At the same time, we observed in chapter 3 that overwhelming majorities agree with such statements as "Better health care, which saves lives and makes the sick healthy, is worth almost any price" (71%) and "We are a rich country and could afford to spend more money to improve the quality of health care" (84%) (Harris, 1978:72, 16). The public complains about higher taxes, but it has supported medical programs for the poor, the aged, and veterans, as well as legislation designed to assist underpriviledged communities to increase their health resources (e.g., Hill-Burton). Since the thirties, public opinion polls have shown that the American public has favored government-sponsored health insurance programs (see Erskine, 1975), and in 1978 a national survey revealed that 70% of the public agreed that the present system of Medicare/Medicaid and private insurance is "adequate," "pretty good," or "excellent," and 50% believed that a national health insurance program would also be "adequate" to "excellent" (Harris, 1978:92–93). The conflict between the provision of medical care and its economic costs is not just a conflict between special interest groups; it is inner conflict based on moral, ethical, and normative precepts of society as experienced by the same individuals.[1] In addition, the integration of large segments of the population in the mainstream of societal activities and the promotion of social cohesion is not just a special group interest. It is a phenomenon in which the present and future well-being of society are at stake.

The nature of the conflict may be seen in the way the expenditures for health services are distributed in the population. Much data indicate that small segments of the population account for a very large proportion of the expenditures. Several studies indicate that from 20% to 30% of the expenditures are spent on about 1% of the population (Andersen, Lion, and Anderson, 1976; Trappel and McFadden, 1977; Newhouse, et al., 1981; U.S. Congressional Budget Office, 1982). These studies indicate that 5% of the population accounts for from 47% to 60% of the total expenditures (Andersen, Lion, Anderson, 1976:96; Trappel and McFadden, 1977; and U.S. Congressional Budget Office, 1982). A survey of 14,000 households reveals that 11.1% of the population accounted for all hospital admissions in 1977 (Taylor, 1983). Other data show that only 11% of the population is chronically ill but accounts for 29% of all expenditures (Berk, Cafferta, and Haga, 1984:7). Analysis of data from the 1982 National Survey of Access to Medical Care of 4,800 households indicates that 4.7% of the population accounted for 80% of annual nights spent in the hospital. In all hospital expenditures accounted for approximately 47% of all personal health service expenditures in 1982 (Gibson, Waldo, and Levit, 1983:6).

Data for persons with specific disabilities also illustrate the concentration of expenditures. In 1982, 159,000 persons underwent coronary artery surgery at a cost of between $2.5 and $3.0 billion, or approximately 1% of all expenditures on health care (Aaron and Schwartz, 1984:64). In 1979, there were 114,000 such operations, and it is estimated that perhaps 5,000 who would have died without this surgery were alive five years later, though about 70,000 of the operations also reduced cardiac pain (Aaron and Schwartz, 1984:64). If the same survival rate attained for 1983, approximately 7,000 of the 159,000 will have survived for five years. The 7,000 survivors constituted only about 0.0003% of the total population.

Treatment for end-stage kidney disease represents another example. In 1976, treatment of 31,731 victims cost $684.2 billion (Rettig, 1976:98). Since we spent a total of $149.7 billion on health services in 1976 (Gibson, Waldo, and Levit, 1983:3), about 0.5% of all expenditures were spent on approximately 0.015% of the population (not all of whom survived or enjoyed a good quality of life). Most of the costs ($573 billion) were paid by Medicare. In 1981, the cost to Medicare is reported to have been $1.8

billion, or 0.62% of all expenditures, for 64,000 survivors or about 0.027% of the total population (*Wall Street Journal*, 1983).

Clearly, then, small percentages of the population account for grossly disproportionately large amounts of health service expenditures. Such expenditures can hardly be accounted for by economic externalities such as increased productivity (e.g., the $2.5 to $3.0 billion for coronary bypass surgery did not yield a comparable increase in gross national product (GNP), even over a five-year period), reductions in infectious disease, or other economic or health benefits for the population as a whole.

The cost of medical care of the elderly is a telling example. For fiscal 1977, persons 65 and over accounted for 29.4% of the health service expenditures but constituted only 10.9% of the population: per capita expenditures for the aged was $2,026, almost three times the expenditure of $753 for the total population (Fisher, 1980:66). Thus, the age sector of the adult population that counts for the most disproportionate share of medical expenses is the same age sector that contributes the least to the economic productivity of society. Further, the large proportion of expenditures is not evenly concentrated among the elderly. In 1983, for example, 72% of Medicare enrollees (90% of whom are 65 or over) received all Medicare benefits (based on figures in Gibson et al., 1984:19). This means that 8.4% of the population accounted for 18.5% of all expenditures for personal health care and 27.4% for hospital care (figures based on Gibson, 1983:19, 20). Further, 5.2% of enrollees who died in 1978 accounted for 28.2% of Medicare expenditures (Lubitz and Prihoda, 1983:72). Data for 1976 also show that of all expenditures for patients in their last year of life, 30% was spent in their final 30 days and 46% in their last 60 days (Lubitz and Prihoda, 1983:73). Clearly those who received the most disproportionate share of medical care contribute the least to the economic productivity of society. Furthermore, treatment of such persons yields little if any positive economic externality since most of the treatment is for chronic disease rather than infectious disease. In 1974, among the aged, 43.1% of females and 49.7% of males had chronic conditions in comparison to much smaller percentages for the more economically productive 45- through 64-year-olds (23.0% and 25.3%) and 17- through 44-year-olds (8.6% and 9.2%) (Fisher, 1980:69).

Such patterns obviously cannot be explained on economic grounds. They do not represent a rational allocation of resources and allocation that is in the interest of the economic welfare of society. One could well argue that the very large proportion of resources spent on a very small proportion of the population could more efficiently and productively be spent on other goods and services and that the economic welfare of society would be served as a result. This, however, would be at the expense of the social welfare of society. It would deny medical services to a minority which needs or is perceived to need them, and this would raise a serious moral conflict for many members of society. It would produce feelings of despair and rejection by those few who account for such a large proportion of expenditures. Furthermore, since a very large proportion of the expense is paid by health insurance (e.g., a very high proportion of the elderly's hospital expense is paid by Medicare, and 90% of all hospital charges are paid by health insurance), insurance reduces the financial burdens of their relatives. Social relations are maintained at a more harmonious level than otherwise. Higher levels of social integration and cohesion are a result. The conflict between economic welfare and social welfare has generally been resolved in favor of the latter, and this has been accomplished largely because of health insurance.

This is not without an economic price, as noted. The price is inflation in the medical sector and ever greater expenditures for health services as a proportion of all expenditures. The very high costs for the few are spread among the many, either in higher insurance premiums (or taxes), higher prices for health services and products, or both.

In writing about the costs of insurance in general, Aharoni (1981:186) states: "At bottom, inflation was caused by the inability of our political institutions to restrain the growth of insurance within tolerable limits. The increased insurance necessitated much higher costs, both in the public and private sectors." While this may overstate the role of insurance, insurance is certainly a contributing factor to inflation; and some economists view it as the single leading cause of inflation in the medical sector (e.g., Feldstein, 1971). But as we have noted, inflation is not the only outcome of health insurance. Health insurance also implements a major value of society, it reduces worry and anxiety about one's own ability to obtain medical care when needed as well as worry and anxiety about the ability of others, and it promotes social integration and cohesion. But, as noted, since insurance contributes to inflation, these social benefits of health insurance are not free.

It is frequently said that inflation is the "cruelest tax of all." It wipes out people's savings and makes the future less secure. But without the "cruelest tax of all" there would be cruel social results. Whether the social benefits of health insurance are worth the additional economic costs of medical care is a question of values. It is also in large measure a political question. In addressing that political question, however, the social utility of health insurance, private no less than public, should be made explicit. While higher costs are due, no doubt, to some inefficiencies and waste, inflation in the health sector cannot be eliminated unless health insurance, private and public, is eliminated or drastically reduced. And this would have disruptive social results.

We have noted that health insurance causes inflation because of moral hazards, not because of its social benefits. People use more medical care and providers perform more tests and conduct more procedures than they would if medical care were altogether an out-of-pocket expense. At the same time, social factors are important in the growth of health insurance. The moral imperative that medical care should be available to all who need it is a contributing factor as is the social definition and public expectations of medicine. Aaron and Schwartz (1984:129) state, "A generation of U.S. patients has come to expect all medical services from which it might [conceivably] benefit." And when people believe there is a danger that this expectation might not be met, they develop methods to try and assure that it is met. Increasing health insurance coverage is the typical American response to this expectation.

The role of social integration and cohesion as a causal factor in health insurance is less clear. While the economic anxiety that one's elderly parents may become seriously ill may lead people to support policies that provide their parents with health insurance coverage, it is questionable if they do do so because they believe the policies would lead to more cohesive family relations. In some instances, however, as with health insurance benefits for the working and lower class, the easing of class tensions may be a motivating factor. Among the beneficiaries (workers and employees) the motivating factor, of course, is to be assured that medical care will be available in time of need without devastating economic consequences. But for those who provide the benefits, such as capitalists, management, and the state, the easing of worker-management and class tensions may be the underlying reason, as it was in Bismarck's program, and in another way, in the fringe benefits provided workers by American business firms today. In addition, as the social benefits of health become recognized, they may increasingly become motivating factors for health insurance among the recipients of medical care. We may see happen with health insurance the same thing that others have observed about other social institutions. While the social *consequences* of health insurance, and particularly the cohesive effects, may not have been major original causes of health insurance, they may become recognized as consequences of health insurance and, therefore, provide a supporting rationale for health insurance programs in the future; and such rationalizations may become major contributing causes of health insurance in the future. Health insurance may generate social consequences that provide significant support for its own existence. As an institution, health insurance may have come full cycle, or be in the process of doing so.[2] Its role in the alleviation of conflict between sectors of the population and the preservation of kinship cohesion may in the future be used as explicit justification for third-party reimbursement. This, of course, may increase the problem of moral hazards and, hence, even higher costs. And higher cost may be cited as reason for extending insurance to cover medical care.

## Moral Hazards, Social Control, and Social Cohesion

The conflict between economic and social outcomes of health insurance may be seen in particular with respect to the relation between moral hazards, social control, and social cohesion. Moral hazards and the preservation of social cohesion are both consequences of health insurance. It would obviously be better if the social benefits could be retained with a reduction in moral hazards, that is, with less excessive and unnecessary use. The problem is that attempts to reduce moral hazards are also apt to reduce the benefits of social cohesion.

Recall that moral hazards derive from the structure of pooled interdependence. This affects the way people respond to the moral hazard problem. Usually when a person's actions have undesirable effects (such as increasing costs) for others, others respond by punishing the individual responsible. This is apt to occur when the connection between the actor's behavior and the outcomes for others is known. A peculiar characteristic of pooled interdependence, particularly as it relates to insurance, is that the relationship between an actor's behavior and the adverse outcomes of others is not known. Consequently, individuals are usually not held responsible for the adverse consequences that their bahavior (moral hazards) has for others.

Observe, also, that the excessive behavior which insurance encourages is not always a moral hazard phenomenon. Members of the same group insurance plan are not equally healthy; members will vary, therefore, in terms of their need for medical care. Hence, the medical expenses of some will be greater, sometimes much greater, than others, which means that some will receive more benefits from the plan than others. The healthier members help to pay for the medical care of the less healthy. This, of couse, is what the plan is intended to do: in return for protection against unexpectedly high medical expenses, the individual agrees to pay a smaller but certain premium. But note that whether the high costs are due to excessive use (moral hazards) or to appropriate use, the connection between behavior and outcome is still usually not visible. A worker usually does not know that increases in his health insurance premium are due to the medical expenses of particular co-workers. This has significant social and economic consequences.

Lester Thurow (1980) contends that we live in a zero-sum society, which means that anytime one person benefits, others lose.[3] This is especially so for insurance. The point is clearly made by Aharoni, though his remarks need not be limited to government programs. He states that "risks cannot be eliminated by passing them to government. Certain risks can be insured against by government, but these entail costs,...[and since] risks are mutually exclusive, not all of them can be eliminated. A worker in a certain workplace can be protected against the risk of losing his or her job only if others are willing to bear the additional costs and additional risk.... [Consequently,] the reduction of risk to one individual can be achieved only by an increased risk somewhere else to someone else.... The risks to one group of individuals often can be eliminated or reduced only by increasing the [costs] to others" (Aharoni, 1981:169, 171, 189). The problem may be viewed in terms of social control.

The problem of moral hazards represents a lack of social control. It is reduced if negative sanctions are directed at the deviants, the excessive users. If sanctions are applied uniformly so that a negative reaction is highly probable, reactions are more apt to have a deterrent effect. In the present case this would necessitate that the connection between behavior and outcome would be visible, and the connection between payment and benefit of all beneficiaries or potential beneficiaries would be known. Individuals who reap high benefits would therefore be identified; they would become known to other policyholders (taxpayers). This itself would be a form of negative social sanction. The certainty of negative sanctions is the most important factor in deterring deviant behavior (Gibbs, 1981), in this case excessive use of medical care. But if high cost policyholders are identified, other policyholders may be less willing for such persons to continue to pay the same premium as they. For example, if an employee and his or her dependents received medical care that were many times the benefits received by co-workers and if this is publicized and made known to co-workers, the recipient of the benefits might be resented. Co-workers may realize that they have to do without goods and services because the large expenditure of another worker has have caused their premiums to increase so much. Also the recipient may feel guilty that the cost of his or her own misfortune is at the expense of others. Resentment and guilt might be especially high when the real benefit from the expenditure is of very limited value (e.g., a worker's dependent may die despite great expense).

Thus, the identification of such persons would probably create pressure to reduce insurance coverage for them or to exclude certain high-risk individuals (those in poor health) from such coverage or else require them to pay higher premiums, in line with their "actuarial experience." Aharoni states (1981:203) that "an essential part of any attempt to assess the cost and benefits of insurance is to identify them and then make them visible. Innovations in the way insurance is organized often can save much unnecessary costs, but this can be found out only if every cost—visible and invisible—is identified and justified by a comparison to the benefit."

Since "the lack of a visible link between behavior and payments tends to increase the costs of the system" (Aharoni, 1981:204), if the link between behavior and payment were visible it would decrease the economic costs. Enhanced visibility would result in better social control. But the social costs would mount. Major beneficiaries of the system, many of whom are *not* the result of moral hazards, might be resented by other policyholders or taxpayers. For example, higher taxes, which are necessary to pay for government insurance programs, would be even more resented by the public if individual beneficiaries were made known. The general point is made by Aharoni (1981:135): "Invisibility makes possible a disbursement of various grants and benefits in ways that are not immediately obvious, and allows a distribution that would not be socially acceptable if it were fully known." What is not recognized in the recommendation that persons who receive benefits be made known is the disruptive social consequences that would result. Then individuals are apt to be set against individuals, group against group, young against the old, healthy against the sick. The lack of visibility helps to prevent this. Because of the zero-sum aspect of insurance programs, private and public, a conflictual relationship is *inherent* between policyholders. The low visibility of the connection between benefit and payment keeps the conflict from being recognized; low visibility makes it possible for individuals and groups to live together in harmony. It conceals conflict and, thus, promotes social cohesion. Significant social benefits exist only because of low visibility and, hence, paradoxically, because there is a low level of social control. The conclusion is not limited to grants and benefits allocated by the federal government, but is a general characteristic of pooled interdependence, and therefore of private insurance as well. Although there are important differences between private and public insurance, only when private insurance increases the premiums for high-risk persons (or reduces their coverage) is the difference of much consequence in this respect.

In summary, to make more visible the link between behavior and payment—of how the benefits and the costs are distributed among policyholders—would no doubt reduce the economic costs associated with insurance programs. It would reduce the problem of moral hazards. In the process, however, many legitimate beneficiaries would also be identified. They may be resented, generating tensions and conflict between them and others. The result would be an increase in *social* costs. Pooled interdependence, by keeping the link between insurance benefits and costs invisible, and hence social control low, helps to preserve cohesion in a zero-sum society, where the large costs of a few are spread among many others. There is important social utility associated with most insurance and with health insurance programs in particular. True, such utility is frequently in conflict with a more efficient economic allocation of resources; from an economic perspective, the danger is that resources are utilized in the medical sector that could be used more "productively" in other sectors. Thus, more efficient use of resources might be accomplished if the individuals and groups on whom such a large proportion of expenditures is spent were more visible to others. From a social perspective, however, the danger is that the minority of people on whom such a disproportionately large share of medical expenditures is spent are resented by others despite the fact that the expenditures are themselves based on legitimate medical need. Lower social cohesion would be the result.

## Implications for Medicare and Social Security

Economic problems of the Social Security program, which includes Medicare, are well publicized and are the joint result of benefits being raised and the proportion of the population aged 65 and above having increased over the past number of years. In general, the trust fund into which the beneficiaries have paid is inadequate to meet the payments required under law so that a major proportion of the concurrent payments is paid by younger generations who are gainfully employed. The problem is serious, and what is said below is not intended to deemphasize the magnitude of the economic issues. It will, instead, be intended to emphasize sociological aspects which are often ignored.

A major issue in the continuing debate about the problems of Social Security concerns the method by which the program is financed. Currently, it is finance by payroll tax deductions. Benefits are paid through deductions from the pay of currently gainfully employed workers as well as from contributions that the beneficiaries have also paid, which have gone into a trust fund. The argument frequently made, and one that has prevailed to this point, is that the program should be financed by the payroll tax rather than by general revenues. The logic for this is that persons who are beneficiaries are persons who have paid into the fund. And there is some social merit to this. If benefits are tied to the payroll tax, then Medicare can be defended in terms of exchange. In return for having contributed to Social Security, individuals receive benefits from it: beneficiaries therefore have a right to their benefits that are based on their economic contributions. This was the rationale for linking Medicare to Social Security: "A program that provided medical care for Social Security beneficiaries under an insurance system that they had contributed to makes that care an earned right" (Harris, 1966:61). Of course, there have already been deviations from this policy since many of the benefits from Social Security do not come from the trust fund but from individuals who are currently employed and paying a payroll tax. Hence, the reference to Social Security as a "contract between generations." The contract, however, is more along the lines of Sahlins' conception of generalized exchange than balanced exchange (see chapter 7), though funding by the payroll tax and limiting benefits to persons who were contributors to Social Security at least a *sense* of balanced exchange. Benefits are still tied to the payroll tax in accordance with the view that only those persons (or their dependents) who have paid into the fund receive benefits from it. Sociologically, however, aside from the belief, which has some symbolic value, that the benefits are an earned benefit (though it seems fewer people believe this anymore), it doesn't matter how the tax is paid. General revenue could accomplish the same thing as the payroll tax. The social benefits may be achieved either way.

There may be adverse economic consequences to using general revenues, however. Unless benefits are tied to the payroll tax, financial restraints on raising the benefits may be weakened (though the linkage to the payroll tax has not deterred politicians in the past from raising benefits).[4] This in turn may lead to an even greater tax to support the needs of the elderly so that, on balance, the tax burden and adverse economic consequences are worse than they would otherwise be. Again, however, sociologically, it makes little if any difference. And keeping the financial restraints on benefits tight may have pervasive adverse effects on social benefits, particularly for kinship units. Titmuss' comments with regard to blood (whether blood is to be treated as a donation or "gift" to strangers—to persons one does not know—or as a commercial commodity) is relevant to this point.

> Once a man begins to say,... "I need no longer experience (or suffer from) a sense of responsibility (or sin) in not giving to my neighbour" then the

consequences are likely to be socially pervasive. There is nothing permanent about expressions of reciprocity. If the bonds of community giving are broken the result is a state of value neutralism. The vacuum is likely to be filled by hostility and social conflict.... *The myth of maximizing economic growth can supplant the growth of social relations* (Titmuss, 1971:198–199; emphasis supplied).

And so it can be with insurance for medical care for the elderly.

The point bears on the low visibility of the connection between premiums (taxes) paid and benefits received. The average Social Security recipient receives more in benefits than he (or she) has paid, with the difference being paid for with the taxes paid by younger generations. As this becomes more widely known, one wonders how many of the younger generations would really accept the contract between generations. To make a big issue of this is politically dangerous, to say the least, but it would likely increase pressures to limit benefits for the elderly and, hence, to lower the premiums (taxes) of the gainfully employed. Economic gain would be at the expense of social loss; "economic growth [would] supplant the growth of social relations."

A weakening of family relations between generations would result. Some people argue, to the contrary, that Social Security weakens rather than strengthens kinship relations across generations. This is because individual welfare is shifted from the responsibility of individuals and families to the state or society. There is logic to this argument, and there may be some validity to it as well. A problem, however, is that the growth of Social Security began after extended kinship ties had already begun to grow weak. An industrial and postindustrial society, with its requirement of extensive geographical mobility, is not conducive to the maintenance of cohesive extended family relations. Also, perhaps the one index that is most reflective of the weakness of the family is the divorce rate. The rate has steadily risen over the years so that today almost 50% of people who marry get divorced (U.S. Department of Health, Education and Welfare, 1979:11). It is hard to see how this could be due to Social Security, welfare assistance, or to any other one factor. The dominance of the isolated small nuclear family and increases in the divorce rate are related to changing norms of lifestyle that are in turn related to an increasingly urban, complex, and mobile society.

Medicare, and health insurance in general, may indeed reduce the motivation of family and relatives to care for and financially assist one of their own during periods of crisis. The question arises, however, of what happens if the motivation has already been reduced by forces over which insurance programs, private and public, have no control. The crises and deprivations that this can generate may reduce the motivation even further by alienating family members and relatives from each other even more unless supportive institutions, such as health insurance, exist. A further deterioration of family cohesion would be the result.

The problem may be viewed further from the vantage point of theories of exchange. In economic exchange theory, one gives up something of monetary value in return for something that is believed to be of equal monetary value. In "classical" social exchange (in contrast to such exchange theories as that of Sahlins), the same general relation is said to obtain, except that the things exchanged are not limited to economic goods and services; they may be purely social, such as social approval. In the case of Medicare, we have a situation in which transactions take place between groups or sectors of the population rather than between individuals. It resembles the type of exchange that Marcel Mauss wrote about with respect to "archaic" societies (Mauss, 1967).

According to Mauss, exchange in such societies is usually between clans, age groups, and sexes rather than between individuals. Individuals may make the transaction but it is done on behalf of a group. Mauss believed such exchange differed from that in classical economic theory or utilitarianism in two senses. The first, as noted, is that the exchange is between groups rather than individuals. More fundamentally, at least at the time Mauss presented his thesis (1925), Mauss' formulation differed from economic theory since the exchange is not limited to things of monetary value, but may also include noneconomic goods (e.g., status or morality). At the same time, when exchanges are made—sometimes as "gifts"—there is usually a self-interested dimension. Something is expected in return. When a tribal leader gives a *potlatch* for another leader, he expects something greater in return, and the receiver is socially obligated to comply with this expectation. The exchange is not simple. "It is a complex notion that inspires the economic actions we have described, a notion neither of purely free and gratuitous presentations [gifts], nor of purely interested utilitarian production and exchange; it is a kind of hybrid" (Mauss, 1967:70).

Some economists would dispute the view that such transactions represent a hybrid. They would contend that the "commodities" exchanged, whether they be social and moral in nature, may be given a monetary value, and hence can be adequately expressed in terms of the economic theory of exchange. (On this point, see Weisskopf, 1971.) A more fundamental point, and one on which Mauss' analysis agrees with economic and classical social exchange theories, concerns the nature of the exchange. While Mauss is not explicit about the balanced nature of the exchange, he does contend that the exchange is bilateral; only to the outsider does the "gift" appear unilateral. Expectation that the "gift" giving be bilateral "at once binds clans together and keeps them separate, which divides their labour and constrains them to exchange" (Mauss, 1967:71). Exchange is a basis for social cohesion between groups. A point on which all exchange theories agree, with the exception of Sahlins (1965), is that relations between groups no less than individuals are based on bilateral transactions. Otherwise, the relations are apt to generate resentment, produce individual or group alienation and withdrawal, and are characteristically unstable.

When we realize that the elderly consume approximately 30% of the health care, constitute only about 11% of the population, and that they contribute little to the economic growth and productivity of society, the health benefits they receive through Medicare are heavily tilted toward Sahlin's conception of generalized exchange. The elderly pay much less for medical care than the cost of the services they receive. Therefore, when viewed from the perspective of classical theories of exchange, the relationship between the elderly and younger sectors of society is under potential strain and consequent instability, alienation, and withdrawal, and, hence, weaker cohesion between generations. Possibilities for the future will be explored in the next chapter.

## Conclusion

The social benefits of health insurance programs are important, but they are not free. The social benefits do not cause the economic costs of medical care to increase, but they are some of the consequences of health insurance, and health insurance does cause medical costs to increase. Consequently, efforts to reduce cost pressures by scaling back health insurance benefits are apt to have serious adverse social effects. Policies designed to lower the economic costs of medical care by reducing the scope of health insurance are apt to be in conflict with policies that produce social benefits.

This is not to say that one set of policies is superior to another—just that efforts to enhance economic objectives are apt to be in conflict with efforts to enhance social objectives, and vice versa. Today, public policy on health insurance poses a deep dilemma for society. A more cohesive society is not necessarily more economically productive, and a society in which economic productivity is high is not necessarily one in which social cohesion is high. It was long a mistaken view, promoted by the so-called human relations school of industry and work organizations, that workers' satisfaction and work-group cohesion would result in more productive workers. After decades of research, it is now known that this is not true (see the review by Berg, Freedman, and Freeman, 1978:35–48). This may hold for society in general. Economic efficiency in the medical area and positive social relations between important sectors of society are, to some extent, inversely related. An increase in one may be at the expense of the other. While social policies may be designed to alleviate this conflict, the conflict will probably never disappear.

## Notes

1. Conclusions in this paragraph draw on the works of Mishan (1967) and Weisskopf (1971). Weisskopf states: "The most glaring external 'diseconomies' (negative externalities) of today involve much more than problems of conflict of interest. The basic problem is usually one of ethics and policy; a conflict between the profitableness of a particular good or service within the existing economic structure on the one hand, and the welfare of society on the other hand. The ethical conflict is aggravated by the problem of measurement: The benefits to special interests (firms, investors, wage earners) are easily measured in terms of money profits, wages, returns: The external 'disamenities' are mostly unquantifiable intangibles. The difficulty in calculating such disamenities can be seen from the efforts of certain economists who, among other devices, 'add to the social costs of motorized traffic...by reckoning the cost of a man killed as the loss of his potential future pecuniary contribution to the national product!' (Mishan, 1967:87)...Problems such as the uglification of cities, the polluting and jamming effects of motorized traffic, 'the dirt and dust, the noise and smell, and the destruction and tenseness...but also the growing dehumanization of the physical environment...' (Mishan, 1967:87) are more than conflict of interest; they are on a different level than the conflict between a noisy laundry and its neighboring residents. The 'interests' of the 'public at large' are not special individual or group interests: They are social goals based on moral, ethical, normative principles. Calling it an 'interest' (and expressing it in monetary units) only serves to obscure its normative character. In an oversimplified, crude but nevertheless practically valid formulation: The problem of external diseconomies involves a conflict between the acquisitive orientation in pursuit of more and more money and possessions on the one hand, and the quality of life in the present and future society on the other. To call them interests is nothing but a propagandistic trick to make these goals acceptable in a culture in which monetary and acquisitive ends reign supreme.... What exists [with respect to despoiling coastal shoreland from oil drilling] is a qualitative conflict between good, which should include a right to unspoiled nature, and monetary interests, which can only be solved by moral judgments and decisions. It is true that behind the monetary interests of corporations there may be a 'public interest' in getting more oil and gasoline. In this case the conflict is between goals: Either more oil, gas, cars, pollution, cementing of land, traffic jams, urban and suburban sprawl, or unspoiled open spaces and nature. Again, this conflict can only be resolved by moral judgment and decision; and such decision is not facilitated by interpreting a moral conflict in terms of a conflict between individual and group interests" Weisskopf, 1971:102–103, 105).

2. Reference here is to those functionalists who view the consequences of social institution as causal to their existence. The position is similar to the Skinnerian view that behavior is a function of its consequences, though most anthropologists and sociologists do not contend that the positive consequences of *soical institutions* are *necessarily* causal in the institutions' existence because such consequences may go unrecognized, as Merton (1957) has observed.

3. Some reject Thurow's thesis of capitalism being a zero-sum game on the grounds that greater overall income (e.g., a larger GNP) results in more income for everyone. Thus, some getting less when others get more is rejected; everyone may gain from increased productivity. This is a correct conclusion, but it is not the point that Thurow makes. Thurow's thesis is based on the *proportionate* distribution of income, or the sociological concept of relative deprivation. If one person doubles his or her income and another only increases his or her income by 25%, the differences between them has increased and the one with the smallest increase, in comparison to the one with the largest increase, *feels* that he or she has lost ground even if in absolute terms he or she has actually gained.

4. One part of Medicare does come from general revenues and requires a premium from the recipient. This is Part B, for nonhospital services.

## References

Aaron, Henry J., and William B. Schwartz. *The Painful Prescription: Rationing Hospital Care.* Washington, DC: The Brookings Institution, 1984.

Aharoni, Yair. *The No-Risk Society.* Chatham, NJ: Chatham House Publishers Inc., 1981.

Andersen, Ronald, Joanna Lion, and Odin W. Anderson. *Two Decades of Health Services: Social Survey Trends in Use and Expenditure.* Cambridge, MA: Ballinger Publishing Co., 1976.

Berg, Ivar, Marcia Freedman, and Michael Freeman. *Managers and Work Reform: A Limited Engagement.* New York: The Free Press, 1978.

Berk, Mark L., Gail Lee Cafferata, and Michael M. Hagan. *Persons with Limitations of Activity: Health Insurance, Expenditures and Use of Services.* Washington, DC: U.S. Department of Health and Human Services, National Center for Health Services Research, Rockville, Maryland, October, 1984.

Erskine, Hazel. "The Polls: Health Insurance." *Public Opinion Quarterly* 39 (1975):128–143.

Feldstein, Martin S. *The Rising Cost of Hospital Care.* Washington, D.C.: Information Resources Press, 1971.

Fisher, Charles R. "Differences by Age Groups in Health Care Spending." *Health Care Financing Review* 1 (Spring 1980):65–90.

Gibbs, Jack P. "The Sociology of Deviance and Social Control." In Morris Rosenberg and Ralph H. Turner (eds.), *Social Psychology: Sociological Perspectives*, pp. 483–522. New York: Basic Books, 1981.

Gibson, Robert M., Daniel R. Waldo, and Katharine R. Levit. "National Health Expenditures, 1982. "*Health Care Financing Review* 5 (Fall 1983):1–31.

Gibson, Robert M., Katharine R. Levit, Helen Lazenby, and Daniel Waldo. "National Health Expenditures, 1983." *Health Care Financing Review* 6 (Winter 1984):1–29.

Harris, Richard. *A Sacred Trust*. Baltimore: Penguin Books, Inc., 1966.

Lubitz, James, and Ronald Prihoda. "Use and Costs of Medicare Services in the Last Years of Life." In U.S. Department of Health and Human Services, *Health—United States*, 1983 pp. 71–77. Washington, DC: U.S. Government Printing Office, 1983.

Mauss, Marcel. *The Gift: Forms and Functions of Exchange in Archaic Society*. Glenco, IL: The Free Press, 1954.

Merton, Robert K. *Social Theory and Social Structure*, rev. and enlr. ed. Glencoe, IL: The Free Press, 1957.

Mishan, E.J. *The Cost of Economic Growth*. London: The Staples Press, 1967.

Newhouse, Joseph, et al. "Some Interim Results from a Controlled Trial of Cost Sharing in Health Insurance." *New England Journal of Medicine* 305 (December 17, 1981):1501–1507.

Rettig, Richard A. "The Policy Debate on Patient Care Financing for Victims of End-Stage Renal Disease." *Law and Contemporary Problems* 40 (December 1976):192–230.

Sahlins, Marshall D. *The Relevance of Models for Social Anthropology*. London: Frederick A. Praeger, Publisher, 1965.

Taylor, Amy. "Inpatient Hospital Services: Use, Expenditures, and Sources of Payment." Rockville, MD: U.S. Department of Health and Human Services, National Center for Health Services Research, May, 1983.

Thurow, Lester. *The Zero-Sum Society: Distribution and the Possibilities for Economic Change*. Middlesex, England: Penguin Books, 1980

Titmuss, Richard M. *The Gift Relationship: From Human Blood to Social Policy*. New York: Vintage Books, 1971.

Trappell, Gordon R., and Frank E. McFadden. *The Rising Cost of Catastrophic Illness*. Falls Church, VA: Actuarial Research Corporation, December, 1977. Final Report to U.S. National Center for Health Services Research, Department of Health, Education, and Welfare, Contract No. HRA 230-75-0143.

U.S. Congressional Budget Office. *Catastrophic Medical Expenses: Patterns in the Non-Elderly, Non-Poor Population*. Washington, DC: Congressional Budget Office, December 1982.

U.S. Department of Health, Education, and Welfare. *Monthly Vital Statistics Report*. Vol. 27 no. 13, 1979.

# 9 HEALTH INSURANCE, COST CONTAINMENT, AND SOCIAL CONFLICT: A FUTURE PERSPECTIVE

In the late 1960s and 1970s much public medical policy in the United States was designed to use public insurance to increase access to medical care for low-income and older people and, thus, to bring about a closer relationship between the need for medical care and the utilization of it. In addition, the increase in private insurance made medical care more accessible to more people. Therefore, the primary method used to assure access to medical care regardless of cost was to extend health insurance coverage to more people. Now, during the 1980s, after more than two decades of rapidly rising expenditures for health services, "cost containment" has begun to replace access as a major policy issue. In order to lower the national cost of medical care, some contend that the scope of government (and private) insurance programs should be reduced; the beneficiaries of such programs should be required to share the cost of those programs more than they do now (e.g., raising the deductible feature of Medicare, taxing the health insurance premium paid by private employers on behalf of their workers, which is not presently taxed). Just as health insurance was the primary mechanism used in policies designed to reduce income barriers to access, its reduction is central in programs of cost containment.

A strong theoretical (economic) argument that insurance is the primary factor in the rise of hospital costs has been made by Martin S. Feldstein (e.g., 1971, 1977), among others. Significantly, cuts were made in government insurance programs during the period in which Feldstein was chairman of the President's Council of Economic Advisors. Reduction in rance coverage has been voiced by others, sometimes in terms of .ioning" medical care (see Aaron and Schwartz, 1984; Mechanic, 1977; and Cooper, 1975). Of course, alternatives besides reducing health insurance have been advocated, and some have been implemented. They include the DRG program (for Diagnostic Related Groups) which sets fixed rates for Medicare patients (hospitals are reimbursed a fixed rate for patients with a particular diagnosis rather than being reimbursed on the basis of hospital charges), the encouragement of competition between alternative delivery systems (particularly between health maintenance organizations [HMOs] and other forms of delivery), and increasing and encouraging local governments and private industry to foster competition. Other steps will probably be taken in the future. Nevertheless, since health insurance is viewed as a basic cause of increases in expenditures, its reduction will no doubt continue to be emphasized by many who think that national expenditures for health services should be reduced.

We have reasoned, however, that while health insurance does increase health service expenditures, it is an adaptive institution and a response to and not just a cause of increases in expenditures. In this last chapter we will examine several factors that will probably continue to exert upward pressure on expenditures and, hence, most probably lead to the demand for more rather than less insurance. We will also examine possible social consequences from reductions in health insurance. A fundamental thesis of this book is that health insurance reduces conflict and promotes harmony in social relations and that this may be a far more signfiicant consequence of health insurance than any improvements in health. Relations between generations have received specific attention. In the final section of this chapter we will examine the possible effect that reductions in health may have on these relations. In the years ahead such relations are viewed as replacing relations between social classes as the arena where health insurance will be most significant from a social perspective.

At the outset, one point should be made absolutely clear. Proponents of health insurance sometimes claim that reductions will lead to a decrease in the health status of the population in general, or of specific subpopulations in particular. As we have seen, except for programs in which the effects of medical care are dramatic, clear, and immediate, such as with the End-Stage Renal Disease program, evidence simply does not exist to prove that health insurance has a major positive effect on the health status of populations. Our focus, however, is not on the medical effects but, rather, on the social consequences that are to be expected from reductions of health insurance.

Before reviewing factors that will put upward pressure on expenditures from health services in the future, it will be useful to recall that from 1955 to 1983 national expenditures for health services in the United States rose from 4.5% to 10.8% of the gross national product (GNP). The trend is not unique to the United States, since substantial increases have also occurred in other industrial countries. No one can say to what extent this trend will continue, but everyone agrees that at some point it will have to level off. If expenditures in the United States continue to increase at the same annual rate they have since 1955 (14.3%), they will constitute approximately 26% of GNP in the year 2008 and 64% in 2033. By about the middle of the twenty-first century, health services would virtually encompass the entire economy! Obviously this will not occur. At some point, movements of some kind will develop to stop if not reverse the trend. No one knows at what point this will be. Probably no one envisioned in 1955 that expenditures would have reached the level they are at today; and most would have also agreed then that steps would be taken to prevent this from happening. It will be instructive, therefore, to examine several factors that have contributed to this increase and that will also continue to exert pressure on additional expenditures in the future.

## Supply of Physicians

A positive relationship between the supply of physicians and expenditures for health services has been recognized for some time but has not been given the attention it deserves. Contrary to general economic process, an increase in physicians (and hospitals) leads to an increase in the demand for their services (see Miqué and Bérlangér, 1974). Economists don't agree on the reasons for this (Newhouse, 1978), and several factors are undoubtedly involved (Rushing, 1985). One is probably that the number of physicians per unit of population gives physicians more time to spend with patients and hence to be more thorough and penetrating in their examinations. This results in the discovery of more rather than fewer conditions that are perceived as requiring medical attention. The result is more testing, more referrals to specialists, more treatment, and more hospitalization—all leading to more expenditures. The relationship between the national supply of physicians and national expenditures for medical care as a proportion of all expenditures may be seen from the trend from 1950 to 1980 (see Rushing, 1985).

In 1950 there were 14.2 active nonfederal physicians per 10,000 population. There was no growth during the fifties (the number remaining at 14.2 in 1960) but grew to 15.5 by 1970, 17.4 by 1975, and 20.2 by 1980

(U.S. Department of Health and Human Services, 1981:177). For the most part, such growth reflected the creation of new medical schools and expansion of existing schools in the sixties and seventies. The percentage of GNP spent on health services grew as the supply of physicians increased, from 5.3 in 1960 to 7.6 (1970), 8.6 (1975), and 9.5 (1980). While the supply of physicians is not the only factor in the escalation of expenditures (for example, it could not have accounted for the increase from 4.5% in 1950 to 5.3% in 1960), results do suggest that it is important.[1] Therefore, if increases in physician manpower occur in the future, pressures on additional expenditures would be expected. The U.S. Department of Health and Human Services (1981:177) estimates that on the basis of existing student capacity of medical schools there will be 24.3 physicians per 10,000 in 1990, and 27.1 by the year 2000. The "physician glut" may have a number of consequences, some good and some bad. If it leads to the needs of more people being met, the increase would be considered in a positive light. Also, the increase in physicians may lead to organizational changes in medicine (e.g., more HMOs), which may help to contain costs with no deterioration in quality of care (Starr, 1982). At the same time, the experience of the past quarter century would indicate that the increase in physician manpower will impose upward pressures on expenditures for medical care. This is apt to create more economic insecurity for individuals and families, thus increasing pressures for additional insurance coverage.

## Medical Technology

The relationship between advances in medical technology and national expenditures for medical services is difficult to show with precision because of problems in constructing a single measure of technology. It is clear from specific examples cited in chapter 5, however, that advances in technology have led to increases in expenditures. A more general indication of the influence of technology on additional expenditures may be seen from the following.

The probability of technological innovation is a function of the scientific base of knowledge and the number of persons who have mastered portions of this knowledge. An indication of both the increase in the base of knowledge as well as the number of persons who have a grasp of that knowledge is the national expenditures allocated for medical research. While exact figures prior to 1947 are not available, the annual publication of "National Health Expenditures," which was originally published in the

*Social Security Bulletin* and in recent years in the *Health Care Financing Review*, reports that in 1940, the earliest years for which a figure is reported, we spent $3 million on medical "research and construction" (Gibson, 1980:22). This excludes all research expenditures for research and development of drug companies and other manufacturers of medical equipment and supplies, though, as noted, it does include construction expense. Comparison of figures reported in this publication with those reported beginning in 1948 by the National Institutes of Health (NIH) (U.S. Department of Health, Education and Welfare, 1978; U.S. Department of Health and Human Services, 1984), which excluded research training and construction, shows that for the three years 1948, 1949, and 1950, the NIH figure averaged about 40% higher than the figure for "research and construction" from "National Health Expenditures." On this basis, approximately $4.2 million may have been spent on medical research in 1940. The figure before 1940 was even lower because the amount was too low to be reported for the two years (1935 and 1929) for which figures are available prior to 1940 in National Health Expenditures. By 1947, $87 million was spent on medical research and development, which is equivalent to $55 million 1940 dollars,[2] for a 1,305% increase in just seven years. This increased to $94 and $137 million (1940 dollars) in 1950 and 1955, and by 1960 the expenditure had increased to $414 million. By 1970, the figure was $1.013 billion. Thus in 30 years, research expenditures had increased over 24,000%, and in 23 years (from 1947 to 1970) they increased by 1,165%. Expenditures in 1940 dollars did not increase so dramatically in the seventies, but still had increased to $1.335 billion 1940 dollars by 1982. Further, as a percentage of research and development in all areas, research and development in medicine increased from about 4% to 5% in the 1950s to 6.5% in 1960 to a peak of 12.9% in 1974; it remained above 12% through 1980 (U.S. Department of Health, Education and Welfare, 1978:139; and U.S. Department of Health and Human Services, 1984:135).

Many of these expenditures led to the training of a large number of biomedical scientists and engineers and to the expansion in the base of biomedical knowledge. Consequently, a high level of activity leading to rapid technological innovation in diagnostic and therapeutic procedures occurred in the sixties and seventies and is assured for many years to come. Indeed, the magnitude of the advance is seen constantly, almost daily, as with organ transplant and artificial implant operations. Of course, most innovations will not be as dramatic or as expensive as these and other forms of "high tech medicine." But the trend toward more sophisticated technology and expensive treatment will continue. This is so even if government support for research and development were reduced substantially. The base of knowledge and the large number (large in comparision to previous decades) of biomedical scientists, engineers, and technicians guarantees that. It will be most difficult to suppress the development of knowledge and the invention of new diagnostic and therapeutic procedures by persons who have mastered that knowledge and developed a high level of technical skill.

Two consequences of technological innovation in medicine are to be noted. First, unlike innovation in other areas, technological innovation in medicine tends to increase costs rather than lower them, though in some instances it does lower the cost (e.g., development of more effective antibiotics for certain illnesses). It often allows for the use of more sophisticated, and hence more expensive, diagnostic and therapeutic procedures for the same illness. The point was noted in chapter 5 by way of several examples, as was the difficulty in slowing the diffusion of new and expensive technology, even when its cost effectiveness is unknown. Second, it frequently allows for the successful treatment of conditions that were previously untreatable. Organ transplants are obvious examples, as are open-heart surgery, hemodialysis, the use of lasers and computers in eye surgery and other forms of microsurgery, and artificial organ implants. These developments, in turn, raise the hopes and aspirations of persons with terminal and debilitating conditions; a dread fate is not something that people with certain illnesses and impairments must necessarily accept anymore. This along with the sophistication and expense of technology will impose upward pressures on expenditures for medical care. While there is always the possibility that in some—perhaps in many—instances new technology will allow for less expensive treatment, experience of the past would indicate that in many other instances it will continue to raise the costs of medical care, and in some instances the increase may be astronomical.[3] Consequently, anxieties as well as hopes and aspirations will be stimulated by these developments, and this will raise pressures for insurance to assure that the cost of treatment is covered. As innovations become routinized—are no longer considered as "experimental"—they qualify for insurance coverage, as is the case with many transplant operations today. If this were not the case, then only those who could afford the innovative treatments would receive them. And this is contrary to the moral imperative that medical care is a fundamental human right and should not depend on an individual's ability to pay. New technology that will almost surely develop will almost guarantee a continuation of upward pressure on the cost of health services in the future. This in turn will exert pressures for additional insurance coverage.

## Trends in Illness and Disability

As noted, an increase in the supply of physicians will lead to the detection of more illnesses (not always accurately) in the population. There are, however, other reasons for expecting the rate of illness, or at least of disability, to increase in the future. We observed in chapter 3 that the proportion of the population reporting activity limitations has increased rather substantially in recent years. This may have occurred because the proportion of persons who survive a chronic and debilitating illness or impairment has been increasing. Such persons need continued medical care. If the increase in disabling conditions continues, it will generate upward pressure on additional expenditures for medical services in the future. And there is every indication that this will continue because death rates from many chronic illnesses are decreasing.

The death rate for heart disease, in particular, has been declining since 1950, and the decline since 1968 has been precipitous (U.S. Department of Health and Human Services, 1983:117; Shapiro, 1983:129–131). The decline in deaths due to ischemic heart disease has been especially large (Stallone, 1980). It is not clear what has caused this decline (see Stallone, 1980; and Shapiro, 1983:129–131), though improvements in diagnosis and treatment may be involved. If these improvements continue, we may expect the decrease in deaths from heart disease to continue. This, however, will not result in a decrease in the rate of heart disease itself; since these improvements lead to more survivors, an increase in the proportion of the population who have a history of heart problems may be expected. This is significant because a higher proportion of this group experiences activity limitations than does any other disease group, with 46.4% of 45 to 64-year-olds with heart conditions reporting in 1972 that their condition caused activity limitations (U.S. Department of Health, Education and Welfare, 1975:489). Significantly, the death rate from diabetes is also decreasing, thus increasing the percentage of the population who have diabetes (2.5% in 1981—U.S. Bureau of the Census, 1984:126). An increase in the proportion with chronic disease and the associated residual disabilities leads, of course, to the need for additional medical services. Additional medical expense is the result, thus creating more economic insecurity and the desire for more health insurance.

## Public Attitudes and Perceptions

The things discussed thus far—trends in the supply of physicians, medical technology, and illness-disability—all point to upward pressures on national expenditures for health services in the future and, thus, more health insurance coverage. Such pressures are not inevitable, however, since changes in public attitudes and perceptions may change so that medical care in our scale of priorities may not be as high in the future. After all, in light of the evidence we have reviewed, particularly in chapter 3, the value placed on medical care is largely a result of social definition and not due solely to health benefits that medical care provides. While pressures will no doubt exist which will heighten concern about health and put upward pressures on expenditures for medical care, such pressures could be reduced by a change in the way medical care is viewed and defined by the public. In this section we will examine this possibility by analyzing data from the 1982 National Survey of Access to Medical Care. As noted in chapter 3, in this survey respondents were asked about their priorities for federal expenditures from a list of 10 categories of spending (e.g., education, defense, health, etc.). Respondents were asked to indicate which of the areas they would choose for spending if they had only one choice. They were asked to make a second choice after giving their first choice. Since there was no followup to the question, we don't know what all respondents had in mind when they chose health over other types of expenditures. However, in light of the fact that such an overwhelming proportion of federal expenditures for health care goes for insurance (Medicare, Medicaid, veterans and veteran-related health programs), insurance coverage of some kind is what a substantial proportion of respondents probably had in mind.

Row one of table 9–1 gives the distribution of choices (the percentage choosing health), by disability. Respondents were asked about the number of days they had to stay in bed or cut back on activities because of illness or injury. (The questions were: "How many days altogether during the past year, that is, since (DATE ONE YEAR AGO) 1981, did you [or other members of the household] stay in bed more than half the day because of illness or injury?" [Days spent in the hospital are excluded]; and "Not counting days in bed, how many days during the past year, that is, since (DATE ONE YEAR AGO) 1981, did you [or other members of your household] have to cut down on things you usually do for more than half of the day because of illness or injury?") In all, persons choosing health for federal spending increases from 40.4% for persons who experience less than eight days of disability days to almost 50% for persons with eight or more days of restricted activity. Apparently, persons who are seriously limited in normal functioning are most apt to favor federal expenditures for health. Consequently, if the proportion of the population who experience activity limitations continues to increase, and evidence from the recent past indicates that it

Table 9–1.   Percentage Choosing Federal Expenditures for Health by Disability
and Demographic Categories

| Disability Days: | | 0–7 | | 8–14 | | 15+ |
|---|---|---|---|---|---|---|
| | | 40.4 | | 48.1 | | 49.7 |
| | | (3167)[1] | | (399) | | (805) |
| Serious Illness in Family: | | | | Yes | | No |
| | | | | 51.5 | | 42.1 |
| | | | | (489) | | (4072) |
| Marital Status: | Single | Divorced | | Separated | Widowed | Married |
| Male | 25.7 | 31.4 | | 33.3 | 35.6 | 40.2 |
| | (456) | (118) | | (39) | (73) | (1205) |
| Female | 42.1 | 42.6 | | 40.0 | 55.9 | 49.0 |
| | (508) | (289) | | (95) | (546) | (1269) |
| Age: | | 18–34 | 35–54 | 55–64 | 65+ | |
| | | 38.8 | 39.5 | 49.7 | 52.0 | |
| | | (1767) | (1164) | (630) | (952) | |

Source of data: 1982 National Survey of Access to Medical Care, courtesy of the Robert
Wood Johnson Foundation.
[1]Figure in parenthesis is number of cases.

will, it would constitute a further source of upward pressure on federal expenditures for health in the future.

Similar findings are presented in row two, which gives the percentage selecting health depending on whether a member of the respondent's household had a serious illness. (The question asked if any family member had a serious illness, were chronically sick, or needed medical treatment or hospitalization on a regular basis.) The fact that chronic disease rates are increasing would indicate that the proportion of families with a seriously ill member is increasing (10.7% of the households were reported to have a serious illness or chronic illness). Since members of these households are more apt to favor federal spending for health, results indicate still another source of pressure for more extensive health insurance coverage in the future.

Comparison of differences in sex-marital status categories in the choice for federal spending proves instructive. Rows three and four show that while women of all marital status categories favor federal spending for health more than men, the difference is especially large for the widowed. There are more widowed women than men in the population (the 1980 census reports 12.1% of women 15 and over are widowed in comparison to 2.5% of men, and for persons 65 and over the percentages are 51.7% for women and 14.6% for men) (U.S. Bureau of the Census 1984:67–68). Because of sex differences in life expectancy, the high priority given to federal spending on health can be expected to grow.

The fifth row of table 9–1 gives the percentage favoring more spending for health by age. As can be seen, the percentage increases rather substantially for the 55–64 age category and slightly again for those 65 and over. Since the population is aging (see below), this is another indication of attitudinal pressure for further increases in expenditures of medical care.

Thus, the patterns in table 9–1 indicate that pressures for future increases in expenditures stemming from attitudes about federal spending on health will reinforce pressures stemming from physician manpower, technology, and illness-disability. The subpopulations that are more supportive of spending for health will increase as a proportion of the total population. All the evidence thus suggests that upward pressures for health insurance will increase rather than decrease in the future. The pressures may be greater than they have been in the recent past. This is not to say that reductions in government (or private) insurance programs cannot be made. If they are, however, they will be made in the face of forces which encourage additional expenditures for health services and against a public which will probably increasingly favor more rather than less health insurance.

While it is altogether possible that the public's valuation of medical care will decline in the future, thus making the success of a rationing strategy more probable than it appears to be at present, rationing strategies to reduce expenditures do not appear to be very promising. They do nothing to eliminate underlying expenditure pressures stemming from manpower, technological, and disability trends. Furthermore, it will be most difficult to reduce health benefits when those benefits are perceived as increasing in value, as they will be as a result of these trends. More illness will be identified, and this will increase the perceived need for medical care, and new forms of treatment will give hope when none or very little existed before. For example, for persons with a terminal heart condition, a successful artificial heart would raise the value of medical care greatly, just as kidney transplants and hemodialysis do for patients with end-stage renal disease; it would be a matter of life and of death. There will be more reasons for people to believe that medical care provides hopes for life and life unimpaired, or less impaired, by disablement. To ration medical care, or attempt to do so, by reducing insurance coverage will be counter to what people have come to expect and could lead to despair for many individuals.

More significantly, from a social perspective, it would raise the potential for social conflict and tension. This is particularly the case for relations between generations and family members.

## Health Insurance: From Conflict Between Classes to Conflict Between Generations

As observed in chapter 4, the early forms of national health insurance were in large part a response to the economic insecurity and anxiety of low-income workers. Health insurance appeared not to be as important in assuring workers of health care, since medicine had so little to offer at the time, as in providing low-income families with income during periods of crisis brought on by illness. Since such a large proportion of the industrial workforce worked for a low wage and were frequently victims of infectious disease which depressed their income even more, health insurance was probably a factor in the alleviation of class tension. Indeed, some believe this was the primary objective of Bismarck when he introduced his program in 1883, since it was the worker's attitude and feelings of discontent, not his welfare, that appeared to have been foremost in Bismarck's mind.

Health insurance has grown since, so that today the masses of the industrial proletariat are well protected from medical expense with health insurance, either through the public sector or private sector, as an aspect of welfare capitalism (Brandes, 1976). In either case, while the very low-income households may have less protection than others in society (e.g., the poor who don't qualify for Medicaid), corporate benefits and economic growth have given most of the industrial working class insurance protection that is not greatly inferior to that of most persons located higher in the class structure. In many instances the insurance coverage provided for the lower-status workers may be equal to that of higher-status workers. For example, the insurance protection of many unskilled industrial workers is at least as good as that enjoyed by many school teachers, and the insurance coverage provided by universities may be the same for the custodial staff as it is for the faculty. Differences between classes do not favor persons higher in the class structure nearly as much as they once did. While the poor and destitute are still vulnerable to cutbacks in public insurance in the United States, the masses of the working class speak with a strong voice and are generally well protected by insurance plans provided by their employers. Furthermore, as noted in chapter 7, conflict between the poor (and their representatives) and the nonpoor that might be the basis for class conflict is muted because the discontent of the masses of workers is eased by private sector programs which may redirect worker discontent to Medicaid recipients (and recipients of other forms of welfare). Class conflict in health insurance is less significant today than in the past.[4] It is being replaced by a conflict between generations.

In chapter 7, Medicare and Social Security in general were viewed as alleviating conflict between the elderly and preretirement generations. Nevertheless, Social Security is becoming the focal point of conflict. At the same time, the relations between generations provide a weak base from which social definitions may evolve to rationalize and justify Social Security. Furthermore, this base will probably get weaker in the future. These points will be discussed in detail.

### Social Security as the Source of Generational Conflict

Protection of the elderly from medical costs is superior today to what it was before Medicare. Medical needs of the elderly have grown as the proportion of the population who are elderly has grown, and the level of insurance coverage necessary to meet those needs has risen accordingly. Economic expenditures on health services for the elderly have increased as a result. This can be expected to continue in the years ahead. Life expectancy can also be expected to continue in the years ahead. Life expectancy has increased—from 13.9 years for a 65-year-old in 1950 to 16.8 years in 1982 (U.S. Department of Health and Human Services, 1983:99). At the same time, the birth rate has decreased in the past two decades. The result is that the proportion of the population 65 and over increased from about 9.2% of the population in 1960 to 11.6% in 1982 (U.S. Bureau of the Census, 1984:31). Although the absolute percentage is not large, the increase represents a 25% increase in 22 years in an age sector of the population that requires the most in the way of health services. The percentage 65 and over in the future will vary depending on changes in life expectancy and the birth rate, increasing as the former increases and decreasing as the latter decreases. Hence, any projection is subject to revision. For example, according to a projection in 1980, the elderly would exceed 12% by the year 2000 (U.S. Department of Human Services, 1981:83), a percentage it has almost reached already. Regardless of the actual figure, the percentage of the population 65 and over will definitely increase. More spending pressure can therefore be expected.

It was observed in chapter 8 that the distribution of medical care is highly concentrated; a very large proportion of national expenditures go for health services for a small proportion of the population. Such persons are potential focal points of social conflict. For example, persons with most forms of chronic diseases (e.g., end-stage renal disease, heart disease, diabetes, and so forth) account for a disproportionate share of expenditures. Still, considering the small numbers involved for each disease, it is not likely that any single category will be viewed by the rest of society as a major cause of increases in national expenditures for health services; although all persons with chronic disease considered together receive a share of expenditure that is far greater than their proportion of the populatin, persons with any particular disease will account for only a small proportion of the total. Observe, however, that the probability of most severe disabling chronic diseases increases in the later years. Diabetes is an example. We observed in chapter 5 that the percentage of the total population with diabetes had increased from 0.4% to 2.5% from the mid-thirties to 1981. We also observed that diabetics require substantially more health services than nondiabetics. The percentage of the population with diabetes is very high for the older sectors of the population, as can be seen from the figures below (from U.S. Bureau of the Census, 1984:126):

| 20–44 | 45–64 | 65+ |
|-------|-------|-----|
| 1.01% | 5.71% | 8.8% |

More generally, the relationship of age to disability, as indexed by the disability days index based on data from the 1982 National Survey of Access to Medical Care, is shown in table 9–2. The average number of disability days due to illness or injury continuously increases with age, with the exception of the decrease from the 55- to 64-year-olds to those over 64 among the poor.[5] As the population ages, the additional medical services per capita will be needed, or perceived to be needed. This will

Table 9–2.  Average Annual Disability Days by Age

|          | 18–34 | 35–54 | 55–64 | 65+ |
|----------|-------|-------|-------|-----|
| Poor     | 16.69 | 28.07 | 55.62 | 48.24 |
|          | (842)[1] | (477) | (287) | (713) |
| Nonpoor  | 8.75  | 10.06 | 21.89 | 32.76 |
|          | (925) | (682) | (332) | (202) |

Source of data: 1982 National Survey of Access to Medical Care, courtesy of the Robert Wood Johnson Foundation.

[1]Figure in parentheses is number of cases.

create upward pressures on expenditures for medical care on behalf of the elderly.

A general indication of future trends in utilization by age may be reflected in the fact that while the number of discharges from hospitals (excluding deliveries) decreased slightly for all age groups from 1974 to 1979, it actually increased for persons 65 years and over (from 254.1 per 1,000 to 269.0 per 1,000). Also, while there was a 10.2% decrease among the total population in days of care in short-stay hospitals, there was only a 1.7% decline for the oldest age group (U.S. Department of Health and Human Services, 1981:168). While the days of care decreased for all age groups, days for the oldest sector as a proportion of all age groups was higher in 1979 than in 1974.

Actually, these and other utilization statistics may be poor gauges of spending pressure coming from the elderly in the future. Demographic factors do not operate in a vacuum. On the one hand, it is possible that changes in the organization and financing of medical service will be such that the pressures from demographic sources can be managed with no increase in actual costs. And it is also possible that major breakthroughs in medical technology will reduce the cost of treating certain chronic illnesses. On the other hand, increases in physician manpower and advances in much medical technology will make expenditure pressures stronger. Thus, as physician manpower and the potential for major (and expensive) advances in technology converge with demographic factors, the upward pressure on expenditures will be greater than if only demographic factors were at work. As a result, demands for insurance coverage from the public sector for the aged may be expected to increase. Obviously, this would only exacerbate the economic aspect of the problem. It would increase the costs (taxes) for persons who are not themselves the major recipients of the care.

The situation with respect to the class structure has been historically different. Until recent years, the development of sophisticated methods for treating illness, chronic and acute, was not dramatic or expensive, by today's standards at least. It was also accompanied by increasing economic growth, so that the health-service needs of the masses of the industrial proletariat have been financed largely by workers themselves, through welfare capitalism. The future promises even more sophisticated and expensive forms of treatment, much of it for the elderly who have chronic disease. Significantly, all the variables in rows 1–4 of table 9–1 that are related to priorities for federal spending are also related to age, and as noted, the priority of health in national expenditures increases with age. Since the population is getting older, results indicate strong support in the future for federal expenditures for health (most probably for health insurance) by the older sector of the population. And this will be at the expense of higher taxes for preretirement generations. Economic conflict between generations will increase.

Conflict between generations is not new, of course. Traditionally, however, such conflict has derived more from social and cultural differences than from economic issues. The lack of economic conflict continues to be true in agrarian societies today. Peasants have large families in order to have cheap labor and to be assured that they will be cared for in old age (e.g., Mamdani, 1972; see also Schultz, 1975). But children who work and care for their parents are themselves assured that their own children will work and care for them. There is, indeed, a contract between generations. While the contract is not formalized legally or reinforced by legislation, it is binding socially (e.g., supported by tradition and mutual trust). Expression of any economic conflict between generations is thereby muted.

With the development of industrial economies and the beginning of social security programs, relations between generations became an explicit contractual matter, and this continues to be the case today. However, in the early industrial period, social security programs were characterized by two overlapping features that are not present today. First, the number of preretirement workers far exceeded the number of retirees; consequently, the tax burden of the aged for the younger generation was not very great. Second, since few workers lived to retirement age anyway, few persons actually received old age assistance. The contrast between generations was largely symbolic. This appears to have been explicit in Bismarck's plan.

The situation changed as the mortality rate declined, life expectancy increased and family size declined. The tax burden on younger generations increased greatly and has become a source of potential conflict. Consequently, more than in class conflict, public insurance for the aged is a potential *source* of conflict. At the same time, the same system serves to alleviate generational conflict. The apparent contradiction may be illustrated with Medicare.

Prior to Medicare legislation, many of the aged had to depend upon their children for financial assistance. This was a potential source of tension and conflict within kinship units. With the mounting costs of medical care and the longer period in which such care was needed (people were living longer), many of the younger generation had to deny themselves and their own immediate families necessities and luxuries in order to assure that medical care was provided for their parents. Medicare reduces this threat. Thus, while in the early stages of industrialization Social Security promoted social cohesion across generations largely on symbolic grounds, today it does so by easing very real economically based interpersonal tensions within family units, as discussed in chapter 7.

At the same time, the tax to support assistance for the aged has become increasingly burdensome, and it will increase in the future. It is already mandated to increase from $2,855 on earnings of $40,500 in 1985 to $4,000 of about $70,000 in 1990. Future levels will depend on the size of the benefits, mortality rates among the elderly, fertility rates, and economic growth. As the medical benefits grow and the tax burden increases, the potential for economic conflict grows. Some believe the overall Social Security tax will approximate 40% of salary at some point in the future (the exact date depends on assumptions about benefit levels, fertility rates, and so forth), in which case the conflict would be extreme. Much of this will be due to Medicare. Thus, although Medicare helps to alleviate conflict between generations, it now also generates conflict, and this is apt to be even more the case in the future.

### Social Relations Between Generations and Social Security

In chapter 7 it was noted that extended kinship ties are weaker today than in the past. If the ties grow weaker and the tax burden on younger generations continues to increase, feelings of responsibility for the medical welfare of one's older relatives may decline. This would weaken support for Medicare (and Social Security in general). Moreover, independent of kinship, there is little basis in existing social relations between the elderly and preretirement generations to sustain values and normative definitions that would support Social Security in its present form. This is because ties of interdependence between generations are weak and will most likely become even weaker in the future.

Almost a century ago, Emile Durkheim (1949) argued that contemporary industrial society was changing from a society based on similarity of values and institutions to differences and diversity. Further, in contrast to a society in which similarities constitute the tie that binds individuals and parts of society, today it is differences that promote social bonds by establishing relations of interdependence. For example, economic activities are divided between employers and employees, and the interdependence leads to reciprocal relations. At the same time, as interdependence increases, the potential for conflict grows. Durkheim felt that conflict was a transitory state; and social definitions would emerge that would regulate relations between different sectors of society. Interdependence would form the basis for the integration of society.

Until recent times the proportion of the population over 65 years was very small, and the relations between such persons and their juniors was usually harmonious. The aged depended on younger generations for economic sustenance, while the younger generations depended on the aged for their wisdom and help with children and grandchildren as well as other domestic duties. In modern society, the aged as a proportion of the population is much larger. Because of changes in the economy and the generally growing complexity of life, the younger generations find the knowledge of the aged less relevant. Economic conflict between the aged and younger generations has grown. At the same time, there is less basis for interdependence on which norms and definitions of accommodations can develop.

There are three forms of interdependence: pooled, sequential, and reciprocal (Thompson, 1967). Pooled interdependence exists, of course, when everyone depends on the same pool of resources, as with insurance where everyone contributes to a pool of funds, usually in roughly equal amounts. Medicare (and more generally Social Security) is a form of insurance program. As with public insurance programs in general, it is often defended on the grounds that medical care is a fundamental human right. Contributions, however, are not equal; members of younger generations pay much more than did the older generation, who receive the benefits. This is no problem as long as the ratio of those receiving benefits to those who pay payroll taxes does not get too high, which it will tend to do if the mortality rates among the elderly and the fertility rates among younger generations decrease. The problem is that both of these rates have decreased in the past quarter century, and may continue in this direction in the years ahead. As a result, the taxes needed to support the pool of funds from which benefits are paid have increased and create a certain dissatisfaction among members of younger generations. Thus the structural support for Social Security as a form of pooled interdependence has weakened, and as a result, rationalizations and moral appeals that the elderly deserve extensive Medicare coverage may be difficult to sustain. Sequential interdependence exists when the actions or outcomes of one person or group depend in the preceding acts of others, and seem to capture the essence of Social Security as "a contract between generations." This works out even if the benefits people receive are greater than their contributions as long as economic growth is sufficiently high. However, with the slow economic growth of the past 15 years or so, along with lower fertility rates, many persons have begun to doubt that they can depend on succeeding generations for their benefits. Consequently, the definition of Social Security as a form of sequential interdependence—a contract between generations—does not have a strong base in social relations.

Reciprocal interdependence involves an exchange between parties. One gets from a transaction what he (she) has paid for or has earned. As we have already seen, Social Security cannot be defended in these terms because the relation is not a form of balanced exchange, and this is increasingly recognized.

To conclude, weak ties of interdependence reveals a weakness in relations between the aged and preretirement generations and thus exposes a fundamental weakness in the structural support for the Social Security program, including Medicare. The social relations needed to sustain motivation for younger generations to care for older persons at current and future costs are getting weaker. Weaker interdependence along with weaker extended kin relations may make it most difficult to get younger generations to accept even definitions based on generalized exchange (e.g., medical care as a human right) which, as noted in chapter 7, appear to be the primary base for defending Social Security.

One way to avoid conflict would be for the elderly to accept less in the form of Social Security benefits. Since history shows that a group fights hard to preserve what it has gained, reductions will probably not occur without serious resistance. Another way would be for the preretirement generations willingly to accept the burden of the elderly, a burden that will increase in the future. Such acceptance might be encouraged by making more explicit in public discussion the positive consequences of Social Security, particularly for the nuclear family. The reduction of kinship tensions, discord, and resentment are not small benefits of Social Security. They provide a basis for assessing Social Security on *social* and not just economic grounds. This may be the strongest basis for rationalizing or justifying the increasing cost of the program.

While such an argument may be persuasive for those who have elderly relatives and feel responsible for them, there is the more general problem of the relation between generations qua generations. Since many members of preretirement generations may have no elderly relatives (and some elderly may have no living children or grandchildren), the argument that Social Security for the elderly helps to maintain family cohesion may not be very persuasive. A strong normative argument is needed that has its base in the nature of the social relations between generations. Unfortunately, that base is weak.

### The Elderly, Social Security, and the Social Control of Conflict

We observed that health insurance has helped society to increase social control over the working and lower class. While the elderly are obviously not prone to disruptive and violent behavior, they do express themselves politically. As their Social Security benefits become a political issue, they may take the position that other interest groups take when threatened, thus widening the breach between themselves and younger generations. They may take the form of political protest. Associations such as the American Association of Retired People (AARP) are organized for the explicit purpose of furthering the interest of older people. At the same time, the elderly are not a homogeneous economic group. While it is not uncommon for public officials to refer to "the poor and the elderly," the fact is that the discretionary income of many of the elderly is far above the poverty level, and wide economic differences exist among them. To what extent this split is reflected in the attitudes of the elderly, one can only guess. A number of institutions, such as AARP and "elderly ghettoes" (e.g., retirement communities and homes) encourage a stronger sense of "age consciousness" than "class consciousness," which would divide the elderly along economic lines. In addition, the elderly are more apt to vote and to be politically more knowledgeable than younger voters (Preston, 1983:446). Since they are also growing faster than the general population, they have become a potentially powerful force. Indeed, as recent political events have shown, the elderly can be a major force in helping to shape public policy in the United States. In this respect they resemble other special interest groups. Of course, many younger members of the electorate may also support policies that enhance the welfare of older members. Nevertheless, the potential for political conflict exists, as others have noted (e.g., Preston, 1983:445–448; Schuck, 1979).

At the same time, there are fundamental differences in the conflict between generations and conflict between other groups, particularly social classes. Relations between generations are far more apt than class relations to intersect with kinship relations. Economic conflict within families is more apt to be personalized and fraught with a deeper sense of resentment or guilt, and its reduction makes for a greater sense of relief. Also, unlike class differences where the more fortunate can rationalize the plight of the underpriviledged as due to the lack of ambition and hard work, older persons cannot be held responsible for the fact that they are old. This does not make the economic burden for younger generations any less, but it does make it harder to oppose.

In addition, the lower physical and social distance between generations (independent of kinship) in comparison to that between classes make generational conflict more difficult for society to manage. Generations are not as apt to be physically removed from each other by residential patterns. Although there has been rapid growth in retirement communities, residential segregation by age is much less than it is by class. In addition, relations between members of different classes are more apt to be impersonal since members of different classes are not usually closely acquainted. This is not true for members of different generations. Persons of different ages are apt to live in the same neighborhood, thus encouraging contact and hence intimacy. They are also often members of the same organization, such as churches and clubs, and to have friends in common, and these tend to strengthen relationships. Relations between classes are often characterized by suspicion, distrust, and dislike, and this makes conflict between classes easier to tolerate.

To conclude, since relations between the elderly and the nonelderly are more apt to be based on affection, trust, and friendship, economic conflict is more difficult to handle emotionally. It is apt to lead to withdrawal, interpersonal alienation and animosity. While these are more or less inherent in class relations, they have not been inherent aspects of relations between generations in the past. As the standard of living and medical care of the elderly become increasingly dependent on subsidies from younger generations, the potential for such developments increases. This is especially the case if the subsidization decreases. Then, among other things, the elderly may have to do without medical care or pay for a higher proportion of it themselves. Worry and concern about the medical needs of the elderly would then increase among many members of society. Conflict between generations is apt to have a more wrenching effect on society than conflict between classes or other groups. It will be more difficult to control.

Whenever one component of society subsidizes the standard of living of another component, the potential for conflict exists. One sector may come to be perceived as receiving something it has not earned, and the sector that helps to subsidize the other may feel it is having to give up too much for what it gets in return. Younger generations have helped to subsidize the Social Security and Medicare payments for the elderly for years, of course. For the most part, however, arguments and debates about this took place in subdued tone. In the late seventies and early eighties, the rhetoric escalated. Recently, it has sometimes taken the form that Social Security benefits (including Medicare) are a burden on the backs of working Americans. Such rhetoric has been accompanied by political action that has reduced the benefits of Medicare. The fact that such reductions were vigorously opposed testifies to the potential for the conflict that adheres in the current situation.[6] Considering the pressure for additional health-service expenditures that can be expected in the future, and the weak ties of interdependence between generations, the conflict will probably get worse and be more openly expressed.

The discussion in chapter 7 would indicate that decreases in the societal subsidy of medical care for the elderly, or even perhaps the failure of society to respond by meeting the additional expenditures that may be expected in the future, would have a particularly disruptive effect on the families of the children and other younger relatives of the elderly. The economic burden in individual cases would be enormous. Because the elderly are living longer and have more chronic diseases that will be increasingly expensive to treat, the potential for deterioration of family relations that are already weak is great. One way to avoid these social disruptions is to assure the payment (or a large proportion thereof) of medical services through insurance, as we do now with Medicare. Since the needs will increase in the future, the same degree of social harmony will require additional expenditures in the future. The economic cost may be great.

## Conclusion

Not much more than half a century ago the medical institution was not particularly important to society, and the role of health insurance has always been viewed only as a financial mechanism to pay for health services or to assure economic subsistence during periods of sickness. Today both are extremely important as social institutions. They are especially important for the relations between generations in which the potential for conflict between economic and social benefits is so great. To preserve the benefits that health insurance has for the relations between the elderly and preretirement generations will involve major economic outlays, and alternatively, decisions to reduce economic expenditures or even not to increase expenditures to meet the mounting economic costs of medical care will involve great social costs. Choices must be made. They will not be easy to make. Further, the basis for decisions, which would favor the elderly, is weaker than in the past because social relations between generations have changed. This, in turn, makes rationalizations which make such choices acceptable most difficult to come by. While economic and medical criteria are usually foremost in discussions and debates as to what the choice should be, far more is involved. The social fabric of the nation is at stake.

## Notes

1. According to the analysis of Sloan and Schwartz (1983), the increase in the supply of physicians accounted for 22% of the increase in expenditures for physician services from 1970 to 1979.

2. To convert figures to 1940 dollars, expenditures for research and development for a particular year are divided by the Consumer Price Index (CPI) for that year and multiplied by 42, which is the CPI for 1940 with 1967 being the base year (when CPI = 100). Source of figures for CPI is Council of Economic Advisors (1983:221).

3. Showstack, Stone, and Schroeder (1985) believe their analysis indicates that costs due directly to technology hardware may have leveled off in the period 1972 through 1979 but that costs due to new treatment, especially surgery, increased. Scitovsky's results are similar (Scitovsky, 1985). However, Scitovsky considers new forms of treatment as aspects of technology. The expensive procedures (e.g., coronary by-pass operations) are considered "big-ticket" technologies, in contrast to the low-cost "little ticket" technologies.

4. This is not to say there are no income-related problems. Economic barriers to access are most serious for many unemployed divorced women, self-employed persons, and workers whose income is low but still too high to qualify for Medicaid assistance (the qualifications vary by state). Such persons have serious problems but do not constitute a basis for organized action in the same sense that members of labor unions, nonunion members of large corporate firms, and government employees do.

5. As noted in chapter 3 (footnote 6), the poor are purposely overrepresented in this study, constituting approximately 50% of the sample.

6. This is reflected in national survey data for 1983 in which 54% support (39% oppose) limiting Medicare "so that only those people who need financial help would actually get benefits" (Health Insurance Association of America, 1984:17). Thus, a majority now believe, contrary to the objectives of many who wanted Medicare tied to the Social Security program, that government insurance for persons 65 and above is not an earned right.

## References

Aaron, Henry J., and William B. Schwartz. *The Painful Prescription: Rationing Hospital Care*. Washington, DC: The Brookings Institution, 1984.

Brandes, Stuart D. *American Welfare Capitalism 1880–1949*. Chicago: University of Chicago Press, 1976.

Council of Economic Advisors. *Economic Report of the President*. Washington, DC: U.S. Government Printing Office, 1983.

Cooper, M.H. *Rationing Health Care*. London: Croom Helm Ltd., 1977.

Durkheim, Emile. *The Division of Labor in Society*. Glencoe, IL: The Free Press, 1949.

Feldstein, Martin S. *The Rising Cost of Hospital Care*. Washington, DC: Information Resources Press, 1971.

————. "The High Cost of Hospitals—and What to do about It." *The Public Interest* 48 (Winter 1977):40–54.

Gibson, Robert M. "National Health Expenditures, 1979." *Health Care Financing Review* 2 (Summer 1980):1–36.

Health Insurance Association of America. *Health and Health Insurance: The Public's View*. Washington, DC: Health Insurance Association of America, 1984.

Mechanic, David. "Approaches to Controlling the Costs of Medical Care: Short-Range and Long-Range Alternatives." *New England Journal of Medicine* 298

(1978) 249–254.

Mamdani, Mahmood. *The Myth of Population Control: Family, Caste, and Class in an Indian Village.* New York: Monthly Review Press, 1972.

Migué, Jean-Luc and Gerard Bélangér. *The Price of Health*, translated from the French by Nicole Fredette and James Robinson. Toronto: The Macmillan Company of Canada Limited, 1974.

Preston, Samuel H. "Children and the Elderly; Divergent Pathe for America's Dependents. *Demography* 21 (November 1984):435–457.

Newhouse, Joseph. *The Economics of Medical Care: A Policy Perspective.* Reading, MA: Addison-Weslay Publishing Company, 1978.

Rushing, William A. "The Supply of Physicians and Expenditures for Health Services with Implications for the Coming Physician Surplus." *Journal of Health and Social Behavior* 26 (December 1985):297–311.

Schuck, Peter H. "The Graying of Civil Rights Law: The Age Discrimination Act of 1975." *The Yale Law Journal* 89 (November 1979):27–93.

Schultz, Theodore W. *Investing in People: The Economics of Population Quality.* Berkeley: University of California Press, 1981.

Scitovsky, Anne A. "Changes in the Costs of Treatment of Selected Illnesses, 1971–1981." *Medical Care* 23 (December 1985):1345–1357.

Shapiro, Sam. "Epidemiology of Ischemic Heart Disease and Cancer." In David Mechanic (ed.), *Handbook of Health, Health Care, and the Health Professions*, pp. 120–156. New York: The Free Press, 1983.

Showstack, Jonathan A., Mary Hughes Stone, and Steven A. Schroeder. "The Role of Changing Clinical Practices in the Rising Costs of Hospital Care." *New England Journal of Medicine* 313 (November 7, 1985):1201–1207.

Sloan, Frank A., and William B. Schwartz. "More Doctors: What Will They Cost?" *Journal of American Medical Association* 249 (Feburary 11, 1983): 766–769.

Stallones, R.A. "The Rise and Fall of Ischemic Heart Disease." *Scientific American* 53 (1980):53–59.

Starr, Paul. *The Social Transformation of American Medicine.* New York: Basic Books, 1982.

Thompson, James W. *Organizations in Action.* New York: McGraw Hill, 1967.

U.S. Bureau of the Census. *Statistical Abstract of the United States.* (104th ed.) Washington, DC: U.S. Government Printing Office, 1984.

U.S. Department of Health, Education, and Welfare. *Health, United States—1975.* Washington, DC: U.S. Government Printing Office, 1975.

————. *1978 NIH Almanac.* Bethesda, MD: National Institutes of Health, 1978.

U.S. Department of Health and Human Services. *Health, United States—1981.* Washington, DC: U.S. Government Printing Office, 1981.

————. *Health, United States—1983.* Washington, DC: U.S. Government Printing Office, 1983.

————. *1984 NIH Almanac.* Bethesda, MD: National Institutes of Health, 1984.

# INDEX